The editor

Jason Ditton is lecturer in sociology at the University of Glasgow. He has previously published *Part-Time Crime* and *Controlology*, and has contributed articles to *Sociological Review, Sociology, New Society, Society Today, Sociology of Work and Occupations,* and *Theory and Society.* He is currently writing *The Goffman Primer*, a companion volume to the present book.

The contributors

Randall Collins is professor of sociology at the University of Virginia.
Steve Crook is lecturer in sociology at the University of York.
Jason Ditton is lecturer in sociology at the University of Glasgow.
George Gonos is professor of sociology at the University of Virginia.
Mike Hepworth is lecturer in sociology at King's College, Old Aberdeen.
John Lofland is professor of sociology at the University of California.
Peter K. Manning is professor of sociology at Michigan State University.
George Psathas is professor of sociology at the College of Liberal Arts, Boston.
Mary Rogers is professor of sociology at the University of West Florida.
Laurie Taylor is professor of sociology at the University of York.
Robin Williams is lecturer in sociology at the University of Durham.

THE VIEW FROM GOFFMAN

THE VIEW FROM GOFFMAN

Edited by

Jason Ditton

St. Martin's Press
New York

Introduction and editorial matter © Jason Ditton 1980;
chapter 1 © John Lofland 1980; chapter 2 © George Psathas
1980;
chapter 3 © Mike Hepworth 1980; chapter 4 © Mary F. Rogers
1980;
chapter 5 © George Gonos 1980; chapter 6 © Randall Collins
1980;
chapter 7 © Robin Williams 1980; chapter 8 © Steve Crook and
Laurie Taylor 1980; chapter 9 © Peter K. Manning 1980

ISBN 0–312–84598–1

Library of Congress Cataloging in Publication Data

Main entry under title:

The view from Goffman.

Bibliography: p.
Includes index.
CONTENTS: Ditton, J.   A bibliographic exegesis of
Goffman's sociology. — Lofland, J.   Early Goffman: style,
structure, substance, soul. — Psathas, G.   Early Goffman
and the analysis of face-to-face interaction in Strategic
interaction.   [etc.]
    1.   Goffman, Erving — Addresses, essays, lectures.
2.   Sociology — Philosophy — Addresses, essays, lectures.
3.   Goffman, Erving — Bibliography.   I.   Ditton, Joseph.
HM26.V53   1980   301'.01   79–25202
ISBN 0–312–84598–1

Contents

Editor's Introduction: A Bibliographic Exegesis of Goffman's Sociology

By Jason Ditton

> Thus a professional man may be willing to take a very modest role in the street, in a shop, or in his home, but, in the social sphere which encompasses his display of professional competency, he will be much concerned to make an effective showing. In mobilising his behaviour to make a showing, he will be concerned not so much with the full round of the different routines he performs but only with the one from which his occupational reputation derives.
> (*The Presentation of Self in Everyday Life*, London, Penguin, 1971, p. 43).

TAKING GOFFMAN SERIOUSLY

Erving Goffman's writings are widely available, and widely read. His books and articles are endlessly reprinted (*Stigma* is currently in its 26th edition), and most of his books have been translated into several languages. *The Presentation of Self in Everyday Life*, for example, is currently available in ten different languages (with Hungarian and Chinese among them), is in its 24th year of almost continuous printing, and has sold over half a million copies. Few sociologists have not read some of his work: indeed, he is also often the only contact with sociology that anthropologists, psychologists, psychiatrists, penologists, criminologists and other social scientists have ever had. His work is constantly mined for the insights buried there, and reviewers consistently describe his style with words selected from a highly appreciative vocabulary.

But whilst the singularity and originality of his contribution is acknowledged, there is a problem. Frequently the presentational eloquence and expositional charm of his writing is allowed to conceal the centrality of its origins, and the potential originality of its contribution to sociology. In his writing, style regularly suppresses structure. And the result? Few people take Goffman seriously as a social theorist with a vital contribution to make to the development of sociology. The papers in this book are designed (in various ways, some expositional, some defensive, and some explanatory) to do just that.

One barrier in particular, the one to which this chapter is addressed, is one that can be laid at Goffman's own door. One reason why his work does not have an obvious coherence and development is that he has chosen not to extensively cross-reference his previous work in later publications, nor to specify openly how his subsequent formulations of selected problems differ from, or extend, his earlier analysis of the same problems. This aspect of his style has undeniable charm for the casual reader, but poses problems for those attempting an academic appreciation. Below, I shall lay down at least the bibliographic groundwork for that sort of study.

After that, in chapter one, John Lofland[1] tackles Goffman's work from the nineteen-fifties to the very early sixties. The relatively small amount of Goffman's work available to Lofland when he first researched and drafted this chapter allows him to assess Goffman's contribution in a number of different ways. Lofland begins with Goffman's hallmark: his *style*, and shows precisely how Goffman is able to squeeze originality from a jaded world by applying a version of Burke's 'perspective by incongruity'. Lofland turns then to the formal *structure* of the early Goffman's work, demonstrating him to be most usually an ethnographic taxonomist with no extensive concern at this stage with specifying the relations between the types he describes. The *substance* of the early published Goffman, Lofland continues, is superficially face-to-face interaction, and more deeply, the self. Goffman's ultimate conception of the latter is his *soul*. The links that Lofland is able to establish here between Goffman's and Sartre's conceptions of the self lead him to finally describe the early Goffman as an existentialist.

George Psathas,[2] in chapter two, instead concentrates upon one text: Goffman's *Strategic Interaction*. His aim is to consider the extent to which Goffman's writing (in that book chiefly, but also elsewhere) can provide a systematic and coherent theory of face-to-face interaction. Psathas contrasts Goffman's version of strategic interaction with a phenomenological alternative which Psathas has himself developed from Schutz. Chapter two is a detailed, comparative, and eventually critical appreciation. Psathas concludes that *Strategic Interaction* is insightful yet structurally eclectic, and confused as to whether its analytic task should be conceptual specification or conceptual development.

Chapter three is as detailed as chapter two – but in a different way. Here, Mike Hepworth[3] assesses Goffman's overall contribution to one specific, substantive topic, rather than, as did Psathas before him, his specific contribution to one specific theoretical field. Mike Hepworth's special interest is social control: specifically in the control of information in everyday life. Hepworth has previously examined the problem of blackmail in a way heavily dependant upon Goffman's work, and in this chapter he analyses the general issue of individual privacy which is exceptionally important, and yet particularly difficult to tackle sociologically without Goffman's poineering work on information management.

In contrast, Mary Rogers[4] uses chapter four to challenge Alvin Gouldner's interpretation and to offer a positive appreciation of Erving Goffman's contribution to an area – power, hierarchy and status – to which he is rarely seen to have offered anything of note. Through a painstaking exhumation of Goffman's writings, Rogers is able to demonstrate the inadequacy and superficiality of Gouldner's early critique, and that Goffman's whole sociology (at least, the interactional world he documents) implicitly depends upon the exercise of power and influence, and more explicitly, upon organisation and control.

Continuing the debate opened by Mary Rogers, in chapter five George Gonos[5] opens with the assertion that 'all social theory is class based', and then attempts to locate the class position of Goffman's theoretical system. Gonos succeeds in separating Goffman's sociology not only from the early criticisms advanced by Gouldner, and the humanism of Cooley, Mead and Dewey – to whom Goffman is frequently and carelessly felt to be attached – but also from the work of Mills and Riesman. Where Mills and Riesman have tended to write from the perspective of the lumpen-bourgeoisie, Gonos shows that Goffman is better viewed as writing from the position of the lumpen-proletariat. Goffman's work is a thorn in the side of bourgeois ideology: not a crown of thorns upon its head. To borrow a Goffman metaphor, middle-class man is the 'mark', and GoffMan is, if anything, the lumpen-bourgeois 'operator'.

Randall Collins,[6] in chapter six, attempts a theoretical rather than pragmatic contextualisation of Goffman's sociology. Initially, to appreciate Goffman's centrality in the development of modern social theory, his popularist presentation has to be separated from his basic scholarly contribution. Collins delineates the several theoretical strands that thread Goffman's work, starting with an early Durkheimian emphasis upon the ritual order, filtered through a Radcliffe-Brown style social anthropology and the Chicagoan version of symbolic interactionism. A little later, Collins sees an almost functionalist version of interaction beginning to emerge in *Encounters, Aslyums, Stigma* and *Behaviour in Public Places*; but one quickly stubbed out when the concern with interaction is relit with an emergent egoistical and calculative emphasis which dominates the slightly later *Strategic Interaction*. Collins sees this as a victory for the utilitarian over the Durkheimian, of the cynical neo-rationalist over the hero-anthropologist. Finally, Collins examines and locates what he refers to as the almost hyper-relativism of *Frame Analysis*.

In chapter seven, Robin Williams[7] offers a different sort of assessment altogether. He considers Goffman on what must, in any technical review, be his home ground: conversational interaction. Further, Williams treats both the continuities and developments of key Goffman concepts through their initial formulation in Goffman's Ph.D thesis to their most recent emergence in the article, 'Replies and Responses'. To do this, Williams takes Goffman's original interactional starting point, the 'occasion', as the basic unit of appreciation, and traces its development through the 'gathering', the 'encounter' and the 'engagement'. He then considers developments in the more technically and linguistically conceived Goffman unit of the conversational 'interchange', together with its contribution to the work of conversation analysts who have so frequently footnoted their indebtedness to Goffman's work.

Steve Crook[8] and Laurie Taylor[9] use chapter eight to trace Goffman's version of reality through his work, and particularly within his most recent and major book, *Frame Analysis*. In particular, they take the tricky issue of untransformed reality and discuss it in terms of Goffman's divergence from James and Schutz. They then contest both Jameson's view that *Frame Analysis* is a form of relativistic semiotics, and George Gonos' previously published discussion of Goffman as a structuralist. They conclude that 'frame' is a device to organise the *accounts* of activities, rather than activity *per se*, and that the energy of frame-analysis derives precisely from its epistemological ambiguity.

Finally, in chapter nine, Peter Manning[10] attempts one of the most difficult exegital tasks of all: a technical appreciation of Goffman's style and structure. Here, he takes up an appreciative tradition established by John Lofland in chapter one, and now extended to cover all of Goffman's major published work. That corpus is treated backwards from *Frame Analysis*: a book not only possessing a stronger structure than most of Goffman's other work, but also containing a method of examining its own style.

WORK BY GOFFMAN: A COMPLEAT BIBLIOGRAPHY

There is no need to provide a *curriculum vitae* of Erving Goffman, since an adequate and accurate one is printed near the beginning of most of his books. I have taken some trouble, on the other hand, to construct an accurate and complete bibliography of his work. Ironically, this was necessary partly because of Professor Goffman's own modest inattention to such things coupled with his professional lack of interest in continually quoting his previously published work in each of his successive volumes, and yet has only been successfully completed because of Professor Goffman's tireless and helpful answers to my transatlantic requests that he correct or verify preliminary attempts at a full bibliography, chase up and despatch odd unpublished pieces to me, find copies of reviews that he had almost forgotten that he had written, and entrust what were often his only copies of particular volumes to the US Mail, the British GPO, and ultimately to myself.

In constructing the bibliography, I have tried to cite every piece of published work written by Erving Goffman. To that list, I have added his two unpublished higher degree dissertations, (1949) and (1953), both of which are of some interest in their own right. Chapter Ten of the M.A. dissertation being both an account of the origin of, and a first example of, Goffman's distinctive form of sociology; and pages 33–41 of his Ph.D dissertation being the first, and also the most succinct, unusual and scholarly account to be discovered anywhere of the sociological model that Goffman has subsequently and consistently followed and developed. There is a common misconception that Goffman's Ph.D dissertation is simply an early yet otherwise indistinguishable version of his first book, *The Presentation of Self in Everyday Life*. In fact, on the contrary, the Ph.D is a highly technical piece of linguistic sociology, and of great value to those who wish to allocate to Erving Goffman a central role in the development of sociological theory. The only other piece of unpublished work I cite is as (1953a), and for two reasons. Firstly, it was produced in limited mimeographed form, and secondly, it is mentioned, albeit without a proper reference, in *The Presentation of Self in Everyday Life*.

I have omitted one publication from the list. It would have read:

(1969d)   *Where the Action Is: Three Essays*, (London; Allen Lane); [*Includes* Goffman (1955), (1961a) and (1967a)].

This reader was only published in hardback, and only in Britain. The essays were selected and the book assembled by the publishers without Professor Goffman's knowledge or consent. All three selections are published elsewhere, and are separately cited in the bibliography. Conversely, I have cited some rather arcane references. Those cited as (1968) and (1968a) are advertising puffs for the British publications of Goffman (1961c), and Goffman (1963), put together by the editor of *New Society*. The references cited as (1956c), (1957a) and (1966) are early drafts of pieces of work refined and republished later. They are cited both to complete the list (for the conscientious and compulsive bibliographile), and described here to prevent the less manic reader from investing time chasing references which will only produce a small return.

I have, in each case, been concerned to discover the original publication date of published material (the year of degree award is taken as the date of unpublished dissertations). Where there is more than one published item for a particular year, the allocation of distinguishing letters: a, b, c, and so on, is arbitrary. It is not always clear which of Goffman's books are to be treated as single works, and which as compendia of collected and thus separably citable items. At one end of the scale, *Interaction Ritual* is clearly a collection of separate papers with the first five being previously published, and the sixth completely new; and at the other end, *Frame Analysis* is a complete work with no previously published antecedants. Of course, it is quite possible to take a completely different view, and see *Interaction Ritual* as a unified contribution to the field of the 'sociology of occasions', and *Frame Analysis* as the stripping, cleaning and reassembly of old ideas. Nevertheless, to construct the bibliography, I have followed the rule that if a single previously published item appears in the main part of a subsequently published Goffman book, then all the parts of that book are separately cited by the date of their first publication, even if that means the occasional and separate citation of one or two previously unpublished book chapters. Thus, I have treated as collections: *Encounters*, *Asylums*, *Interaction Ritual*, and *Strategic Interaction*. And as single works: *The Presentation of Self in Everyday Life*, (although there are two sufficiently different editions), *Behaviour in Public Places*, *Stigma*, *Relations in Public*, (although one paper was previously published, it is here published as an Appendix, and not in the main part of the book), *Frame Analysis*, and *Gender Advertisements*, (as a single work because it contains nothing but one previously published piece).

For the citation of all of Goffman's books, I have given the place and name of the publisher responsible for the first American impression, then followed (in brackets) by the place and name of the publisher producing the first British impression, together with the date of the first British impression if that differs from that of the first American one. There was no American impression of the first edition of *The Presentation of Self in Everyday Life*, and no British one for *Behaviour in Public Places*. Overall, this has usually meant the citation of hardback versions, although in all cases paperback imprints are still available. Thus forearmed, the bibliography:

(1949)   *Some Characteristics of Response to Depicted Experience*, M.A. Dissertation (Unpublished), University of Chicago.

(1951)   'Symbols of Class Status', *British Journal of Sociology*, Vol. II, pp. 294–304.

(1952)   'On Cooling the Mark Out: Some Aspects of Adaptation to Failure', *Psychiatry*, Vol. 15, No. 4, (November) pp. 451–63.

(1953)   *Communication Conduct in an Island Community*, Ph.D Dissertation (Unpublished), University of Chicago.

8 *The View from Goffman*

(1953a) 'The Service Station Dealer: The Man and His Work', (Prepared for the American Petroleum Institute), *Mimeographed*, Chicago; Social Research Incorporated.

(1955) 'On Face-Work: An Analysis of Ritual Elements in Social Interaction', *Psychiatry*, Vol. 18, No. 3, (August) pp. 213–31; [*In* Goffman (1967)].

(1955a) *Review* (of: *Tobati: Paraguayan Town*, by Elman R. Service and Helen S. Service, Chicago; University of Chicago Press, 1954), *American Journal of Sociology*, Vol. 61, 1955–6, pp. 186–7.

(1956 Edition) *The Presentation of Self in Everyday Life*, Edinburgh; University of Edinburgh Social Sciences Research Centre, Monograph No. 2.

(1956a) 'The Nature of Deference and Demeanor', *American Anthropologist*, Vol. 58, (June) pp. 473–502; [*In* Goffman (1967)].

(1956b) 'Embarrassment and Social Organisation', *American Journal of Sociology*, Vol. 62, No. 3, (November) pp. 264–71; [*In* Goffman (1967)].

(1956c) 'Interpersonal Persuasion', *in* Bertram Schaffner (ed) *Group Processes* (New York; Josiah Macy Foundation, 1956) pp. 117–193; [*Revised as* Goffman (1957a)].

(1957) 'Alienation from Interaction', *Human Relations*, Vol. 10, No. 1, pp. 47–60; [*In* Goffman (1967)].

(1957a) 'Characteristics of Total Institutions', *in Symposium on Preventative and Social Psychiatry*, Sponsored by the Walter Reed Army Institute of Research, the Walter Reed Army Medical Centre, and the National Research Council, Washington, (Government Printing Office, 1957) pp. 43–93; [*Revision of* Goffman (1956c), *Revised as* Goffman (1961e)].

(1957b) 'On Some Convergences of Sociology and Psychiatry: A

Sociologist's View', *Psychiatry*, Vol. 20, No. 3, (August) pp. 201–3.

(1957c)   Review (of: *Other People's Money*, by Donald R. Cressey, Glencoe; The Free Press, 1953), *Psychiatry*, Vol. 20, No. 3, (August) pp. 321–6.

(1957d)   *Review*: (of: *Human Problems of a State Mental Hospital*, by Ivan Belknap, New York; McGraw-Hill, 1956), *Administrative Science Quarterly*, Vol. 2, No. 1, (June) pp. 120–1.

(1959 Edition)   *The Presentation of Self in Everyday Life*, New York; Doubleday Anchor, (London; Allen Lane, 1969).

(1959a)   'The Moral Career of the Mental Patient', *Psychiatry*, Vol. 22, No. 2, (May) pp. 123–42; [*In* Goffman (1961c)].

(1961)   *Encounters: Two Studies in the Sociology of Interaction*, Indianapolis; Bobbs-Merrill, (London; Allen Lane, 1972); [*Includes* Goffman (1961a) and Goffman (1961b)].

(1961a)   'Role Distance'; [*in* Goffman (1961)].

(1961b)   'Fun in Games'; [*in* Goffman (1961)].

(1961c)   *Asylums: Essays on the Social Situation of Mental Patients and Other Inmates*, New York; Doubleday Anchor, (Harmondsworth; Penguin, 1968); [*Includes* Goffman (1959a), (1961d), (1961e), and (1961f)].

(1961d)   'The Medical Model and Mental Hospitalisation: Some Notes on the Vicissitudes of the Tinkering Trades'; [*In* Goffman (1961c)].

(1961e)   'On The Characteristics of Total Institutions'; [*Revision of* Goffman (1957a), and *in* Goffman (1961c)].

(1961f)   'The Underlife of a Public Institution: A Study of Ways of Making Out in a Mental Hospital'; [*In* Goffman (1961c)].

(1963)   *Stigma: Notes on the Management of Spoiled Identity*,
          Englewood   Cliffs,   New   Jersey;   Prentice-Hall
          (Harmondsworth; Penguin, 1968).

(1963a)   *Behaviour in Public Places: Notes on the Social Organisation of
          Gatherings*, Glencoe; The Free Press.

(1964)   'Mental Symptoms and Public Order', Chapter XVIII,
          pp. 262–9, *in Disorders in Communication*, Vol. XLII of the
          Research Publications of the Association for Research in
          Nervous and Mental Disease; [*In* Goffman (1967)].

(1964a)   'The Neglected Situation', *American Anthropologist*, Vol.
          66, No. 6, Part II (Special Issue) pp. 133–6.

(1966)   'Communication   and   Enforcement   Systems',   *in*
          Kathleen Archibald (ed) *Strategic Interaction and Conflict*,
          (Berkeley; Institute of International Studies, University
          of California, 1966) pp. 198–220; [*Revised as* Goffman
          (1969b)].

(1967)   *Interaction Ritual: Essays on Face-to-Face Behaviour*, New
          York; Doubleday Anchor, (London; Allen Lane, 1972);
          [*Includes* Goffman (1955), (1956a), (1956b), (1957),
          (1964), and (1967a)].

(1967a)   'Where the Action Is'; [*In* Goffman (1967)].

(1968)   'The Staff World', *New Society*, 21st November, pp. 757–
          9; [*Edited Extract from* Goffman (1961c)].

(1968a)   'Marked for Life', *New Society*, 28th November, pp. 795–
          7; [*Edited Extract from* Goffman (1963)].

(1969)   *Strategic   Interaction*,   Philadelphia;   University   of
          Pennsylvania Press, (Oxford; Basil Blackwell, 1970);
          [*Includes* Goffman (1969a) and (1969b)].

(1969a)   'Strategic Interaction'; [*In* Goffman (1969)].

(1969b)   'Expression Games: An Analysis of Doubts at Play',

[*Revision of* Goffman (1966), and *in* Goffman (1969)].

(1969c)   'The Insanity of Place', *Psychiatry*, Vol. 32, No. 4, (November) pp. 357–87; [*In* Goffman (1971)].

(1971)   *Relations in Public: Microstudies of the Public Order*, New York: Basic Books, (London; Allen Lane).

(1974)   *Frame Analysis: An Essay on the Organisation of Experience*, New York; Harper and Row, (Harmondsworth; Penguin, 1975).

(1976)   'Gender Advertisements', *Studies in the Anthropology of Visual Communication*, Vol. 3, No. 2, (Fall) pp. 69–154; [*Republished as* Goffman (1979)].

(1976a)   'Replies and Responses', *Language in Society*, Vol. 5, No. 3, (December) pp. 257–313.

(1977)   'The Arrangement Between the Sexes', *Theory and Society*, Vol. 4, No. 3, (Fall) pp. 301–31.

(1978)   'Response Cries', *Language*, Vol. 54, No. 4, (December), pp. 787–815.

(1979)   *Gender Advertisements*, New York; Harper and Row, (London, Macmillan); [*Reprint of* Goffman (1976)].

(1979a)   'Footing', *Semiotica*, Vol. 25, Nos. 1/2, pp. 1–29.

Let me add a brief note here on how Goffman's work has been cited in the chapters that follow. Firstly, citations are either *by* date, eg, (1959), of first publication of the work in question for quotations; or, if the citation is less specific, and no pagination necessary, by title alone. In the latter case, because some of Goffman's book and article titles are rather long, yet because most of them are perforated by a colon, I have chosen the words preceeding the colon as the title citation wherever possible. Thus, Goffman's third published article would be cited as, eg, (1955, p. 216) for a quotation, and as 'On Face-Work', for a general mention. Where no colon appears in the title of an article or book, then the whole title, eg,

The Presentation of Self in Everyday Life, is given.

Secondly, paginated citations of both books and articles are *from* various editions of Goffman's books and articles. I have decided not to render every single quotation to its pagination in a particular edition of each work. To do so would have been overly laborious, and possibly counter-productive. As things stand, about half the quotations are from popular English editions, and the rest from popular American ones. However, in case a reader should wish to check a particular quotation, the editions used in each chapter are listed at its end, following the date of each book or article's first publication as provided in this bibliography, and *not* the date of the edition or impression used by that chapter author. For example, every quotation from *The Presentation of Self in Everyday Life* will be dated as (1959), although the page number following the date will refer to the impression used by the chapter author, that impression being specified in the list appended to every chapter.

WORK ON GOFFMAN: REVIEWS, APPRECIATION AND CRITICISM

I have excluded from citation here the massive number of petty mentions of Goffman's work, and include only substantial contributions. I have divided that latter category firstly into *A Selection of Appreciation and Criticism*, and have only listed selections that I am aware of, being also those where Goffman is the major or sole target of attention. The second category, *A Sampler of Reviews*, is a list of all the reviews of Goffman's work that I have encountered. I have not been the least bit selective in this latter category. To list reviews at all may seem absurdly conscientious. I have provided this list because most potential critics have chosen a review (and often an extended one) as the forum for their opinions. I can see no grounds for excluding the shorter reviews, as they are often the most perceptive.

The authors of some of the pieces entered in this second list might well feel that their work should properly be cited as a full article in the first list, rather than as a mere review in the second. I hope I have not trodden upon too many untenured toes by following the rule of citing everything that has apparently been prompted by a free copy of one of Goffman's books as a review.

A SELECTION OF APPRECIATION AND CRITICISM

There is not a great deal to choose from. Typically, Goffman is cited by many yet examined by few. Of those few, an even smaller number have concentrated their examination upon Goffman alone, most being content to unthinkingly locate Goffman in a tradition established by Mead and perpetuated by Blumer. The list that follows here is, accordingly, of those pieces of work which are about Goffman alone (except in a few cases, eg, Cioffi, Hall, and Young where Goffman is fruitfully compared to some non symbolic interactionists; and a few others, eg, Clarke, Coser, and Stebbins, where some technical issues are discussed). It is an idiosyncratic list, rather than a systematically produced or necessarily extensive one. It does not so much represent favoured or valuable items as purely available ones, and then only those known (and rather haphazardly) to this bibliographer.

CIOFFI, Frank 'Information, Contemplation and Social Life', *The Royal Institute of Philosophy Lectures*, Vol. 4, (1969–70) pp. 103–31.

CLARKE, Michael 'Total Institutions: Some Dimensions of Analysis', *New Sociology*, Vol. 1, No. 4, (September 1974) pp. 53–80.

COLLINS, Randall and MAKOWSKY, Michael 'Erving Goffman and the Theatre of Social Encounters', Chapter 12 in their book, *The Discovery of Society*, (New York; Random House, 1972).

COSER, Rose Laub 'Role Distance, Sociological Ambivalence and Traditional Status Systems', *American Journal of Sociology*, Vol. 72, (1966–7) pp. 173–87.

CUZZORT, Richard P. 'Humanity as the Big Con: The Human Views of Erving Goffman', Chapter 9 in his book, *Humanity and Modern Sociological Thought*, (New York; Holt, Rinehart and Winston, 1969).

GONOS, George ' "Situation" versus "Frame": The "Interactionist" and the "Structuralist" Analyses of Everday

Life', *American Sociological Review*, Vol. 42, (December 1977) pp. 854–67.

GOULDNER, Alvin W. 'Other Symptoms of the Crisis: Goffman's Dramaturgy and Other New Theories', pp. 378–90, in Chapter 10 of his book, *The Coming Crisis of Western Sociology*, (London; Heinemann, 1970).

HALL, J. A. 'Sincerity and Politics: "Existentialists" vs. Goffman and Proust', *Sociological Review*, Vol. 25, No. 3, (August 1977) pp. 535–50.

MANNING, Peter K. 'The Decline of Civility: A Comment on Erving Goffman's Sociology', *Canadian Review of Sociology and Anthropology*, Vol. 13, No. 1, (1976) pp. 13–25.

MESSINGER, Sheldon E., SAMPSON, Harold, and TOWNE, Robert D. 'Life as Theater: Some Notes on the Dramaturgic Approach to Social Reality', *Sociometry*, Vol. 25, (September 1962) pp. 98–110.

PSATHAS, George 'Goffman's Image of Man', *Humanity and Society*, Vol. 1, No. 1, (1977) pp. 84–94.

ROGERS, Mary 'Goffman on Power', *American Sociologist*, Vol. 12, No. 2, (April 1977), pp. 88–95.

ROSE, Jerry D. *The Presentation of Self in Everyday Life: A Critical Commentary*, (New York; R.D.M. Corporation, 1966).

RYAN, Alan 'Maximising, Moralising and Dramatising', in Christopher Hookway and Philip Pettit (eds), *Action and Interpretation: Studies in the Philosophy of the Social Sciences*, (Cambridge; Cambridge University Press, 1978) pp. 65–81.

STEBBINS, Robert A. 'A Note on the Concept Role Distance', *American Journal of Sociology*, Vol. 73, (1967–8) pp. 247–50.

TAYLOR, Laurie 'Erving Goffman', *New Society*, (5th December, 1968) pp. 835–7.

WEDEL, Janet M. 'Ladies, We've Been Framed! Observations on Erving Goffman's "The Arrangement Between the Sexes"', *Theory and Society*, Vol. 5, No. 1, (January 1978) pp. 113–25.

YOUNG, T. R. 'The Politics of Sociology: Gouldner, Goffman and Garfinkel', *American Sociologist*, Vol. 6, (November 1971) pp. 276–81.

ZEITLIN, Irving 'The Social Psychology of Erving Goffman', Chapter 15 of his book, *Rethinking Sociology*, (New York; Appleton-Century-Crofts, 1973).

A SAMPLER OF REVIEWS

Again, this is not a systematic or extensive list. Because of the lack of much alternative critical examination of Goffman's work, reviews are often cited in the chapters that follow. Accordingly, I have thought it convenient to list those cited, together with some others, roughly chronologically here. Goffman's books are listed in proper temporal sequence, although the individual numbering of reviews, eg, R2, is an arbitrary shorthand.

(i) *Review Essays*: [i.e., reviews of more than one Goffman book. In the chapters that follow, these three review essays will be cited as full articles, eg, as Dawe (1973, p. 250).]

DAWE, Alan 'The Underworld View of Erving Goffman', [Review of Goffman, (1961), (1967), (1969), and (1971)]; *British Journal of Sociology*, Vol. 24, (1973) pp. 246–53.

MACINTYRE, Alasdair 'The Self as a Work of Art', [Review of Goffman, (1959) and (1967)]; *New Statesman*, (28th March 1969), pp. 447–8.

SENNETT, Richard 'Two on the Aisle', [Review of Goffman, (1959), (1961), (1961c) and (1971)]; *New York Review of Books*, Vol. 20, (1973–4) pp. 29–31. [This is also a review of Jerzy Grotowski, *Towards a Poor Theater*, (New York; Simon and Schuster, 1972).]

(ii) *Reviews*: [i.e., includes extended reviews, and review articles, both of which are indicated by the presence of a review title, or, in some cases, purely by the number of pages of the review. In the chapters that follow, these reviews will be cited as : (*date* of original publication of Goffman book, Review *number* from the following list).]

The Presentation of Self in Everyday Life

(1956, R1)   STONE, Gregory P., *American Journal of Sociology*, Vol. 63, No. 1, (July, 1957–8) p. 105.

(1956, R2)   NAEGELE, Kaspar D., *American Sociological Review*, Vol. 21, No. 5, (October, 1956) pp. 631–2.

(1956, R3)   PERRY, Helen S., *Psychiatry*, Vol. 19, No. 2, (May, 1956) pp. 209–11.

(1959, R1)   MILLER, Daniel R., *Contemporary Psychology*, Vol. 6, (1961) pp. 432–4.

(1959, R2)   BOLTANSKI, Luc, 'Erving Goffman et le Temps du Soupçon: Apropos de la Publication en Francais de *La Représentation de Sois dans la Vie Quotidienne*', *Information sur les Sciences Sociales*, Vol. 12, No. 3, (June, 1973) pp. 127–47.

(1959, R3)   FALLERS, Lloyd, *American Anthropologist*, Vol. 64, (1962) pp. 190–1.

Encounters

(1961, R1)   POTTER, Robert J., *American Journal of Sociology*, Vol. 68, No. 1, (July, 1962–3) pp. 125–6.

(1961, R2)   BLOOMBAUM, Milton, *American Sociological Review*, Vol. 27, No. 3, (June, 1962) pp. 436–7.

(1961, R3)   KELLY, Harold H., *Contemporary Psychology*, Vol. 8, (1963) pp. 71–2.

(1961, R4)   DYE, Sister Mary Elizabeth, *Sociological Quarterly*, Vol. 5, Part I, (1965) p. 95.

(1961, R5)   BRUNER, Edward M., *American Anthropologist*, Vol. 65, (1963) pp. 1416–7.

Asylums

(1961c, R1)   CAUDHILL, William, *American Journal of Sociology*, Vol. 68, No. 3, (November, 1962–3) pp. 366–9.

(1961c, R2)   PFAUTZ, Harold W. *American Sociological Review*, Vol. 27, No. 4, (August, 1962) pp. 555–6.

(1961c, R3)   HOLLINGSHEAD, August B., *Annals of the American Academy of Political and Social Science*, Vol. 344, (1962) p. 185.

Stigma

(1963, R1)   WEINSTEIN, Eugene, *American Journal of Sociology*, Vol. 70, No. 5, (March, 1964–5) p. 636.

(1963, R2)   SEEMAN, Melvin, *American Sociological Review*, Vol. 29, No. 5, (October, 1964) pp. 770–1.

(1963, R3)   TYLER, Leona, *Contemporary Psychology*, Vol. 10, (1965) pp. 30–1.

(1963, R4)   DEFLEUR, Melvin L., *Social Forces*, Vol. 43, No. 1, (October, 1964) pp. 127–8.

(1963, R5)   BERKOWITZ, Leonard, *Annals of the American Academy of Political and Social Sciences*, Vol. 357, (1965) pp. 148–50. [This is also a review of W. W. Lambert and W. E. Lambert, *Social Psychology*, (Englewood Cliffs, New Jersey; Prentice-Hall, 1963).]

Behaviour in Public Places

(1963a, R1)   STINCHCOMBE, Arthur L., *American Journal of Sociology*, Vol. 69, No. 6, (May, 1963–4) pp. 679–80.

(1963a, R2) SCHNEIDER, Louis, *American Sociological Review*, Vol. 29, No. 3, (June, 1964) pp. 427–8.

(1963a, R3) BLOOM, Samuel W., *Annals of the American Academy of Political and Social Sciences*, Vol. 355, (1964) pp. 140–1.

Interaction Ritual

(1967, R1) HUGHES, Everett C., *American Journal of Sociology*, Vol. 76, No. 3, (November, 1969–70) pp. 725–6.

(1967, R2) STRODBECK, Fred L., *American Journal of Sociology*, Vol. 77, No. 1, (July, 1970–1) pp. 177–9.

(1967, R3) TIRYAKIAN, Edward A., *American Sociological Review*, Vol. 33, No. 3, (June, 1968) pp. 462–3.

(1967, R4) MELTZER, Bernard N., *Social Forces*, Vol. 47, No. 1, (September, 1968) pp. 110–111.

Strategic Interaction

(1969, R1) TAYLOR, Laurie, *Sociology*, Vol. 6, No. 2, (May, 1972) pp. 311–13.

(1969, R2) LOFLAND, John, 'The Morals are the Message: The Work of Erving Goffman', *Psychiatry and Social Science Review*, Vol. 4, No. 9, (July, 1970) pp. 17–19.

(1969, R3) COUCH, Carl J., *American Sociological Review*, Vol. 36, No. 1, (February, 1971) pp. 135–6.

(1969, R4) SWANSON, Guy E., *American Journal of Sociology*, Vol. 79, No. 4, (January, 1974) pp. 1004–8.

(1969, R5) CARSON, Robert C., *Contemporary Psychology*, Vol. 15, (1970) pp. 722–4.

(1969, R6)   LEMERT, Edwin, *American Anthropologist*, Vol. 74, (1972) pp. 8–10.

Relations in Public

(1971, R1)   LYMAN, Stanford M., 'Civilisation: Contents, Discontents, Malcontents', *Contemporary Sociology*, Vol. 2, No. 4, (July, 1973) pp. 360–6.

(1971, R2)   BERMAN, Marshall, 'Weird but Brilliant Light on the Way We Live Now', *New York Times Book Review*, (February 27th, 1972) Section 7, pp. 1, 2, 10, 12, 14, 16, and 18.

(1971, R3)   HARRE, Rom, *Sociology*, Vol. 7, No. 3, (September, 1973) pp. 468–9.

(1971, R4)   ROTHSTEIN, David, *American Journal of Sociology*, Vol. 79, No. 5, (March, 1973–4) pp. 1339–41.

(1971, R5)   BLUMER, Herbert, 'Action vs. Interaction', *Society*, Vol. 9, (April, 1972) pp. 50–3.

(1971, R6)   MANNING, Peter K., *Sociological Quarterly*, Vol. 14, (Winter, 1973) pp. 135–7.

(1971, R7)   COLLINS, Randall, *Sociological Quarterly*, Vol. 14, (Winter, 1973) pp. 137–42.

(1971, R8)   ARONOFF, Joel, *Sociological Quarterly*, Vol. 14, (Winter, 1973) pp. 142–3.

(1971, R9)   GERGEN, Kenneth J., *Contemporary Psychology*, Vol. 18, (1973) pp. 305–7.

(1971, R10)   TURNER, Ralph H., *Social Forces*, Vol. 51, No. 4, (June, 1973) pp. 504–5.

(1971, R11)   BLACK, Kurt W., *Annals of the American Academy of Political and Social Sciences*, Vol. 401, (1972) p. 206.

(1971, R12)   BRAROE, Niels W., *American Anthropologist*, Vol.
               75, (1973) pp. 945–7.

(1971, R13)   CLASS, Loretta, *Bulletin of the Menninger Clinic*,
               Vol. 37, No. 6, (1973) pp. 645–8.

Frame Analysis

(1974, R1)   JAMESON, Frederic, 'On Goffman's Frame
               Analysis', *Theory and Society*, Vol. 3, No. 1, (Spring,
               1976) pp. 119–33.

(1974, R2)   TAYLOR, Laurie, *New Society*, (15th January,
               1976) pp. 117–8.

(1974, R3)   MANNING, Peter K., *American Journal of
               Sociology*, Vol. 82, (1977) pp. 1361–4.

(1974, R4)   DITTON, Jason, *Sociology*, Vol. 10, No. 2, (May,
               1976) pp. 329–32.

(1974, R5)   SHARROCK, W. W., *Sociology*, Vol. 10, No. 2,
               (May, 1976) pp. 332–4.

(1974, R6)   DAVIS, Murray S., *Contemporary Sociology*, Vol. 4,
               No. 6, (November, 1975) pp. 599–603.

(1974, R7)   GAMSON, William A., *Contemporary Socio-
               logy*, Vol. 4, No. 6, (November, 1975) pp.
               603–7.

(1974, R8)   CRAIB, Ian, 'Erving Goffman: Frame Analysis'
               Philosophy of the Social Sciences, Vol. 8, (1978) pp.
               79–86.

(1974, R9)   POSNER, Judith, 'Erving Goffman: His
               Presentation of Self', *Philosophy of the Social Sciences*,
               Vol. 8, (1978) pp. 67–78.

(1974, R10)   ROSENBERG, Philip, *New York Times Book
               Review*, (16th February, 1975) pp. 21–6.

(1974, R11)   BRAROE, Niels W., *American Anthropologist*, Vol. 78, (1976) pp. 866–70. [This is also a review of Shirley Weitz, *Nonverbal Communication*, (London; Oxford University Press, 1974); and of Lyn H. Lofland, *A World of Strangers*, (New York; Basic Books, 1973).]

(1974, R12)   WEINSTEIN, Eugene, *Contemporary Psychology*, Vol. 21, No. 5, (1976) pp. 332–3.

(1974, R13)   SWANSON, Guy E., *Annals of the American Academy of Political and Social Science*, Vol. 420, (July, 1975) pp. 218–20.

(1974, R14)   SCHNEIDER, Irving, *American Journal of Psychiatry*, Vol. 132, No. 10, (1975) pp. 1093–4.

(1974, R15)   GLASER, Daniel, *Sociology and Social Research*, Vol. 61, No. 2, (1977) pp. 246–7.

(1974, R16)   HACKETT, Ed., *Cornell Journal of Social Relations*, Vol. 9, No. 2, (Fall, 1974) pp. 277–9.

(1974, R17)   JARY, David and SMITH, Gregory, *Sociological Review*, Vol. 24, No. 4, (1976) pp. 917–927.

(1974, R18)   LITTLEJOHN, Stephen W., *Communication Research*, Vol. 4, No. 4, (1977) pp. 485–92.

CHAPTER ENDNOTES

1. John Lofland is Professor of Sociology at the University of California, Davis. His publications include *Doomsday Cult, Deviance and Identity* (assisted by L. Lofland), *Analysing Social Settings, Doing Social Life, State Executions* (with H. Bleackley), and *Interaction in Everyday Life* (editor). He has served as founding editor of *Urban Life*, consulting editor to the *American Journal of Sociology*, and associate editor of the *American Sociological Review*. His current research focuses on display presentations of self as seen in protest demonstrations and other ostentations in the display arena of the California Capitol.

2. George Psathas is Professor of Sociology at Boston University and has taught at

Indiana University and Washington University (St. Louis). He is founder and editor of *Human Studies*, a quarterly journal for philosophy and the social sciences devoted to phenomenological, existential and ethnomethodological approaches and perspectives in those fields. His published work includes *Phenomenological Sociology* and *Language Analysis: Studies in Ethnomethodology*, both of which he edited, as well as numerous articles and research papers. He is currently studying the uses and applications of photography and video recording methods in sociological research.

3. Mike Hepworth is Lecturer in Sociology at the University of Aberdeen. He is the author of *Blackmail: Publicity and Secrecy in Everyday Life*, and has published a number of papers on other aspects of the sociology of deviance. His interests include the study of privacy and secrecy; historical criminology; mass communication and popular culture; and he is currently working with Mike Featherstone on a study of changing perceptions of middle age. He is a founder of the Mid Life Study Group.

4. Mary Rogers (Ph.D, University of Massachusetts, Amherst, 1972) is an Associate Professor of Sociology at the University of West Florida, Pensacola. To date, her research has focused on theoretical analyses of power. Her current research is in the area of phenomenological sociology. She is presently writing a monograph which offers an exposition of phenomenology for social scientists, a phenomenological critique of ethnomethodology, and a delineation of the boundaries of a phenomenological sociology focused on the matter of social action.

5. George Gonos is Instructor of Sociology at Queens College, City University of New York. He has published articles in the *American Sociological Review*, *Urban Life*, and *Journal of American Folklore*, and is currently writing a Ph.D thesis on the sociology of Erving Goffman. His main areas of interest are sociological theory, the sociology of education, and mass culture.

6. Randall Collins is Professor of Sociology, and member of the Center for Advanced Studies, at the University of Virginia. He was educated at Harvard, Standford, and the University of California at Berkeley. He is the author of *Conflict Sociology*, *The Discovery of Society* (with Michael Makowsky), and *The Credential Society: An Historical Sociology of Education and Stratification*.

7. Robin Williams is Lecturer in Sociology at the University of Durham. He was educated at the London School of Economics, and has taught at the Universities of Southampton and Manchester. He is the author of several articles on symbolic interactionism and social research. He is currently working on the sociology of exclusion and is writing a book on interpretative research in sociology.

8. Steve Crook grduated in philosophy at the University of York in 1973, and is currently Lecturer II in Sociology at the College of St. Mark and St. John, Plymouth. His Ph.D concerns the problem of validation in Marxist social theory, but he has also worked for a while as a research fellow on a study of alcohol use, and has interests in the sociologies of the individual, work, and literature.

9. Laurie Taylor, now Professor of Sociology at the University of York, graduated in psychology from Birkbeck College, University of London, and then completed his postgraduate studies at the University of Leicester. His books include *Psychological Survival* (with Stanley Cohen), *Deviance and Society*, *Crime Deviance and*

Socio-Legal Control (with Roland Robertson), *Escape Attempts: The Theory and Practice of Resistance to Everyday Life* (with Stanley Cohen), and *Prison Secrets* (with Stanley Cohen). He has also edited *Politics and Deviance* (with Ian Taylor), and *Young People and Civil Conflict in Northern Ireland* (with Sarah Nelson).

10. Peter K. Manning (Ph.D from Duke University, 1966) is Professor of Sociology and Psychiatry at Michigan State University, where he has taught since 1966. He has done fieldwork on the logic of disease and illness in Mexico and Peru, and on the police in London and the United States, and recently completed a six-city study of narcotics enforcement. His publications report research in organisations, occupations, field work methods, socialisation and deviance and control. He has edited or written five books and has three in press. The former include *Police Work*, and the latter, *The Narc's Game: Organisational and Informational Limits upon Drug Law Enforcement*.

1: Early Goffman: Style, Structure, Substance, Soul

By John Lofland

In the early nineteen sixties a happy chorus began to chant adulations around the work of Erving Goffman. The litany included such endearments as 'remarkable', 'brilliant', 'insightful', 'meaningful', 'trenchant', 'landmarking', 'fascinating', and 'masterful'.[1] I want in this chapter to ask: About what was there suddenly so much enthusiasm? My answer takes the form of delineating what appear to be the main features of Erving Goffman's early sociological work, the work he published in the fifties and early sixties.[2]

My analysis is divided into four main parts. First, what are prominent features of Goffman's early *style* that helped to make it so attractive? How does he go about viewing social life so as to wring out new insights? Second, what is the formal *structure* of the analysis he offers and what is the relation of that structure to more standard matters of theory building and empirical testing? Third, what is the *substance* of his early work, the major questions around which his writing revolves? Fourth, what appear to have been his underlying existential and moral concerns? What, as was said in the high sixties, was his '*soul*'?

STYLE

What stylistic features of Goffman's early work functioned to make it so widely appealing? The material offered by Goffman is somewhat new, but is not as startling as some of his readers seem to believe. The fascination with Goffman rests, rather, upon the peculiar way he goes about his work rather than on the mere naked content of what he is saying.

The 'Goffmanesque touch' is achieved, as first pointed out to me by Marvin B. Scott, by what Kenneth Burke has called 'perspective by incongruity'.[3] This is the trick of 'taking a word usually applied in one setting and transferring its use to another setting'. Thus:

> It is a 'perspective by incongruity', since it is established by violating the 'proprieties' of the word in its previous linkages.

> Nietzsche establishes his perspectives by a constant juxtaposing of incongruous words, attaching to some name a qualifying epithet which had heretofore gone with a different order of names. He writes by the same constant reordering of categories that we find in the Shakespearean metaphor.[4]

This is the art that the early Goffman practices. It is practiced in two forms: firstly, by sprinkling the text with incongruous phrases, and secondly, by applying an entire incongruous model to a phenomenon to achieve a new perspective. Consider these examples of incongruous phrases:

> We must all carry within ourselves something of the sweet guild of conspirators. (1959, p. 105)

> Those who break the rules of interaction commit their crimes in jail. (1957, p. 48)

> Universal human nature is not a very human thing. (1955, p. 231)

> The world, in truth, is a wedding. (1959, p. 36)

> The dead are sorted but not segregated, and continue to walk among the living. (1952, p. 505)

> If the many are to be pleased, then the few may have to sacrifice themselves to the occasion, allowing their bodies to be cast into the blend to make the bell sound sweet. (1961, p. 79)

While phrases such as these give his pages a 'sparkling' quality, the broader fascination springs from his thoroughgoing application of incongruous models to social life. A model is taken as prototype, various concepts associated with it are specified and this apparatus is then applied to all manner of additional situations in a relatively systematic fashion. It is a strategy of metaphor and is therefore not new, especially in literary traditions. Here are some prime instances from Goffman's early writings:

1. The Con Game: Social life is seen in terms of marks, operators and coolers. (1952)

2. The Chinese Conception of Face: Face-to-face conduct is viewed in terms of work that is done to save one's own and others' face. (1955)

3. Ritual Treatment of Deities in Preliterate Religion: Persons are seen as ritually sacred objects. (1956a)

4. The Theater: Social life is viewed in terms of performers and teams who utilise front and back regions to foster an impression on an audience. Persons are seen as performers of characters. (1959)

5. The Total Institution: A category of organisations is created and seen as a place to study the profanation of selves and the response of selves to profanation. (1961c)

6. The Career: The concept of career is applied to a patient's stay in a mental hospital. (1961c)

7. Theories of Human Nature: Mental hospitals (and all organisations) are seen as entities with theories of human nature. (1961c)

8. The Service Occupation: The relationship between the psychotherapist and the client is seen as 'a kind of grotesque of the service relationship' (1961c, p. 369), in which the effort is 'to transform the patient in his own eyes into a closed system in need of servicing.' (1961c, p. 376)

9. The Game: Face-to-face conduct is conceived in certain ways as a game in order to label some properties of an 'encounter.' The sources of 'fun in games' is used to derive 'euphoria' in an encounter. (1961, p. 79)

Some of the fascination with Goffman's work flows from his taking situations or concepts and applying them in contexts which slightly violate conventional conceptions of what labels apply to what kind of phenomena. In many ways, Goffman takes Burke's preachments on perspective by incongruity seriously:

Planned incongruity should be deliberately cultivated for the purpose of experimentally wrenching apart all those molecular combinations of adjective and noun, substantive and verb, which still remain with us.

Let us contrive . . . [a] multitude of imperfect matching, giving scientific terms for words usually treated sentimentally, or poetic terms for the concepts of science, or discussing disease as an accomplishment, or great structures of thought as an oversight, or considering intense ambition or mighty planetary movements as a mere following of the line of least resistance, a kind of glorified laziness.[5]

Why does Goffman seem even to go out of his way to contrive perspectives by incongruity? As Burke well notes, by looking at the familiar through a new set of conc⌐μɨ₃ the taken for granted becomes problematic. Thus, Goffman's analysis of 'cooling the mark out' views the handling of failure as something concertedly to be coped with. The arrangements of everyday life contain built in cooling processes which are not easily seen as problematic. But, the application of the cooling notion to a wide range of social life makes the handling of failure consciously problematic *to Goffman*. Just as foreign travellers and anthropologists often see things as problematic that some circle of natives does not, so Goffman becomes a foreign traveller in his own land by assuming the perspective of a special social process and looking for that process in a variety of places. Messinger *et al*. have made much the same point when they note that by looking at social life through the perspective of the theatre, Goffman is able to stop taking for granted what his subjects do take for granted.[6] Goffman is never very explicit about what he is up to, but sometimes he hints:

Now it should be admitted that this attempt to press a mere analogy so far was in part a rhetoric and a maneuver.

This report is not concerned with aspects of theater that creep into everyday life. It is concerned with the structure of social encounters. (1959, p. 254)[7]

Perspective by incongruity has, however, its liabilities. It is rather easy simply to misread his intentions.[8] And, associated with misreading, is *ambiguity* in trying to pin down exactly what a given concept might mean. Thus, what is really meant in referring to people as Goffman does in his article, "The Nature of Deference and Demeanor", as 'ritually sacred objects'? Or, in *Encounters*, what can really be meant by saying there is a 'membrane' around an encounter?

STRUCTURE

Having described one of the more obvious features of Goffman's early work, we turn to the meaty business of formal structure. By the term 'formal structure' I refer to the range of concerns conventionally considered in the logic of theory building and testing. What is Goffman doing when viewed from a conventional perspective on theory construction?

DEFINITIONS

Most fundamentally he is propounding large numbers of (many new) terms and definitions. These are mostly concepts that denote some aspect of interpersonal conduct. For example, 'The Nature of Deference and Demeanor' opens with definitions and illustrations of rule, obligation, expectation, symmetrical and asymmetrical rules, substance, ceremony, ceremonial idiom, and the like. The essay, 'On Face-work', opens with several pages of definitions and illustrations of line, face, have or be in face, to be in wrong face, to be out of face, to lose face, to give face, expressive order, face-work, and the like. Some of these concepts are then used in the sections that follow, but, often, many are simply 'dropped' into the text and *not* taken up at a later point. Sometimes terms are introduced, defined and illustrated in the middle of an analysis and then ignored. For example, in that essay the following is 'dropped' but not used:

> When a person manifests these compunctions primarily from duty to himself, one speaks in our society of *pride*; when he does so because of duty to wider social units, and receives support from these units in doing so, one speaks of *honor*. When these compunctions have to do with postural events derived from the way in which a person handles his body, his emotions and the things with which he has physical contact, one speaks of *dignity*. (1955, p. 215, emphasis added)

INSIGHTS

There are also occasional paragraphs which begin an idea that is not developed further in that particular publication. These simply lie there, or are brushed aside with a phrase such as 'these are questions for more refined analysis', (1956a, p. 476). Such embryonic ideas usually occur at the beginning of a paper such that one forms the impression of a page virtually bristling with insights.

TYPES

The bulk of any given piece of Goffman's work is taken up with more or less elaborate enumerations of types and kinds of things that can happen in a situation.[9] These types and kinds are assigned names that usually derive from an incongruous model and from the more flashy portions of the English language. Typically, at least three-quarters of the space in any one piece is devoted to laying out categories of kinds of *sources* of occurrences, *forms* of occurrences, kinds of *consequences* of occurrences, ways of *preventing* occurrences, and forms of *dealing* with occurrences. Some pieces do not focus on occurrences, but explicate kinds of rules in face-to-face conduct. Consider the structure manifest in but these two illustrations:

'On Face-Work' (1955)

3 Types of face (pp. 213–14).
4 Consequences of being out of or in wrong face (p. 214).
2 Basic kinds of face-work (pp. 217–21).
5 Kinds of avoidance processes (pp. 217–19).
3 Phases of the Corrective Process (pp. 219–22).
5 Ways an offering can be accepted (p. 221).

The Presentation of Self in Everyday Life (1959)

4 Types of precaution practices (pp. 13–14).
2 Parts of front (pp. 22–25).
2 Alternative parts of front (pp. 22–25).
6 Discrepancies between appearances and reality (pp. 43–48).
3 Groups of minor events which can disrupt a projected definition (p. 52).

2 Functions which must be performed on a team (pp. 98–99).
3 Dimensions of variation of a position on a team (pp. 99–104).
2 Types of regions (p. 107).
2 Types of standards in the front region (pp. 107–8).
6 Forms of decorum (ends list with "etc.") (pp. 109–10).
3 Limitations on backstage informality (pp. 129–32).
3 Controls over access to the front region (pp. 137–39).
4 Ways of managing breakdown in audience segregation (pp. 139–40).
6 Types of team secrets (pp. 141–44).
11 Discrepant roles (pp. 144–61).
4 Types of communication incompatible with the fostered impression (pp. 169–207).
7 Ways of derogating the audience (pp. 171–75).
5 Types of staging cues (pp. 177–84).
5 Subtypes of one type of team collusion (pp. 186–87).
4 Principal forms of performance disruptions (pp. 208–11).
4 Types of scenes (pp. 210–11).
3 Defensive attributes and practices to insure the show (pp. 212–28).

The main effort is clearly that of delineating categories of types and kinds of events, roles, rules, and so on. Each category is usually given one or more illustrations, sometimes drawing from a wide variety of contexts and historical periods, bringing together seemingly disparate incidents, activities and reflections into a single model of interest at the moment.[10]

Most of the types Goffman describes seem to have the status of *postulation*. It is asserted there are X kinds of a given phenomenon. For example the statement that when a person enters an encounter he takes on three involvement obligations (1957, p. 47–9) does not seem to be a statement to be tested, but rather an assertion, firstly, that these can be identified, and secondly, that they are important considerations in looking at an encounter. This kind of activity seems to have the same logical status as asserting that there are norms, social groups, and the like. They are not assertions to be proven or 'tested' in the conventional sense. They are, rather, postulates upon which an analysis is based. They are, presumably, retained or not depending upon how fruitful a slice they seem to make in approaching solutions to given theoretical problems.

Recognising this extensive positing of types we can go on to raise some of the problems of this procedure. When one engages in the building of types a decision must be made as to how concerned one is going to be about the logical relations *among* the types. In one direction, the types can become almost dictated by a concern that there be a logical relation among them. This is manifest in the procedure of *typologising* so extensively practiced by Talcott Parsons at a relatively abstract level and by certain survey analysts at a less abstract level. Typology has the elegance of deriving a discrete and finite number of types from a given number of dimensions. The other direction is to be unconcerned with the dimensions which specify the relations among categories. One is concerned, rather, with staying 'close to the data' and letting the material dictate the categories, without much concern with the underlying relations among the types. The implicit assertion seems to be that there is no reason to assume that the world comes in logically interrelated categories, or in the number of categories dictated by a procedure such as typologising. The early Goffman seems strongly to move in this latter direction, a direction called, derisively, 'type atomism'. It is worthy of note, however, that pieces of reality come in only two, three, four or a few more forms for Goffman. Are these smaller numbers reflective of 'raw reality' itself or simply of Goffman's preferences?

THEORY

These considerations bring us to the question of what is a theory and whether or not the early Goffman is constructing theory. I will here refer to a 'theory' as a set of substantively interrelated propositions which purport to specify the conditions under which some determinate phenomenon varies. On this understanding, it is necessary to suggest that Goffman delineates various types of phenomenon but he does not very much offer reasons why one rather than another type will occur. Put another way, he engages in explicating sources of outcomes, outcomes themselves, and modes of dealing with outcomes, but he rarely offers reasons (propositions) for the appearance of an outcome. It is the typical absence of such statements that deny the early Goffman's analyses the status of theory. Let us examine Goffman's essay, 'On Cooling the Mark Out', in this light. The phenomenon addressed is loss of a role which involves humiliation for the person deprived. Goffman sees this as posing four problems about the 'self in society', two of which are:

1. What are the ways in which persons are 'cooled out'? (1952, pp. 492–6)
2. What can happen if a person refuses to be cooled? (1952, pp. 496–8)

The first question is answered by listing six 'common ways in which individuals are cooled out' (1952, p. 492). These ways become necessary because the 'mark' has defined himself in a way that it is impossible for the facts to support within his existing frame of reference. The job of the cooler is to supply the mark with a 'new set of apologies'. These ways are: (1) giving the cooling job to someone with a 'status relative to the mark's' which will 'serve to ease the situation in some way' (1952, p. 493); (2) providing the mark with an alternative status, a something to become; (3) offering him another chance to qualify; (4) allowing the mark to explode and simmer down; (5) stalling the mark by giving him no target at which to direct his feelings, thus giving him time to become accustomed to his new conception of self; and (6) bribing the mark by maintaining the fiction of voluntary removal from the role.

Four possible lines of action are offered as ways the mark can act if he refuses to be cooled: (1) go into sustained personal disorganisation; (2) raise a squawk to the authorities; (3) turn sour by accepting the alternative role offered but withdrawing all enthusiasm from playing it; and (4) go into business for himself by creating a new group in which he has a status similar to the one he has lost.

This is as far as an analysis by the early Goffman typically goes. He does not go on to ask: 'What are the conditions under which one or another way of cooling the mark will be employed?', but, rather and simply: 'What are the ways in which a mark can be cooled?'. He does not ask: 'What are the conditions under which the mark will refuse to be cooled?' and, 'What are the conditions under which one way rather than another will be the mode of refusing to be cooled?', but, rather, and simply: 'What are the ways the mark can act in refusing to be cooled?'.

This is not to say that he *should* pose these 'conditional' questions. He is explicit in never setting such tasks for himself. It is to say, instead, that under the conception of theory used here, the early

Goffman is not propounding full theory. Nonetheless, the step he does take is a necessary first step in developing theory. He may, in this sense, be making important contributions in the *direction* of theory.

PROPOSITIONS

Although there may be little theory in this strict sense, there remains a question of whether or not propositions or empirical generalisations are present. As indicated, there are very many empirical assertions on the order of 'X exists', but these are not propositions in the narrow theoretical sense.[11] Rather, I am asking, are there propositions in the sense of assertions containing two concepts (or variables) said to be correlated? There do not seem to be many, but they do occur. They are difficult to find, at first, because they are not stated as explicit hypotheses. They emerge as the overall argument of a paper or section that has been devoted to documenting kinds of things. Thus:

1. *If* persons are embedded in situated activity systems, *then* they will inject other identities into the system to show they are not only what the situation implies. (1961a, 1961c)

2. *If* persons are to abide by the rules of interaction and treat one another relatively well, *then* they must treat each other as ritually sacred objects. (1955, p. 227; 1956a, p. 497)

3. *If* a fostered impression is to survive, *then* the audience must exercise tact in receiving it. (1959, pp. 229–34)

4. *If* persons are placed in total institutions, *then* their selves will be mortified. (1961c, pp. 3–169)

5. *If* persons are placed in total institutions, *then* they will develop secondary adjustments to protect themselves from the identity implications of the organisation's theory of human nature. (1961c, pp. 186–9)

6. *If* an impression is to be fostered without large disruption, *then* the performers must be loyal, disciplined, and practice circumspection. (1959, Ch. VI)

7. *If* a situation does not allow a person to present any of his selves appropriately, *then* there will be an oscillation of selves

presented and this oscillation will give rise to embarrassment.
(1956b)

8. *If* a person defines himself in a way that cannot be supported
   by the facts of the situation, *then* he will be humiliated and
   have to be offered a set of apologies with which to adapt
   himself to his humiliation and his new role (he will have to be
   cooled out). (1952)

To summarise, it seems reasonable to conclude that even though
there are a number of propositions, the central pre-occupation is
with sociological taxonomy,[12] rather than sociological theory. It is
taxonomy in the sense that the subject of inquiry is dimensions of
social life, rather than laws (propositions) about social life. The unit
of the typical sentence is a definition rather than a proposition
(A = df B, rather than If X then Y). The overall system is a
conceptual scheme or frame of reference rather than a theory. Early
Goffman provides us with something like a long 'shopping list' with
which to perform sociological analysis. And, he performs a kind of
abstract ethnography organised around his own concepts rather
than around those of a particular set of 'natives'.

FORMALISM AND NATURALISM

A final comment. The 'naturalistic' position the early Goffman
seems at times to espouse is in one significant respect not as 'natural'
as he sometimes appears to believe.[13] He may 'stand close' to his
data and have relatively little concern with the logical derivation of
his categories, but precisely because the bulk of his work is the
spinning out of categories, it might be suggested that even the early
Goffman is a formalist of the first rank. Indeed, insofar as there is
simple spinning of categories without much use of them to solve
theoretical problems, one might argue that the early Goffman was
the most formalistic sociologist of his time, surpassing even his chief
competitor, Tarcott Parsons.

SUBSTANCE

What substance is the early Goffman talking about, and what
imagery is he employing in going about it? There appear to be two

basic sets of questions or substantive areas of concern. One is obvious enough; the study of face-to-face conduct, or the encounter. The other is perhaps less apparent; the study of the self in society.

THE ENCOUNTER

In the early period, Goffman believes that sociologists have not dealt with the phenomenon of persons coming together for rather short periods of time and maintaining a 'continuous engrossment in [an] official focus of activity'. (1961, p. 11). In·a series of papers and monographs[14] he argues that situations of face-to-face talk are 'members of a single natural class, amenable to a single framework of analysis'.[15] He calls this unit the encounter.

I will not here review the elaborate collection of categories and properties pertaining to the encounter. My purpose, instead, is to explicate the imagery in terms of which it is conceived and to ferret out the main classes of questions that are posed regarding it.

Although Goffman's work is unique and unusual in some ways, his main question about that tiny social system, the encounter, is an ancient and honoured puzzlement. Digging under the incongruities and categories, we find him posing the Hobbesian problem of social order.[16] But, instead of asking how society in general is possible, he asks: how is sustained social interaction possible? How are encounters possible and how are they maintained?

> The conventions regarding the structure of occasions of talk represent an effective solution to the problem of organising a flow of spoken messages. In attempting to discover *how it is that these conventions are maintained in force* as guides to action, one finds evidence to suggest a functional relationship between the structure of the self and the structure of spoken interaction. (1955, p. 227, emphasis added)

> If he and the others were not socialised in this way, interaction in most societies, and most situations would be a much more hazardous thing for feelings and faces. The person would find it impractical to be oriented to symbolically conveyed appraisals of social worth, or to be possessed of feelings – that is, it would be impractical for him to be a ritually delicate object. And as I shall suggest, *if the person were not a ritually delicate object, occasions of talk could not be organised in the way they usually are.* (1955, pp. 224–5, emphasis added)

I am not so much concerned with Goffman's solution to the problem of face-to-face order as with noting that it lurks at the bottom of his conceptualisation of the encounter. Lurking there, it renders more intelligible the further modes of his analysis. *One part* of his solution, however, does not seem substantially to differ from the one offered by Durkheim, and Parsons after him. Persons much of the time act according to shared and internalised rules. Much of the writing on the encounter is a documentation of kinds of rules.[17]

Nonetheless, Goffman does not fully adopt the Durkheimian solution. Order in the encounter remains *almost* fundamentally problematic. And herein lies the dynamic of the face-to-face contact. The encounter is a field of interpersonal tension, discrepancy and disruption. For Goffman, organised talk remains a difficult task, labouring under a constant barrage of forces striving to break down any current organisation. There is, indeed, an implicit assertion that encounters have a 'natural' tendency to break down and become disorganised. Hard labour must be put into this little interpersonal system in order to keep it going:

> These two tendencies . . . form the bridge that people *build to one another*, allowing them to meet for a moment of talk in a communion of reciprocally sustained involvement. (1957, p. 49, emphasis added)

> Conjoint involvement appears to be a *fragile* thing, with standard points of *weakness and decay*, a *precarious unsteady state* that is likely at any time to lead the individual into some form of alienation. (1957, p. 49, emphasis added)

> Given the fact that the individual effectively projects a definition of the situation when he enters the presence of others, we can assume that events will occur within the interaction which *contradict, discredit, or otherwise throw doubt upon this projection*. (1959, p. 12, emphasis added)

The dependent variable becomes the maintenance of a given face-to-face activity system (an encounter). Attention turns to the independent variables of factors breaking down a definition of the situation, or a given reality. Note that he might instead focus on factors sustaining or maintaining an encounter. But the choice is, by and large, to approach maintenance from the opposite direction. He looks for tension, discrepancy and disruption.

By listening for this dissonance [embarrassment], the sociologist can generalise about the ways in which interaction can go awry and, by implication, the conditions necessary for interaction to be right. (1956b, p. 265)

Detailed analysis appears to be organised around the following sets of questions. These are questions that come up in each piece regardless of the substantive dimensions of the encounter being posited at the moment:

1. What are *sources* of given kinds of tensions, discrepancy or disruption? What are the kinds of things which beset a given mutually sustained reality? Each piece gives somewhat different answers to these questions, but the general answer is, usually, the existence of a discrepancy between the persons' actual focus of cognitive attention and the official focus being maintained in the encounter at the time, (1961, pp. 41–5, 54). Dimensions of this discrepancy appear to be alienation (1957, pp. 49–53), embarrassment (1956b, pp. 268–9), aggressive face-work (1955, pp. 221–2), and the like. A somewhat different kind of source resides in the fact that in maintaining a definition of the situation, 'representation of an activity will vary in some degree from the activity itself and therefore inevitably misrepresent it' (1959, p. 65). This gives rise to various types of 'discrepant facts' which threaten the system (1959, pp. 43–6).

2. What are the *kinds* of tension, discrepancy or disruption? The sources tend to be transformed into kinds of tensions existing within the encounter. They now have a different status. They are no longer incipient, but are lodged in the ongoing system itself. Whatever may be the source of disruption, they subsequently appear in the encounter, transformed and existing anew in their own right, (1959, pp. 208–12). There are, thus, kinds of threat to face (1955, pp. 217–19; 221–2) and forms of alienation (1957, pp. 49–53).

3. What are *consequences* of tension, discrepancy and disruption, and what are ways in which the participants in the encounter *prevent, reduce and cope with* these problems? If these kinds of things erupt into the encounter (#2 above), what are the kinds of things that can happen to the person felt to be responsible for them, and to the others present who witness the disruption? This leads to delineating consequences such as 'the repercussive character of involvement offenses' (1957, pp. 53–4); 'flooding out' (1961b, p. 55); and discrediting.

The consequences of unchecked tension, discrepancy or disruption are seen as most severe:

> Unless the disturbance is checked, unless the interactants regain their proper involvement, the illusion of reality will be shattered, the minute social system that is brought into being with each encounter will be disorganised, and the participants will feel unruled, unreal and anomic. (1957, p. 59)

But, the system is viewed as constantly at work to insure that the problems which beset it never become acute. There are, on the one hand, activities carried on to insure that sources never get activated. If they are activated, mechanisms operate to prevent their eruption into the system itself. Thus,

> One cannot judge the importance of definitional disruptions by the frequency with which they occur, for apparently they would occur more frequently were not constant precautions taken. We find that preventive practices are constantly employed to avoid these embarrassments. (1959, p. 13)

Among these 'preventive practices' are careful instilling of discipline, loyalty, and circumspection into the interactants (1959, pp. 212-28). Another form is cooperative work in which each person engages in letting each other person sustain the self he has projected into the encounter (e.g. 1955, pp. 223-5). These, however, seem assigned less importance in maintaining the system than practices of coping with problems once they have erupted. Persons thus act to protect the system from the problem they are causing. They act, for example, to conceal embarrassment (1956b, pp. 266-8), or affect involvement even though they are alienated in one or another way (1957, pp. 54-6).

Even more important than what a person alone can do to protect the reality being sustained, are the actions taken by the others present. The encounter is viewed as *mutually* sustained and as requiring the cooperation of others if it is to exist at all. Thus, others are said to act in a tactful way by overlooking or ignoring disruptions or by not taking actions which cause them (e.g. 1959, pp. 14, 229-33) and for responses to 'flooding out' (1961b, pp. 58-60).

If it becomes impossible to employ these practices and some

official (open) cognizance must be given the tension or disruption, the participants can engage in 'corrective practices'. The offense is acknowledged by the offender and others, and promises offered and accepted to produce no further threat (1955, pp. 220–1). If the load on the system is very great, threat may be 'integrated' into the encounter, causing the system to take on a new structure with a new set of rules (1961b, pp. 48–55).

This, then, stripped of its embroidery is the way in which this unit called the encounter is conceived. It would seem to be, fundamentally, a boundary-maintaining system'.[18]

THE SELF

Recognising the encounter, I want now to suggest that attention given it is but another of the indirections employed by Goffman in getting at what is, in fact, the central concern of his early work: the self in society.

The concept of self seems to be the only one that appears throughout his early work. It is in its terms that the early corpus of his writing is most unified and explicable. His seemingly disparate writings on adaptation to failure, class symbols, the mental hospital, the encounter, stigma and other topics are part of a single effort unified by a small set of abiding ideas about the self.

Conceptions of the 'self' travel under a variety of names in Goffman's early work, but refer to only two basic notions. One of these is the 'official self' called also the 'situated self', 'the virtual self in context', 'character', and 'face'. These various names refer to selves as located and contained in the social situation. This official self is conceived as existing apart from persons. Persons only perform them or play them out. The theatrical model in *The Presentation of Self in Everyday Life* (1959) is perhaps the most obvious rendition of the 'official self'. But it is otherwise ubiquitous. Referring to formal organisations:

> The self . . . can be seen as something that resides in the arrangements prevailing in a social system for its members. The self in this sense is not a property of the persons to whom it is attributed, but dwells rather in the pattern of social control that is exerted in connection with the person by himself and those around him. This special kind of institutional arrangement does not so much support the self as constitute it. (1961c, p. 168).

Selves reside in roles:

> Personal qualities effectively imputed and effectively claimed, combine with a position's title, when there is one, to provide a basis of *self-image* for the incumbent and a basis for the image that his role others will have of him. A self, then, virtually awaits the individual entering a position; he need only conform to the pressures on him and he will find a *me* ready-made for him. In the language of Kenneth Burke doing is being. (1961a, pp. 87–8).

Even in what is sometimes seen as the flow, flux and spontaneity of face-to-face interaction, there are selves awaiting those who enter it:

> The person's face [*viz*, official self] clearly is something that is not lodged in or on his body, but rather something that is diffusely located in the flow of events in the encounter. (1955, p. 214)

> During interaction the individual is expected to possess certain attributes, capacities, and information which, taken together, fit together into a self that is at once coherently unified and appropriate for the occasion. (1956b, p. 268).

Underlying, or over against, this official self is a second conception of the self, called variously the 'self as performer', 'our all-too-human selves', and 'self as player'. This second conception is always spoken of in contrast to the official self. There is:

> A crucial discrepancy between our all-too-human selves and our socialised selves. As human beings we are presumably creatures of variable impulse with moods and energies that change from one moment to the next. As characters put on for an audience, however, we must not be subject to ups and downs, (1959, p. 56).

Whenever the playing out of an official self is in some way disrupted

> The individual who performs the character will be seen for what he largely is, a solitary player involved in a harried concern for his production. Behind many masks and many characters, each performer tends to wear a single look, a naked unsocialised look,

a look of concentration, a look of one who is privately engaged in
a difficult treacherous task, (1959, p. 235).

The performing self is seen as a rather sullen, plodding being. He is,
in his 'back region' moments, an a-social creature who lapses into
'silent irritability', (1959, p. 132).[19]

Beginning with these two conceptions of self, two basic problems
form the conceptual substrata of Goffman's early work: (1) What
are the conditions of being able to perform and sustain a given
official self? Stated in reverse, what are the things that disrupt the
maintenance of a given official self? (2) Somehow, the official and
performing selves never quite 'fit'. What are the consequences of
this discrepancy?

   1. It can now be seen why the encounter is a major focus. Even
though the encounter is a system which strives to maintain itself,
official selves are built into it. Anything, therefore, that threatens
the stability of the encounter *also* threatens the selves residing in the
encounter.

> The elements of a social encounter . . . . . . consist of effectively
> projected claims to an acceptable self and the confirmation of like
> claims on the part of others. (1956b, p. 268)

> The organisation of an encounter and the definition of the
> situation it provides turn upon the conceptions the participants
> have concerning the identity of the participants and the identity
> of the social occasion of which the encounter is seen as a part.
> These identities are the organisational hub of the encounter.
> Events which cause trouble do not merely add disruptive noise
> but often convey information that threatens to discredit or
> supplant the organising identities of the interaction. Hence, such
> events, however small in themselves, can weaken the whole
> design of the encounter, leaving the participants bewildered
> about what next to do, *or what next to try to be.* (1961, pp. 43–4,
> emphasis added)

Among the sustaining work contributed to an encounter is the
performing self's standing guard on the expressive implications of
each occurrence, making sure that each occurrence is consistent
with the official self that has been assumed or alloted. (1961, p. 99;
1955, p. 215) Another sustaining factor has to do with what Goffman

calls 'a characteristic obligation of many social relationships' wherein each participant 'guarantees' to support the official self that each of the other participants has assumed (1955, p. 229; also, 1955, p. 215; 1956b, p. 268).

But Goffman is not so much concerned with conditions sustaining official selves as with circumstances which disrupt them. Much of his work on encounters is most usefully read as an elaborate listing of ways in which official selves can become disorganised in interaction, and ways in which performing selves can prevent or correct for the disorganisation. The focus of *The Presentation of Self in Everyday Life*, (1959) is phrased in terms of the fostering and disruption of impressions. That phrasing can, as well, be read as the fostering and disruption of official selves. The essay, 'On Cooling the Mark Out', likewise addresses the disruption of official selves: 'He has defined himself as possessing a certain set of qualities then proven to himself that he is miserably lacking in them. This is a process of self-destruction of the self.' (1952, p. 485). The concern with official and performing selves is, of course, clearest and most explicit in the work on mental hospitals, or, more generally, 'total institutions' . Total institutions assume importance precisely because they are places in which selves are assaulted and disrupted. Such places make profoundly problematic relations between official selves and the performing self. The papers on total institutions are documentations of ways in which official selves are both attacked and laid on and of ways in which the performers deal with these assaults, (1961c, esp. pp. 23, 35, 179–81, 186–89, 248, 318–20, 358, 376–7).

One synthesis of these concerns occurs in the essay, 'The Nature of Deference and Demeanor', (1956a). Interpersonal conduct is discussed, note, with particular reference to a mental hospital setting. The official self is conceived as a sacred object, a ceremonial thing which has to be treated with proper ritual care if it is to be sustained. Therefore:

As a means through which this self is established, the individual acts with proper demeanor while in contact with others and is treated by others with deference. It is just as important to see that if the individual is to play this kind of sacred game, then the field must be suited to it. The environment must ensure that the individual will not pay too high a price for acting with good demeanor and that deference will be accorded him. Deference and demeanor practices must be institutionalised so that the individual will be able to project a viable, sacred self and stay in the game on a proper ritual basis. (1956a, p. 497)

Goffman then suggests that some mental hospitals are places in which those persons who are least ready to take up appropriate, social adult (official) selves 'are lodged in a milieu where it is practically impossible to do so' (1956a, p. 497). To be an appropriately demeaned person giving appropriate deference requires a range of self-determination and access to a variety of 'identity equipment'. When these are absent the grounds for sustaining an adult official self are absent. (1956a, p. 498; see also; 1961c, pp. 168–9)

This, then, is one of the central problems around which Goffman's work seems to revolve.

2. The way Goffman seems to see it, there is never much of a 'fit' between the official self offered in a situation and the person's performing self. Persons are always straining at the boundaries of the official self provided for them. They constantly attempt to express something more, or something else, than the situation officially requires or allows. Goffman has given particular attention to two forms of this straining: role distance and organisational underlives.[20]

Role distance is the interposition or interjection into a situation of elements of 'officially irrelevant official selves' in order to demonstrate that the performer is not only what the current official self implies:

> This 'effectively' expressed pointed separateness between the individual and his putative role I shall call *role distance*. A shorthand is involved here: the individual is actually denying not the role but the virtual self that is implied in the role for all accepting performers, (1961, p. 108).

> The image of him that is generated for him by the routine entailed in his mere participation – his virtual self in the context – is an image from which he apparently withdraws by actively manipulating the situation, (1961, p. 107).

When one watches the performance of any official self, he will see not only the performance of that official self, but the juggling of a

whole range of selves within the context of the officially activated
self. 'One ends up by watching a dance of identification'. (1961,
p. 144)

Another form of straining appears whenever the official selves
available to the participants are covertly or overtly denied by the
persons who have had the given official selves laid on them. All
organisations (especially total institutions) are conceived as places
where programmes of expected activity are laid down and contain
within them a theory of the nature of the performers (an 'organisational theory of human nature'). Compliance, therefore, has this
meaning: 'To engage in a particular activity in the prescribed spirit
is to accept being a particular kind of person in a particular kind of
world' (1961c, p. 186). And so, in every 'social establishment' there
is likely to be some opposition to the programme of officially
available selves:

> We find that the participants decline in some way to accept the
> official view of what they should be putting into and getting out of
> the organisation and, behind this, of what sort of self and world
> they are to accept for themselves. (1961c, p. 304)

Defaulting from the official self and its world is the way in which the
performing selves 'dodge' the identities offered to them. The
counter-official activities carried on in organisations are seen as
ways in which extra-official identities are generated and maintained as a form of opposition to official identities.

> To forego prescribed activities, or to engage in them in unpre-
> scribed ways or for unprescribed purposes is to withdraw from the
> official self and the world officially available to it. To prescribe
> activity is to prescribe a world, to dodge a prescription can be to
> dodge an identity. (1961c, p. 187)

In organisations 'we find a multitude of homely little histories, each
in its way a movement of liberty. Whenever worlds are laid on,
underlives develop.' (1961c, p. 305)

These two sets of concerns about the self would seem, then, to be
at least a part of the abiding and underlying concerns of early
Goffman.

SOUL

We must go on, however, to see that at least a third conception of the self has crept into the discussion of official and performing selves. This implicit third notion is bound up with a consideration of Goffman's root image of human life and functioning. To assert continuing default from the official self is to make assumptions about the nature of the creature doing the defaulting. Traditionally, sociologists have dealt with defaulting by reference to such ideas as incomplete socialisation or role conflict. They have tried to explain it within a sociological framework *via* the assumption that persons are only what social life makes them. Goffman questions these explanations and their assumptions and removes the explanation from the preserve of sociology, even though he is, at other times, quite concerned to press to the ultimate a sociological conception of persons.[21] At crucial concluding moments, Goffman suddenly becomes extra-sociological and asserts it to be the nature of humans to be recalcitrant. The human should be defined:

> As a stance-taking entity, a something that takes up a position somewhere between identification with an organisation and opposition to it, and is ready at the slightest pressure to regain its balance by shifting its involvement in either direction, (1961c, p. 320).

A third notion of the self is involved in this imagery of humankind's nature. It is this third notion that Goffman refers to as 'selfhood' or 'personal identity'. Out of the conflict between official selves laid on and the performing self comes the 'sense of selfhood', 'conception of one's self', or 'personal identity'. The idea of selfhood is implicit when he says that 'it is . . . *against something* that the self can emerge'. (1961c, p. 320) Further:

> Our sense of being a person can come from being drawn into a wider social unit; our sense of selfhood can arise through the little ways in which we resist the pull. Our status is backed by the solid buildings of the world, while our sense of personal identity often resides in the cracks, (1961c, p. 320).

Personal identity is also, perhaps, the most important result of role distance:

If an individual is to show he is a 'nice guy' or, by contrast, one much less nice than a human being need be, then it is through his using or not using role distance that this is likely to be done. It is right here, in manifestations of role distance, that the individual's personal style is to be found, (1961, p. 152).

The idea of the human as a 'stance-taking entity' may seem foreign to sociology. It is appropriate, therefore, to trace further what kind of philosophical roots the idea may have, and what sort of sociology it may represent.

Although Goffman's intellectual ancestors are primarily sociologists, his work shares much with existentialism, particularly the variety propounded by Sartre. This can be seen from the congruence of their conceptions of humans. Abraham Kaplan has succinctly summarised the existentialist image. Note the similarity between this imagery and the notion of a 'stance-taking entity'.

Because man's existence precedes his essence, no definition of man is possible. This is the core of the existentialist's conception of human nature. If man is to be defined, it must be as the being who defies definition. If a philosopher were to define man as being of such and such a kind, man, on hearing the definition, would surely make something else of himself, if for no other reason than to spite the philosopher. The fact that man is capable of such an act of spite is just what constitutes his humanity.[22]

Further, for Goffman, action is being. To engage in a particular kind of activity is to be that kind of person. (eg., 1961c, pp. 187–8) On this, Sartre and Goffman are inseparable. These famous sentences by Sartre could as well be by Goffman:

Man is nothing else but that which he makes of himself. That is the first principle of existentialism.

What we mean to say is that a man is no other than a series of undertakings, that he is the sum, the organisation, the set of relations that constitute these undertakings.[23]

If being is defined by action, then qualities imputed to persons are the result of action. They need not be seen as somehow adhering 'to' or 'inside' the person. Thus, in the existentialist view, ' . . . the coward makes himself cowardly, the hero makes himself heroic; and . . . there is always a possibility for the coward to give up cowardice and for the hero to stop being a hero'.[24] Qualities reside in definitions of acts, not in the character of the persons who perform acts. Goffman parallels these ideas in his notion of the blank, performer self who is, after all, *nothing*. He performs given official selves and is presumed, by Goffman, to be free to project almost any available self.

Such congruences make it possible, then, to suggest that early Goffman's work represents, at least in part, an existentialist sociology[25]

Allow me to conclude with a suggestion of a different kind, one relating more to moral impulses than to images of humans and action. The protection and fostering of human dignity and freedom is a central concern of existentialism. The problems posed by early Goffman and the comments sprinkled throughout his texts point strongly to human freedom and dignity as animating moral impulses. It is difficult to view his extended concern with disruption of selves, personal identity, and the like, as a dispassionate, merely professional pursuit. His treatments of psychiatry, mental hospitals and the problems of the stigmatised continue to stand as some of the most sophisticated and most penetrating social criticism and commentary. *Asylums* (1961c) has even become a standard reference in the work of criticising the psychiatric establishment, and the 'medical model'. It has become so, it would seem, not only because of its sheer reportage and analysis, but also because of the cool, controlled moral outrage with which it is suffused, the persistent (but not shrill) demand for human dignity that it makes. Even the most mundane of his dissections of everyday life are shot through with a critical stance. He deals deftly with what is conventionally identified as hypocrisy, sham and covert coercion.

I suspect I am not alone in knowing people who have been deeply moved upon reading *Stigma* (1963) and other of his works. These people recognised themselves and others and saw that Goffman was articulating some of the most fundamental and painful of human social experiences. He showed them suddenly that they were not alone, that someone else understood what they know and felt. *He* knew and expressed it beautifully, producing in them joy over pain understood and appreciated, an inextricable mixture of happiness and sadness, expressed in tears.

I suspect that I am not alone in knowing people who have gained from his writings, too, an exhilarating sense of their own possibilities for personal freedom, the existential vision that the social order is after all constructed and can therefore be dealt with like other constructions.

Humans may be 'nothings', blank ciphers, but they can act to promote and protect their dignity and freedom. In many ways, then, the work of early Goffman can be viewed as a search for the conditions under which mere people can be persons. And, in engaging in that quest, through intimately depicting the quality of human experience, his early work is properly thought of as an existentialist sociology.

EDITIONS OF GOFFMAN'S WORK USED IN THIS CHAPTER

(The dates are taken from the bibliography provided in the *Editor's Introduction*; the pagination for quotations cited in this chapter from the editions shown below).

(1951)   'Symbols of Class Status', *British Journal of Sociology*, Volume II, pp. 294–304.

(1952)   'On Cooling the Mark Out: Some Aspects of Adaptation to Failure', in Arnold M. Rose (ed) *Human Behaviour and Social Processes*, (London; Routledge and Kegan Paul, 1962) pp. 482–505.

(1955)   'On Face-Work: An Analysis of Ritual Elements in Social Interaction', *Psychiatry*, Volume 18, No. 3, (August) pp. 213–231.

(1956a)   'The Nature of Deference and Demeanor', *American Anthropologist*, Volume 58, (June) pp. 473–502.

(1956b)   'Embarrassment and Social Organisation', *American Journal of Sociology*, Volume 62, No. 3, (November) pp. 264–271.

(1957)   'Alienation from Interaction', *Human Relations*, Volume 10, No. 1, pp. 47–60.

(1959)   *The Presentation of Self in Everyday Life*, (Garden City, New York; Doubleday Anchor).

(1961)   *Encounters: Two Studies in the Sociology of Interaction*, (Indianapolis; Bobbs-Merrill).

(1961a)   'Role Distance', in *Encounters* (Goffman, 1961).

(1961b)   'Fun in Games', in *Encounters* (Goffman, 1961).

(1961c)   *Asylums: Essays on the Social Situation of Mental Patients and Other Inmates*, (Garden City, New York; Doubleday Anchor).

(1963)   *Stigma: Notes on the Management of Spoiled Identity*, (Englewood Cliffs; Prentice-Hall).

CHAPTER ENDNOTES

1. See, for example: Victor A. Thompson, *Modern Organization*, (New York: Knopf, 1961) p. 138; Reviews of Goffman by Naegele (1956, R2), and Perry (1956, R3) [see: *Editor's Introduction* for a fuller list in *A Sampler of Reviews*]; Ernest Becker, 'Socialization, Command Performance and Mental Illness', *American Journal of Sociology*, volume LXVII: p. 495 (March, 1962); announcement of the MacIver Award of the American Sociological Association, *American Sociological Review*, Volume 26: p. 834 (December, 1961); Alvin W. Gouldner, 'Anti-Minotaur: The Myth of a Value-Free Sociology', *Social Problems*, Volume 9: p. 208 (Winter, 1962); Sheldon L. Messinger, *et al.*, 'Life as Theater', *Sociometry*, Volume 25: pp. 98–109 (September, 1962).

2. Indeed, this chapter was originally researched and drafted in the Spring of 1962, and is presented here in substantially its original form. An early version is often cited, but the chapter has not, until now, been published. The picture of the style, structure, substance and soul I have drawn here serves only to capture aspects of the relatively youthful Goffman.

3. In conversation, Berkeley, California, March, 1962.

4. Kenneth Burke, *Permanence and Change*, (New York; New Republic, Inc., 1936) p. 119.

5. Burke, op. cit., p. 157, 161.

6. Messinger, *et al.*, op. cit., p. 108.

7. See, also, Goffman (1961c, p. xiv).

8. See Messinger, *et al.*, op. cit.

9. The 'situation' may be an encounter, a situated activity system, a mental hospital (total institution), and so on.

10. Curiously, the stating of the categories laid out in any piece serves rather well as a summary of that piece.

11. For example, the assertion that there are rules of irrelevance that govern what can enter an encounter at any given time, (1961, p. 19).

12. Hans L. Zetterberg, *On Theory and Verification in Sociology*, (New York; Tressler, 1954).

13. Consider these comments:

> Focused gatherings do have unique and significant properties which a *formalistic* game-theoretical view of interaction tends to overlook, (1961, p. 37, emphasis added).

> When *seen up close*, the individual bringing together in various ways all the connections that he has in life, becomes a blur . . . Many who have analysed role have *stood across the street* from the source of their data oriented by William James' *abstract view* of human action, instead of the *lovingly empirical view* established by his younger brother, (1961, p. 143, emphasis added).

> Small group experimenters have certainly *stood up close* to their data but have used a considerable amount of this opportunity to adjust their equipment, (1961, fn. 46, p. 143, emphasis added).

14. In particular, Goffman (1955), (1956a), (1956b), (1957), (1959), and (1961).

15. (1956b, p. 25). See also, (1961, pp. 7–14) for the rationale of this category.

16. Talcott Parsons, *The Structure of Social Action*, (Glencoe; The Free Press, 1949) esp. pp. 89–94.

17. See, especially, the model set out in the 'Formalisations' section of Goffman (1961b).

18. In the sense used by Talcott Parsons, *The Social System*, (Glencoe; The Free Press, 1950) fn. 7, p. 36.

19. See also, (1955, p. 225), where the performing self is seen as 'a kind of player in a ritual game'. There are also a few assertions on the way in which the performing self is itself built up so that it will play and be concerned about official selves: the cipher that is the human is *taught*:

> . . . to have feelings attached to self and a self expressed through face, to have pride, honor, and dignity, to have considerateness, to have tact and a certain amount of poise. These are some of the elements of behaviour which must be built into the person if practical use is to be made of him as an interactant, and it is these elements that are referred to in part when one speaks of universal human nature, (1955, p. 231).

Universal human nature is not a very human thing. By acquiring it, the person becomes a kind of construct, built up not from inner psychic propensities but from moral rules that are impressed on him from without, (1955, p. 231).

20. See also, the (1959) distinction between 'character' and 'performer' (pp. 252–4) and the discussion in Chapters III and IV of the same volume.

21. See, e.g., his discussion of getting 'the ego back into society'. (1961, pp. 120–32) Reference for the discussion above is (1961c, pp. 319–20.

22. Abraham Kaplan, *The New World of Philosophy*, (New York: Random House, 1961) p. 104.

23. Jean Paul Sartre, 'Existentialism as a Humanism', in W. Kaufmann, (ed), *Existentialism from Dostoevsky to Sartre*, (New York: Meridian Books, 1956) p. 291, 301.

24. Sartre, ibid., p. 302.

25. For others, see Kaplan, op. cit., esp. p. 117, on the rich ambiguity of life and 'the masks which all things wear belong to the truth'.

2: Early Goffman and the Analysis of Face-to-Face Interaction in *Strategic Interaction*

By George Psathas

Goffman (1969, p. ix) has told us that his 'ultimate interest [is] . . . to develop the study of face-to-face interaction as a naturally bounded analytically coherent field – a sub-area of sociology.' Given this ultimate interest and acknowledging that the concepts he has presented have been widely used and cited by others in the discipline, I wish to consider how and in what ways his studies develop the field of face-to-face interaction.[1]

I shall examine closely one of his works, *Strategic Interaction*, published in 1969, in order to assess the extent to which his formulations of interaction provide a systematic, coherent and clarifying approach to a theory of face-to-face interaction.[2] The difficulties which are found in this book are, in my view, similar to the confusions found in most of his other treatments of face-to-face interaction. This infrequently cited book contains numerous examples of interaction and proposes some key concepts for the analysis of one type of interaction which is called 'strategic'. Because it is a relatively concise and well-organised statement it is a particularly attractive candidate for analysis. However, it must be noted that Goffman considers his main works in the study of face-to-face interaction to be *Encounters* (1961), *Behavior in Public Places* (1963a), *Interaction Ritual* (1967) and *Relations in Public* (1971). A thorough analysis of his work will require careful study of these and other works in order to adequately represent his position and determine what concepts he has contributed.[3] Such a large undertaking, though long overdue, is nevertheless beyond the scope of this chapter.[4]

Goffman himself tells us that his manner of attack on the subject is not consistent[5] and it is perhaps as true of all his works as it is for the specific papers in *Relations in Public* of which and in which he says:

> Each (paper) develops its own perspective starting from conceptual scratch. And taken together, the six do not purport to cover systematically, exhaustively and without repetition what is common to them. I snipe at a target from six different positions unevenly spaced; there is no pretence at laying down a barrage. The result is chapters, but wayward ones. (1971, Author's Note)

What is the target of these wayward snipings? And is there any integrating framework which could pull them together? Perhaps we should rest content with Goffman's contributions, as the book jacket of *Relations in Public* tells us:

> Like the work of a fine novelist or filmmaker whose descriptive power and eye for significant detail teaches us to see our social world for the first time, this major new book . . . enriches our understanding of our daily lives.

If the intent is to present a novel or film-like view of social life, then criticism can be concerned with style, exposition, faithfulness to reality and the artist's statement about the observed reality. And certainly comments on Goffman's work have considered these aspects of his presentation.[6] Yet Goffman writes as a sociologist and his work is read as sociological work. Therefore, the contributions made to the distinct body of theory and knowledge that are considered sociology also need to be assessed. My major concern is with the basic concepts used to describe and analyse face-to-face interaction since any lack of faithfulness to the phenomena referred to be such concepts can produce a distortion of social reality rather than an accurate reporting.

The failings of Goffman, as I see it, are the failings of field researchers in the symbolic interactionist tradition. Insights are based on commonsense understandings of daily life occurrences, ethnographic descriptions of particular social occasions and settings, the use of broad theoretical concepts, and relatively little development of concepts which can be used transsituationally to analyse the patterns and forms, the routines and their variations, the grounded assumptions made by social actors about themselves, others, and situations which provide the facticity of the world of everyday life.[7]

In contrast, a phenomenologically grounded investigation of face-to-face interaction can contribute to the description and analysis of the occasions, situations, and patterns and elements of interaction and to the concepts to be used to refer to these. The major concern of this paper is with some of the basic concepts developed by Goffman to describe and analyse face-to-face interaction. I shall consider five concepts used to describe the basic moves in 'expression games' and argue that a phenomenological analysis as presented by Schutz, and elaborated by Psathas and Waksler, can contribute to their clarification.[8]

The discussion is restricted to the case of two actors, not only because Goffman does so most frequently but also because the exposition is simplified.

First, it is necessary to distinguish between: (a) the perspective of the acting subject and the sociological observer, (b) the characteristics of the actor, (c) the characteristics of the relation between the actors, (d) the characteristics of the situation, (e) the performance of an act, (f) the interpretation of the other's act and (g) the interpretive schemas which the actors may use to determine the meaning of one another's act. All of these are distinctions which Goffman fails to make theoretically.

When reference is made to the observation of interaction or when it is clear that observations from the viewpoint of a sociological observer are being presented, we must be aware that this situation is analytically different from the actor's perspective of the same interaction.

For example, the sociological observer may attribute to one actor a conscious awareness of the other actor. However, the actual actor may not be aware of the other. In adopting an observer's perspective, it must be kept in mind that it is his judgments and beliefs about the actors and the situation (what constitutes 'knowledge' for him) that is being presented. There may be discrepancies between what he 'knows' and what the actual actors in an existential situation 'know'. The 'observer's perspective on interaction' requires making assumptions about his own (observer's) consciousness *and* both of the actors being observed.

The actor's perspective, on the other hand, requires making assumptions about his own (actor's) consciousness and the other actor. The actor knows his own consciousness directly and the other's indirectly. The observer knows *both* actors only indirectly.

Further, in those situations where interaction is being directly observed, the observer's presence and his identity as observer may or may not be known. Knowledge-of-an-other's-presence is not equivalent to knowledge-of-the-presence-of-the-other-as-observer. Observations reported by observers may need to take into account whether those they observe are aware of their presence and what social identity they attribute to them. But furthermore, concepts developed by observers need to clearly specify whether they apply to both perspectives or only to one. Goffman fails to distinguish clearly and consistently between these two perspectives. Consequently, ambiguities result and the reader is not certain at times whose perspective on the interaction is being taken and whether the shift in perspective has any analytic significance. We shall examine this later when looking at his concept of *unwitting moves*.

In order to clarify a number of issues, I shall present a framework for the analysis of face-to-face interaction developed by Psathas and Waksler based on the conceptual and phenomenological analyses of Schutz.[9] The perspective adopted in this framework is that of the observer and it is the observer who is attributing characteristics to the actors, the situation and the action. The framework considers each of these characteristics separately and shows that a number of elements are attributed by the observer when judgment is made that actors are co-present and interacting. This analysis is based on extensive considerations of face-to-face interaction which are not presented here. My contention is that concepts, developed by observers such as Goffman about face-to-face interaction, must explicitly or do implicitly involve these elements. This is because these elements are present, that is to say, can be analytically differentiated on all occasions when the judgment is made that an actor and an other are involved in face-to-face interaction. I hold that it cannot be otherwise and if the observer does not make some of these attributions then the phenomenon reportedly being studied is not face-to-face interaction.

I. *Characteristics of the Actors*

(Two actors are observed to be present).
A. Each actor is conscious (wide-awake) and aware of his own consciousness.
B. Each actor has constituted a self.
C. Each has acquired and is able to use a stock of knowledge and systems of relevance.
D. Each is able to communicate ('transmit information' in Goffman's terms) and to use (for both transmitting and receiving information) a symbolic system of meaning.
E. Each is motivated to develop and carry out a project of action.
F. Each is aware of his own body as a field of experience.

(In Goffman's terms, expressive messages are known to be 'exuded', whether intended or not, by the body, e.g., eyes, lips, face, gestures.) These pre-conditions refer to the characteristics of the actors as judged by the observer.

II. *Characteristics of the Relation between the Actors*

With regard to the relation between the actors, for face-to-face interaction between consociates:
A. Both actors are present, i.e., share the same time and space. We may wish to describe their interaction when they become contemporaries (sharing time but not space) rather than consociates. However, only consociates can be in the face-to-face situation.
B. Each is aware of the other's bodily presence.
C. Each is aware of the other as a person (with all the characteristics previously described for actors). (Here, it is possible to differentiate those situations when one actor is aware of the other but the other is not aware of him from the situation when they are mutually or reciprocally aware.)
D. Each is aware that the other is conscious of his own bodily presence. (Again, this may be either one-sided or reciprocal.)
E. Each is aware that the other constitutes him as a person, that is, with all the features of an actor previously enumerated.

Under these conditions when awareness is reciprocated, each

actor is able to receive information (whether intended or unintended) about the other's subjective experiences *at the same time that they are occurring*.

We have now described the characteristics of the relation between the actors. When these conditions are present we may refer to the 'face-to-face situation' though interaction has not yet occurred.

III. *Characteristics of the Action*

Now with regard to the action of the actors, we must make some further analytic distinctions. A project of action will be defined, as in Schutz, as a formulated plan of acts known to the actor, imagined as performed, but not yet performed.[10] An act will refer to the completed, performed action arising out of a previously formulated project. When the actor has as an in-order-to motive the bringing about of certain conscious experiences in the other, his project is called an 'affecting-the-other' type of project.[11]

A. Each actor is able to and actually does formulate a project of action of an affecting-the-other type. This may include 'affecting-the-other' such that he will perceive the in-order-to motive only as it is presented and that the other will not look for concealed motives.

B. Each develops an act based on his project of action. Now, we are prepared for the first completed act, manifested in behaviour, by the actor. Up to this point, only unintended expressive messages, not controlled by any formulated project of action may have been generated by one actor and perceived and interpreted by the other.

C. An act is performed. The other perceives the act and interprets it as arising from a project of action. That is, the act is seen as meaningful and an effort is made to understand its meaning. Whether the interpretation is congruent in the sense of being consistent with the intent of the originator in terms of his affecting-the-other project of action or discrepant in the sense of disbelieving the intended interpretation of the act, is another matter.

D. An act is performed by the other. Insofar as the first actor is aware of this act, he also interprets it as arising from a project of action.

Now, I shall consider whether Goffman explicitly or implicitly considers these elements of face-to-face interaction in his analysis of strategic interaction.

In one short section of his essay on expressive games in *Strategic Interaction*, Goffman (1969b) presents concepts to be used in analysing the interaction between two actors, called subject and observer. Although he subsequently uses these same concepts to discuss interaction between persons *not* face-to-face, he does not indicate how such situations differ. He says (1969, p. 140):

> Important applications of strategic interaction involve participants who are not present to each other, and sequences of moves which are not closely bound by time, whereas, generically, face-to-face gatherings entail mutual presence and brief continuities in time. Here, surely is a source of confusion in the social psychological literature. The applicability of the gaming framework to relationships and gatherings, and its great value in helping to formulate a model of the actor who relates and who foregathers, has led to conceptualisations which, too quickly, intermingle matters which must be kept apart, at least initially. Social relationships and social gatherings are two separate and distinct substantive areas; strategic interaction is an analytical perspective which illuminates both but coincides with neither.

Social relationships can be found between individuals whether they are co-present or not whereas the gathering requires the sharing of space and time. Therefore, the framework of strategic interaction can be applied to social relationships which occur or do not occur in social gatherings. We shall have to keep this in mind but for the purposes of this paper focus only on those discussions and analyses of strategic interaction occuring in the face-to-face situation, i.e., when persons are co-present, sharing time and space (as described in II A-E above).

First I shall briefly note that Goffman does not make conceptual and analytical distinctions between the orientation of the actors, the situation, the relation of each actor to the other, and social interaction.

Both Schutz's, and Psathas and Waksler's analyses clearly show that these distinctions are important. Orientation refers to an attitude on the part of the actor, e.g., an 'other orientation'. It is prior to interaction and can be determined only through interpretations made by the observer. It does not necessarily lead to or result in interaction but when interaction of a certain kind occurs it can then become apparent.[12] Goffman lacks such a concept though he assumes that the Other is there for the actor, who, in turn, must be an other for the Other. Since orientation involves awareness and may or may not lead to a formulated and completed action, it is possible to determine that an other-orientation exists for each of the actors, as they can so determine for one another, although interaction does not occur. An other-orientation exists for the actor when he is aware of the other and aware of the other's attention to him. The observer would have to make a judgment about both of the actors in order to say that each has an other orientation.

Situation refers to the presence or absence of others in particular ways. A social gathering, in Goffman's use, involves a situation in which persons are co-present, sharing time and space, and are aware of each other's presence. Copresence for Goffman involves: 'persons must sense that they are close enough to be perceived in whatever they are doing, including their experiencing of others, and close enough to be perceived in this sensing of being perceived' (1963a, p. 17). Gathering refers to 'any set of two or more individuals whose members include all and only those who are at the moment in one another's immediate presence'. Situation refers to 'the full spatial environment anywhere within which an entering person becomes a member of the gathering that is (or does then become) present. Situations begin when mutual monitoring occurs and lapse when the second last person has left', (1963a, p. 18).

A social occasion refers to 'a wider social affair, undertaking, or event, bounded in regard to place and time and typically facilitated by fixed equipment. . . . (it) provides the structuring social context in which many situations and their gatherings are likely to form, dissolve and reform while a pattern of conduct tends to be recognised as the appropriate and (often) official or intended one – examples are a social party . . . a picnic or a night at the opera' (1963a, p. 18).

It seems that Goffman assumes that for the two person gathering, each person is aware of the other's presence and that their action is known to one another. The social gathering involves awareness, an other-orientation, and is interrelated to situation. But awareness and other-orientation do not require copresence whereas situation does. Thus, for Goffman the social gathering and the situation are inextricable and he has difficulty, because he lacks the concept of social relationship, in extricating social relationships from gatherings and situations. The problem this produces will become more apparent when discussing strategic interaction. In other of his writings it is apparent that he lacks a concept of orientation and does not differentiate the characteristics of the social relationship from pre-conditions for interaction. A particularly confusing example is his reference to interaction as involving a single visual and cognitive focus of attention, 'a mutual and preferential openness to communication, an eye-to-eye ecological huddle that maximises each participant's monitoring of him, and a we-rationale, that is, a sense of the single thing that *we* are doing together at the time', (1961, p. 18). Clearly, as Schutz, and Psathas and Waksler show, a visual focus of attention and communication are not necessary for interaction and a 'we-rationale' involves a social relationship which does not necessarily require copresence. His failure to analyse and present the criteria underlying these classifications makes it difficult for us to either advance the taxonomy or extend his analytic schema to new observations.

Turning now to some of the specific concepts which Goffman uses in analysing strategic interaction, I wish to show in detail some of these analytic inconsistencies. First a detailed presentation of some of his key concepts is necessary.

The basic moves which actors can make and which are necessary to understand before concluding that strategic interaction is occurring or has occurred are the following. All quotations are from Goffman's *Strategic Interaction*:

1) *Unwitting move* – 'a subject's observable behavior that is unoriented to the assessment an observer might be making of it' (1969, p. 11).
2) *Naïve move* – 'the assessment an observer makes of a subject when the observer believes that the subject can be taken as he appears, that is, that he is involved in an unwitting move. . . . . . . This is the second move in expression games. It is restricted to observers and is not available to informants, and it is a move that does not distinguish between animate and inanimate subjects' (1969, p. 11).
3) *Control move* – 'The intentional effort of an informant to produce expressions that he thinks will improve his situation if they are gleaned by the observer. . . . . . . Among humans the process is self-conscious and calculated' (1969, p. 12).

'The various processes of control do not strike at the observer's capacity to receive messages, but at . . . his ability to read expressions . . . (since) the observer will have to attend to the expressive aspects of the transmission as a check upon semantic content,' (1969, p. 13).[13]

4) *Uncovering move* – This is performed by the observer who, suspicious of possible deception and misrepresentation by the subject 'attempts to pierce, penetrate, and otherwise get behind the apparent facts in order to uncover the real ones,' (1969, pp. 17–18).

He then proceeds to list and illustrate several types of uncovering moves ranging from interviews and interrogations to body examinations and inquisitions.

5) *Counter-uncovering moves* – subjects, appreciating that they may be suspected of covering may meet uncovering moves with countering actions.

So, here we have 5 basic moves:

Subject	Observer
(1) unwitting move	(2) naïve move
(3) control move	(4) uncovering move
(5) counter-uncovering move	

These are not proposed as a sequence but only that sequences are possible and that certain moves are the subject's and others the observer's.

Using the terminology and analytic distinctions presented above, we can say that Goffman, without direct specification or elaboration, attributes to both actors in the face-to-face situation all the characteristics of the actor and all the characteristics of the relation between the actors which have been presented in Sections I and II above. However, he is ambiguous as to whether he attributes to the actor an awareness that an observer (other) is present *and* observing him in the *unwitting move*. Goffman includes both of these as possibilities and does not consider that the distinction matters.

In Goffman's discussion, there are at times three persons involved – the subject, the other, and a (sociologist) observer.

Goffman considers explicitly only two persons, whom he refers to as 'subject' and 'observer', because it is these persons' efforts to determine what each one's real intentions are that enables a third person, the sociologist observer, to decide if strategic interaction is occurring. The judgment of 'strategic' interaction of various types is a third party's judgment since the actors themselves are not formulating their projects in the same terms or with the same meanings which Goffman (who is the third party) sees in their actions. However, since Goffman refers to one of the parties as 'observer' and says that each is both subject and observer, presumably as one shifts from performing one's own acts to attending to the others' acts, there is a possible confusion introduced. Since the concept 'observer' can be used by Goffman to refer to one of the actors, he can claim to be taking the actor's perspective and presenting only what appears to the actor to be true for him within the situation. Yet, as sociologist observer he must also be present in the situation in order to perceive it. Either he must be referring to situations in which he was the actor and subsequently reflected on his observations of his own and the other's actions, or he has observed two other persons engaged in interaction. Of course, both are possible. However, if one of the actors is referred to as 'observer' it should be noted that this 'observation' is restricted to his awareness and monitoring of the other person with whom he is engaged in interaction and not to the formulation of sociological observations. It is we – and Goffman – who are self-conscious sociologist observers, undertaking to examine the actions of *both* parties with our own in-order-to motives operating. Namely, we are not interested in 'affecting-the-other' type of action but only in remaining oriented to the others' actions and attempting to understand the projects of action which each is formulating and enacting. Our relationship to the actors is a social relationship only if they are aware of us; otherwise it is a non-reciprocated or one sided 'other-orientation'. Our observation is not undertaken in order to then formulate a project of action of an 'affecting-the other' type. Our intentions as (sociologist) third party observers are to understand the actors' relationships and interactions. Our motives, as observers, therefore, are different from those of the actor-as-observer.

But it does matter whether the subject is *aware* of the observer and deliberately does *not* orient his behaviour to the interpretation an observer might make or whether he is *unaware* of the observer and therefore does not orient his behaviour to him. In fact, as Goffman's later discussion shows, it can matter a great deal whether the observer (other) believes the subject knew or did not know of his presence. The subject can be aware of an other person but not be aware of that person's identity as an observer. Thus, when one believes he is alone versus when others are believed to be present constitute, from the standpoint of the acting subject, phenomenologically different situations. And, of course, it matters whether the observer referred to is a potential subject in the ensuing interaction or a third party observer or whether the situation is one in which two rather than three persons are present. The confusion introduced in Goffman's use of the term 'observer' serves to obscure the differences between the two types of observers and the different types of situations which may be involved.

Consider another concept, that of 'unwitting move'.

An *unwitting move*, from the actor's perspective, is not a 'move' because it is genuinely not oriented to an observer's detection; from the other's perspective, it is considered a 'move' because it is observed and interpreted as unoriented to the other's presence. If the other (observer) interprets it as unwitting, then he (the observer) is committing a *naïve move*. Thus, the concepts *unwitting* and *naïve* are used to refer to two different persons but are based on the perspective of only one of them, namely the other (or observer). That is, whether the subject is aware or unaware of an observer and orients or does not orient his acts to the observer does not really matter (as Goffman uses these terms) so long as the observer believes the subject is or is not so oriented. When the observer believes the subject is not so oriented, he considers the subject *unwitting* and is himself *naïve*; when he believes the subject is oriented to an observer, he considers that the subject is engaged in *control moves* and he is himself 'non-naïve'.

However, which observer is involved here? It is the third party observer, the sociologist in this case, who is judging that the one actor is unwitting and the other is naïve. An actor cannot judge himself to be naïve because, by Goffman's definition, only an observer can make this interpretation of a subject's observable behaviour. Furthermore, a naïve 'move' is not an action or 'observable behaviour' in the same sense as an unwitting 'move' is intended by Goffman. Rather it is an act of interpretation and involves no project of action or act performed by the person. Thus, not only is the perspective of the third party observer obscured by

Goffman when he speaks only of two parties, subject and observer, engaged in unwitting and naïve 'moves' but the notion of 'move' also obscures the difference between an observable behaviour and an act of interpretation.

A *control move* by the subject is, according to Goffman, made only when the subject is aware of an observer. Such a move involves what Schutz calls 'affecting-the-other' action, that is, the subject intends that the other attend to and make a certain interpretation of his act(s).

An *uncovering move* does not require that the observer actually perform an observable act or, if he does act, that his act be observed by the subject. Uncovering can involve acts of passive interpretation by the observer. The observer's project of action is to uncover the subject's motives and intent. Here again Goffman does not distinguish between acts of interpretation and behavioural acts. The examples of uncovering which he uses to refer to what he means, for face-to-face situations, are interviewing (covert or overt), medical examinations, courtroom testimonials, inquisitions, and inter-rogations. Examples that can occur in non-face-to-face situations are observing the subject's track or leavings, spying into the subject's possessions and concealment places or monitoring the subject directly but without his awareness. *Uncovering moves* can be interpreted as such by the actor-subject only when they are detected. Since they may be acts of interpretation rather than observable actions by the actor-observer, they are also not 'moves' in the same sense as unwitting 'moves'.

Goffman's confusion is again apparent as he shifts from an examination of the actor-subject to the actor-observer. The subject performs an action which the observer interprets. If the observer is aware of the subject and of his action, then Goffman considers the observer's interpretation a 'move'. But a 'move' for the subject cannot be an act of interpretation. It must, by definition, involve 'observable behaviour'. Thus, only subjects' 'moves' are necessarily observable behaviours whereas only observers can make 'moves' of interpretation. Clearly, it is the third party observer's perspective that enables a judgment to be made for both actors in these matters.

How would a 'move' look to the actual participating actors? If the actor has an other-orientation and formulates a project of action which is to result in acts of an affecting-the-other type he would be aware not only of the other but also that the other is capable of making interpretations of his acts. The responses of the other-as-observer to the performed act would then be examined by the subject to determine whether the act was a) noticed, b) interpreted and c) what the interpretation was as this interpretation may eventually be manifested in the observer's actions. Only if the observer gave indications that allowed the subject to make interpretations that he, the observer, had noticed and interpreted the subject's action would the observer be judged, *from the actor's perspective*, to have 'moved'. A consistent position by Goffman, if he were to take the actor's perspective, would require that his notion of 'naïve move' be changed. The subject, if he were to make a 'move' (overt behaviour) which was genuinely unoriented to the other's presence and to the other as observer, could, when and if he subsequently became aware of the other's presence and identity, examine the observer's signs to determine whether the observer was aware of his action and whether he took the action at 'face value'. If he believes this to be the case, he may undertake no further action to affect the other's interpretation. The subject, from his own perspective is now judging the observer to be 'genuinely naïve'.

The subject could, on the other hand, undertake an action which was intended to produce an interpretation by the observer that the subject was unoriented to his presence and/or to his identity as observer. In such a case the subject *is* oriented to the observer and is engaged in affecting-the-other projects of action. However, in this case, if the observer is judged by the subject to have been 'taken in' by the deception, the subject may consider the observer to be 'mistakenly naïve', or 'deceived'.

If Goffman maintained the perspective of the actor-subject, who knows his own in-order-to motives and is involved in assessing the observer's actions and interpretations of his (the subject's) acts, the concepts which would be developed would have to be based on the following possibilities.

The actor-subject:

1. considers himself to be unobserved and acts as though there is no other person observing him.

   Here he is genuinely unaware of an other's presence. He has no intention to deceive an other and is not engaged in any affecting-the-other project of action.

2. considers himself to be unobserved but acts as though he is being observed.

Here he is genuinely unaware of an other's presence but takes precautions in the event that he should be mistaken. His intent is to deceive a possible other into interpreting his acts as based on affecting-the-other projects of action.

3. considers himself to be observed but acts as though he is unobserved.

Here he is genuinely aware of the other's presence but acts so as to deceive the other into believing that he is unaware. He is engaged in affecting-the-other types of action with his primary intention being to affect the other's interpretations.

4. considers himself to be observed and acts as though he is being observed.

Here he is genuinely aware of the other's presence and is engaged in acts based on affecting-the-other projects of action. The interpretations he intends the observer to make may be of various kinds including that the subject is not aware of his presence or identity, and, if his intention is to deceive the subject into believing that he is unaware, then this resembles (3) above.

From the actor-subject's perspective, he may be engaged in 'control moves' when he seeks to produce an interpretation by the actor-observer that he believes himself to be either unobserved *or* observed. The concept of 'control move' does not differentiate between these two because 'control', when Goffman uses it, refers to the effort to produce certain kind of impressions on the actor-observer, namely, those that 'will improve his situation if gleaned by the observer'. On occasion his situation may improve when he produces the impression that he considers himself to be unobserved and at other times when he considers himself to be observed. Goffman confuses the matter of judging whether one is observed or not observed with the substantive matters of the kinds of interpretations that are desired by the actor-subject. Awareness of the other, acting with awareness, and acting so as to indicate to the other that awareness, are three distinct matters. Similarly, *un*awareness, acting with *un*awareness, and acting so as to indicate *un*awareness, involve different matters. The combinations of these various elements will produce analytically different circumstances, for both the actor-subject and the actor-observer. The schema I have outlined is better able to capture these distinctions as well as provide a consistent terminology for the analysis. The perspective of the third party observer is consistently maintained and the confusions resulting from shifts in perspective are minimised.

As an example of what such an analysis would look like I will consider Goffman's concepts of 'unwitting move', 'naïve move', and 'control move'.

First take the unwitting move. Here, a third party observer is able to directly observe the behaviour of two actors, A and O. Goffman notes that for A and O, the following holds.

I *A and O both*:

    i are conscious,

    ii have constituted selves,

    iii have, and are able to use a stock of knowledge and systems of relevance,

    iv are able to communicate, and to use a symbolic system of meaning,

    v are motivated to develop and carry out projects of action,

    vi are aware of their bodies as fields of experience.

II *In terms of awareness*:

    i A and O are co-present—as judged by the third party observer,

    ii A is *unaware* of O's presence, but O is aware of A's presence,

    iii A is *unaware* of O as person, yet O is aware of A as person,

    iv A is *unaware* that O is conscious of A's bodily presence, and O is aware that A is not conscious of O's bodily presence,

    v A is *unaware* that O constitutes him as a person, and O is aware that A does not constitute him as a person.

III *For future action*:

    i A does not formulate a project of action as of an "affecting-the-other" type where O is the "other" whom he wishes to affect; and O does not formulate a project of action of an "affecting-the-other" type unless he wants A to become aware of him, or for whatever other reason,

    ii A does not develop an act based on a project of action of an "affecting-the-other" type in which O is the one to be affected,

    iii neither does O for A unless, etc. (as noted in III, ii), iv Any acts can then be judged by the third party observer as being "unwitting" as far as A is concerned and as long as O regards them as "unwitting".

We can now see that O, as judged by our third party observer, is taking the actor-subject 'as he appears' – O's interpretation is what Goffman calls a 'naïve move'. In our terminology, 'A is unaware of O, un-oriented in his action to O, and does not undertake action of an "affecting-the-other" type with O as the other'. The concept of 'naïve move' is unnecessary if we simply add the qualifier in front of the above sentence 'O considers that A' . . . . (is unaware of O, un-oriented in his action to O, and does not . . . etc.)[14]

In this way, the terminology becomes more descriptive and more closely reflects the complexity of the two persons' awareness, interpretations, and acting.

We can proceed in a similar fashion to examine 'control moves'. Here what we find is that actor-subject A, again as judged by the third party observer, is now aware of O, (I i–vi, above), is aware of O's presence, etc. (II i–v) and formulates a project of action which has a particular intent, namely, to control the impression which O will have of A. He formulates a project of action of an 'affecting-the-other' type where O is 'the other'. A develops an act based on this project and performs the act. O, on his part, is monitoring these acts and interpreting the project of action that underlies them.

What Goffman is most interested in is whether O is 'taken in' by these intended interpretations and if not, whether he attempts to 'counter' these moves with moves, acts of interpretation or performed acts based on a project of action designed to 'uncover' or discover that which A sought to cover. Similarly, A can respond to O with 'counter-uncovering' projects of action and performed acts.

In covering, uncovering, or counter-uncovering moves, as Goffman formulates these, both parties are aware of each other (see I i–vi, II i–v above) though there will be variations in terms of features described under section III, characteristics of the action, because some 'moves' may or may not involve performed acts. Acts of interpretation may not be visible or discernible to the other actor, whether it is A considering O, or O considering A, again, as judged by the third party observer. The specific content of these interpretations and the performed acts are not considered here but do constitute the main interest of the analysis of strategic interaction. Goffman's main point is that action is 'strategic' when the actor and the other are engaged in impression management, discovery, concealment, and counter discovery. This process is potentially an infinite cycle and an infinite series of 'moves'. Thus, even that which is judged by O to be 'unwitting' becomes suspect when and if O suspects that A may manipulate his expressions so as to convey the impression that he (A) is unaware, un-oriented, etc.

'Strategic' interaction becomes an interpretive 'set' whereby the actor undertakes to examine or consider the 'strategic' possibilities in all of what the other says or does – and, likewise, may undertake to deliberately manage his own expressions. It is perhaps best characterised as a hyper-conscious awareness of the other, an awareness of the potential 'strategic' interpretations of one's own acts and an awareness that the other may also be interpreted as behaving strategically at any or all times.

In this sense, Goffman's analysis in this work has similarities to his other discussions of deception, discovery, impression management, manipulation, and revelation found in *The Presentation of Self in Everyday Life, Interaction Ritual*, and *Relations in Public*. It is what led me to consider *Strategic Interaction* as part of the same cloth – the effort by Goffman to study face-to-face interaction as a naturally bounded analytically coherent field – a sub-area of sociology. However, in *Strategic Interaction* as in his other works, Goffman fails to develop a set of analytic concepts which will provide us with the tools to advance this sub-area of sociology. The framework originally presented by Schutz, and advanced by Psathas and Waksler, in contrast, lends itself to the description of a variety of situations of face-to-face interaction.[15] Perhaps the efforts to systematise a field can be better advanced when each strategy becomes informed by the other – the phenomenological approach to the clarification of concepts used to describe the complexity of social action, social relationships, situation and the characteristics of the actors on the one hand and the examination of the concrete projects of action and performed acts by particular actors in the everyday situations of social occasions and gatherings on the other.

If we were to examine closely what Goffman himself says about his book, we would find additional difficulties. In concluding the book, Goffman says he has 'attempted to formulate a definition of strategic interaction and clarify the special perspective this concept implies' (1969, p. 138).

He then relates the concept to symbolic interaction theory by saying he has advanced the symbolic interactionist approach in two ways. The first is that strategic interaction analytically excludes merely any kind of interdependence from the study of interaction since the conditions of strategic interaction require *full* interdependence of outcomes, mutual awareness of this fact by the parties involved, and the capacity to make use of this knowledge. Presumably, non-strategic interaction does not involve these conditions.

Second, strategic interaction he says 'addresses itself directly to the dynamics of interdependence involving mutual awareness; . . . seeks out basic moves and . . . natural stopping points in the potentially infinite cycle of two players taking into consideration their consideration of each other's consideration . . .' (1969, p. 137) Presumably, he has analyzed the basic moves and sequences involved and developed concepts to be used in subsequent analyses (see his discussion of moves in 'Expression Games', 1969b, pp. 11–28). These concepts would therefore represent an addition to symbolic interaction theory.

Then, perhaps aware of the broad scope of his examples and descriptions of strategic interaction and the loose application of the concepts he has presented, he says (1969, p. 137) he wishes to caution us about 'the limits of this application' of the framework of strategic interaction since, as a formal framework, 'no limit is placed on its application including the type of pay-off involved as long as the participants are locked in what they perceive as mutual fatefulness and are obliged to take some of the available highly structured courses of action'. He disarms his critics by admitting that this inclusion of any kind of pay off seems to allow the game approach to be applied to 'almost everything that is considered under the ill-defined rubric "interaction"'. (1969, p. 137)

He also is aware that the characteristics of 'gamesman' may be found in actors in almost any kind of interaction.

The limits he lists are in relation to social relationships, and to social gatherings. He cautions us that although strategic analysis can be applied and can illuminate facets of social relationships (e.g. how relationships are avoided, created, maintained, deepened, attenuated, terminated) a 'generalised picture of relationship formation and the resulting structures cannot be fully delineated in strategic terms'. (1969, p. 137–8)

Moreover, since relationship pay offs are only instances of a larger class, no *special* contribution to strategic analysis game theory can be made by analysing relationships. In other words, the theory is to be applied to and not developed from the study of relationships.

In his view, there is no qualitative difference, from the actor's perspective, of relationship pay offs as compared with profit and loss of possessions and goods. This is sweepingly stated without demonstration. It is a statement consistent with the fact that Goffman adopts an observer's perspective in studying interactants. How else could a game theory perspective be used to cover all the instances cited in his studies? The actors themselves may not conceptualise their actions in a similar fashion, never consider that they are being 'strategic' when involved in life and death struggles (cf. Harry, in Harry and the lion) nor even be possessed with the faculty of conceptualizing abstract symbols (cf. the lion in Harry and the lion). Nevertheless, according to Goffman, they are involved in strategic interaction.

As for social gatherings, decisions of actors can also be analysed according to strategic interaction theory (e.g. whether to attend a party, whether to talk to persons of low rank or remain unengaged, etc.) but the rules that guide their conduct in gatherings are part of the set of norms 'that regulate socially organized co-mingling' and not of the set of rules of 'strategy'. (1969, p. 139) Therefore, the analysis of social gatherings requires an analysis of the social norms which regulate them. Here, we may distinguish between form and content, though Goffman does not use these terms. Strategic interaction seems to refer to the form whereas social norms refer to the content of the conduct of actors. Norms are specific and context bound whereas strategic interaction, as an analytic framework, cuts across the situations of conduct between actors. Whether, in Goffman's view, norms exist with regard to the handling of strategic interaction is not clear, (i.e. whether one should or should not operate as a gamesman, how far he should carry strategic conduct, at what gain or cost, how counter moves should be developed, etc.).

Now Goffman adds an interesting qualification. He notes that there are 'strategic moves which directly depend on their player being face-to-face with his opponent'. But, considering that he has not analysed interaction in the face-to-face situation as a distinct situation or tried to show what the nature of such moves in this situation may be, he only tells us that he is aware of this distinction. Strategic interaction, he says, can involve participants who are not face-to-face, and their moves may not be closely bound by time and space. Therefore, the study of strategic interaction should not be limited to the face-to-face situation alone.

Moreover, others, who are unnamed, have applied the gaming framework to social relationships and social gatherings 'too easily' and conceptualisations have resulted which have mixed issues that should be kept separate. 'Social relationships and social gatherings are two separate and distinct substantive areas; strategic interaction is an analytical perspective which illuminates both but coincides with neither,' says Goffman.

This surprising statement in effect says that, although he is aware of the special features of the face-to-face situation and that strategic moves may have distinctive properties in this situation, he can ignore these distinctions because he is trying to show the possibilities as well as the limits of the application of the strategic interaction framework. However, it is precisely this systematic ignoring of the specific features of the face-to-face situation which leads to the same result, in Goffman's *own* work which he attributes to others, namely, 'conceptualizations which, too quickly, intermingle matters which must be kept apart, at least initially.' (1969, p. 140). It is his use of the same concepts, across all situations, which blurs the distinctions between interaction in the face-to-face situation versus that between contemporaries who may never be co-present, or the distinction between interaction between individuals not acting on behalf of or representing any other social unit than themselves versus their being agents of larger social units which plan their moves and make them pawns in a game. He merely warns us of the necessity for making clear distinctions – he, himself, does not make them.

A similar point can be made with regard to his discussion of the concept of communication (1969, pp. 140–144) which he says is 'even easier to confuse with strategic interaction' than are social relationships and social gatherings. Communication systems must function under particular conditions (e.g. concealment of the agent's location when transmitting, guardedness, authentication and avoidance of equipment malfunction) and operate within particular 'frames' or contexts within which the content they transmit is to be interpreted. Communication systems can also be examined with regard to their strategic implications and with regard to the bearing which social relationships and face-to-face interaction have on the system used. However, Goffman does not do this; ('in this paper . . . communication was not a central subject matter', 1969, p. 143). Therefore, we cannot hold him responsible for the failure to clarify the concept and to improve on what he claims is a problem namely that 'in practice, when the term *communication* is used, little clarity and consistency is found as to just what it is that is being investigated' (1969, p. 143). Even in these concluding paragraphs he merely informs us that he is aware of these distinctions and refers back to the discussion in which he presumably clarified the distinctions, without ever systematising the analysis so as to present the typology or the criteria underlying the classifications.

The last concluding sections of the study can be interpreted as a confession and a plea. He confesses that he has not been consistent, has not clarified the distinctions between the phenomena being studied, has not provided the reader with a model for proceeding with additional research and in fact is aware that some confusions may result from possible indiscriminate applications of the concepts presented (as he himself has already demonstrated). Yet, he asks the reader to recognise the 'difficult' task involved, the 'little clarity and consistency' in the use of some of these concepts by others, and the possible 'easy application' of the framework to 'almost everything' considered under the 'ill-defined rubric of "interaction"'. He is therefore not to blame for the lack of precision and clarity of concepts in the field yet he asks that his work be considered as a contribution to the development of 'a naturally bounded, analytically coherent field', the study of face-to-face interaction.

Now the issue is, if Goffman himself will not provide the analysis and clarification so needed and if his work contributes to the continung confusion between such phenomena as relation, situation, interaction and communication by the presentation and development of new concepts, can an 'analytically coherent field' be developed by additional studies such as these?

The answer it seems to me is clearly 'no'. A thorough analysis of the basic phenomena being studied is necessary and Goffman's method is unable to provide such analysis. Further ethnographic descriptions and efforts to apply frameworks from other fields (e.g. game theory) even though simultaneousy pointing to their limitations, add to the confusion. The apparent illuminaion in the reader's mind is based on his unquestioned assumption of commonsense reasoning, evidence and example, and the stipulative definitions of concepts. The reader's impression that he has gained an understanding of previously perceived but un-understandable complex events serves merely to keep him ignorant of the basis of his 'understanding' and to keep him dependent on Goffman to provide further 'illumination'. He is furthermore unable to assess critically

Goffman's method or his epistemological assumptions since these are never discussed or presented. The reader can only infer that he is fortunate to have a keen and insightful guide in Goffman whom he must trust to lead him by the hand to newer gardens with evermore exciting vistas of the fruits of human performances, presentations, and interactions.

The risk, however, for a social sceince of everyday life, particularly of a 'field of face-to-face interaction', is that we will accept his classifications without further examination to determine the criteria used to group situations into categories.[16] Moreover, as I have shown, conceptual clarification may come only if close examination of interaction is first undertaken without regard to the substantive matter of what the actors are trying to accomplish, with a regard instead for interaction as a phenomenon on its own right.

Although the encyclopedic collections and ethnographic details of a variety of situations and types of interaction offer illuminating insights, they do not a) systematise a field, b) present basic concepts which can be used to develop a theory of face-to-face interaction, or c) develop and use a theoretical framework consistently over a variety of studies. Goffman tends to confuse the task of conceptual analysis with the development of concepts. He is more concerned with developing and assigning concepts and categories to the phenomena observed than with analysing the properties of the phenomena themselves. His own observations and the studies which he extensively quotes or draws upon as data assume that the elements of face-to-face interaction are already understood; face-to-face interaction is generally used as a primitive term and by repeatedly shifting from an observer's to a subject's perspective he fails to indicate the theoretical as well as practical significance of such perspectival differences.

EDITIONS OF GOFFMAN'S WORK USED IN THIS CHAPTER

(The dates are taken from the bibliography provided in the *Editor's Introduction*; the pagination for quotations cited in this chapter from the editions shown below).

(1959)   *The Presentation of Self in Everyday Life*, (Garden City, New York; Doubleday Anchor).

(1961)   *Encounters: Two Studies in the Sociology of Interaction*, (Indianapolis; Bobbs-Merrill).

(1963a)   *Behaviour in Public Places: Notes on the Social Organisation of Gatherings*, (New York; Free Press of Glencoe).

(1967)   *Interaction Ritual: Essays on Face-to-Face Behaviour*, (Garden City, New York; Doubleday Anchor).

(1969)   *Strategic Interaction*, (Philadelphia; University of Pennsylvania Press).

(1969a)   'Strategic Interaction', in Goffman, (1969).

(1969b)   'Expression Games: An Analysis of Doubts at Play', in Goffman, (1969).

(1971)   *Relations in Public: Microstudies of the Public Order*, (New York; Basic Books).

CHAPTER ENDNOTES

1. This is a much revised version of a paper originally presented at the meetings of the American Sociological Association, New York, 1973. I wish to thank Peter Manning and Jerry Jacobs for their comments and W. G. Carson for the opportunity to present an earlier draft of the chapter at his seminar at Bedford College, University of London.

2. His aims for the two essays ('Expression Games: An Analysis of Doubts at Play' and 'Strategic Interaction') in the book are several and I believe can be summarized as follows (Goffman, 1969):

   a) his ultimate aim is to 'develop the study of face-to-face interaction as a naturally bounded, analytically coherent field – a sub-area of sociology' (1969, p. ix),
   b) to clarify some central concepts, e.g., communication, and to show that communication, though believed to be a concept which would illuminate the field has been of doubtful value,
   c) drawing from theoretic work in game theory, to examine what has been discussed as communicative behavior,

   d) to show that a game theoretic perspective can be used to illuminate the study
of interaction thus providing an alternative or additional theory to
communication theory,

   e) to examine strategic interaction in its own right and clarify its properties,

   f) to contribute to the use of a game theoretic (strategic interaction) perspective
in the analysis of face-to-face interaction, and

   g) to contribute to the field of face-to-face interaction the use of basic analytic
concepts developed in other fields while at the same time pointing out the
limitations of such efforts.

These are varied and ambitious aims and I shall consider his analysis of strategic
interaction only in terms of the first of the above-mentioned.

   3. Goffman's own assessment of his work places it within the tradition of Meadian
social psychology – a broader theoretical perspective than the one I am considering
here. He says (1969, p. 136):

> It should be noted that strategic interaction is, of course, close to Meadian social
> psychology and to what has come to be called 'symbolic interaction' – since
> nowhere more than in game analysis does one see the actor as putting himself in
> the place of the other and seeing things, temporarily at least, from his point of
> view.

   4. The lack of an index in all his books (except *Relations in Public*) makes it difficult
for the reader to assess the extent of consistency and the development of concepts in
his work. For example, a brief survey shows that total institutions, underlife and
face-work do not appear in *Strategic Interaction*; engagement, gathering, focused and
unfocused interaction developed in *Behavior in Public Places* are not used in *Strategic
Interaction* or *Relations in Public*; performances, teams, regions, and staging
developed in *The Presentation of Self in Everyday Life* are not used in *Strategic Interaction*
or in *Relations in Public*.

   5. Examples (Goffman, 1971) can be found to show that he uses different concepts
to describe situations that contain similar elements. Concepts to be used to analyze
pedestrian interaction in public places (e.g., body check, collision course, early-
warning system, gallantry, intention display, lanes rules, passing rules, scanning)
are not used to analyze 'co-waiting' or 'elevator behavior', situations in which
similar patterns might be found. For example, in discussing pedestrians, Goffman
says:

> a simple 'body check' is involved . . . when the individual making it can
> introduce a large directional change through a small and therefore undemean-
> ing angular correction. Once others have been checked out satisfactorily, they
> can be allowed to come close without this being cause for concern. . . . And
> further, since he does not concern himself with oncomers who are separated from
> him by others, he can, in dense traffic, be unconcerned about persons who are
> actually very close to him. Therefore, the scanning area is not a circle but an
> elongated oval, narrow to either side of the individual and longest in front of him,
> constantly changing in area depending on traffic density around him. Note that
> even as the individual is checking out those who are just coming into range, so

they will be checking him out, which means that oncomers will be eyeing each other at something of the same moment and that this moment will be similarly located in the course of both; yet this act is almost entirely out of awareness. (1971, p. 12)

In discussing co-waiting, he says:

. . . to stand or sit next to a stranger when the setting is all but empty is more of an intrusion than the same act would be when the place is packed and all can see that only this niche remains. . . . arrival creates sequential allocation but departure leads to somewhat more complex behavior, . . . a departure may leave an empty place and no change in the remaining allocation, or at least an appropriator may wait for some tactful moment before making use of the newly available resource. . . . moving in on someone or having oneself moved in on is a less delicate task than removing oneself from proximity to him. (1971, p. 31)

And, in discussing behaviour in elevators, he notes:

The first few individuals can enter without anyone present having to rearrange himself but very shortly each new entrant – up to a certain number – causes all those present to shift position and reorient themselves in sequence. Leave-taking introduces a tendency to reverse the cycle, but this is tempered by the countervailing resistance to appearing uncomfortable in an established distance from another. Thus, as the car empties, passengers acquire a sense of uneasiness caught between two opposite inclinations – to obtain maximum distance from others and to inhibit avoidance behaviour that might give offense. (1971, p. 32)

In each of these interaction settings, problems of contact and avoidance of contact, entering and leaving spatial locations, management of a course of movement through space, indications of awareness of others, among other matters, are involved. Yet each is treated as somehow unique and therefore presumably requiring different descriptive concepts.

6. See, for example, Herbert Blumer's review of Goffman's *Relations in Public*, [cited as (1971, R5) in the section entitled *A Sampler of Reviews*, (in the *Editor's Introduction*)]; and also John O'Neill's essay, 'Self-Prescription and Social Machiavellianism', in his *Sociology as a Skin Trade*, (New York; Harper Torchbooks, 1972).

7. On this point, compare the remarks made by Egon Bittner in his essay, 'Objectivity and Realism in Sociology', pp. 109–125, in G. Psathas (ed), *Phenomenological Sociology*, (New York; Wiley-Interscience, 1973) concerning the risks of naive realism among field researchers:

Characteristically, to carry out their studies the researchers rely exclusively on those competences and resources they possess as members of society, (p. 117).

The concentration on how to do field work well and how to get it done, laudable as it is, not only fails to cast light on the epistemological problem underlying realism but actually obscures it. The greater the effort to enhance the adequacy of observation on counts such as acceptance, transfer of trust, subtlety, perspicacity, open-mindedness, patience, and scope, the less likely that serious, searching questions will be asked about that which has come to view by means of all this loving care. . . . The nature of the reality the field worker attends to and, by extension, the realism embodied in his observations have nothing at all to do with the particulars of research technique. It is not whether he observes well or poorly that matters but the circumstance of his being an outside observer with all the consequences issuing from it, (p. 119).

And further:

> even when (the field worker) dwells on the fact that this reality is to 'them' incontrovertibly real in just the way 'they' perceive it, he knows that to some 'others' it may seem altogether different, and that, in fact, the most impressive feature of 'the' social world is its colourful plurality. Indeed, the more seriously he takes this observation, the more he relies on his sensitivity as an observer who has seen firsthand how variously things can be perceived, the less likely he is to perceive those traits of depth, stability and necessity that people recognise as actually inherent in the circumstances of their existence, (p. 123).

8. See, Alfred Schutz, *The Phenomenology of the Social World*, (Mouton; The Hague, 1967); and G. Psathas and F. Waksler, 'The Essential Features of Face-to-Face Interaction', pp. 159–183, in G. Psathas (ed), op. cit.

9. Ibid.

10. Schutz, op. cit., pp. 59–63.

11. Ibid. pp. 144–150.

12. Ibid. pp. 154–156.

13. He then lists three control moves: 1) concealment or cover, 2) accentuated revealment, and 3) misrepresentation. He discusses the first of these as 'the most important'. The various sub-types discussed are: 'open secrecy and privacy' where the subject 'does not try to keep observers from perceiving that they are being kept in the dark'; covert concealment as in masking or camouflaging; and feigning and feinting where the latter refers to 'faked courses of action' and the former to 'beliefs, attitudes, and preferences misrepresented strategically'; and accounts and explanations.

14. In the analysis of strategic interaction, moves are central . . . During occasions of strategic interaction a move consists of a structured course of action available to a player which, when taken, objectively alters the situation of the participants'. (1969, p. 145) Yet, as I have shown, a 'more' is not a 'structured course of action' when Goffman speaks of a 'naïve move' which suggests that he does indeed confuse acts of interpretation and performed acts based on a project of action.

15. See: fn. 8., above.

16. Another criticism of Goffman's work, presumably on methodological grounds, is that despite careful study of his work it is not possible to either replicate or extend

it. This may be the difference between reading and appreciating a novel and writing one – or viewing a film and producing one. Goffman does not present methodological discussions. His studies of face-to-face interaction situations present classifications but do not reveal the procedures followed in developing the classes or the criteria underlying the classes.

3: Deviance and Control in Everyday Life: The Contribution of Erving Goffman

By Mike Hepworth

Even the critics of Goffman agree he is 'an extremely sensitive and acute observer of human interaction'.[1] His declared interest is 'ordinary, actual behaviour' (1974, p. 564), and his main concern that sociologists should never lose sight of the significance of the observable complexities of concrete conduct for an understanding of human nature and social order.[2] Throughout his work Goffman presents himself in the role of a committed social scientist, engaged in the business of unravelling the tangled skein of micro-interaction in an attempt to bring us closer to an awareness of the intricate principles of social organisation upon which orderly lives depend. In this chapter I shall consider certain of the insights his particular brand of sociology offers into processes of social control, and some of their implications for a fuller appreciation of the delicate balance we daily maintain between deviance and normality.

I must first of all stress that, as a sociologist, Goffman never departs radically from the accepted canons of the profession. The 'core matters of sociology', he writes (1974, p. 13), are 'social organisation and social structure'. As human beings we necessarily inhabit a socially organised 'working world' which requires us to spend considerable time in the presence of others and thus, whether we like it or not, to enter into some sort of relationship with them. The basic ingredients of life are processes of interaction and communication and these are organised according to certain rules.

The point is the old one that social order does not just happen, but is actively created by human beings gathered together in various kinds of association. The central argument of interactionist sociology is that in the course of relating one to another we produce not only externally observable social order or structure but also our public and private identities and, equally important, our identities are created for us.

A poignant illustration of the tension these processes can produce occurs in the diary of a fifteen years old white, middle class, American girl, now dead from an overdose of drugs. At one stage of her life, before she became involved with the drug scene, she wrote:

> I'm partly somebody else trying to fit in and say the right things and do the right thing and be in the right place and wear what everybody else is wearing. Sometimes I think we're all trying to be shadows of each other, trying to buy the same records and everything even if we don't like them. Kids are like robots, off an assembly line, and I don't want to be a robot. [A few days later she wrote] Oh dear God, help me adjust, help me be accepted, help me belong, don't let me be a social outcast and a drag on my family.[3]

This tension between inner consciousness and outward conformity is, I think, something we all recognise whatever our social status. In order to be in the right place at the right time, to do the right things, say the right things and wear the right clothes, we must subordinate ourselves to the demands of others. As Goffman has amply demonstrated, everyday life is made up of a series of sometimes subtle pressures to which we adjust with varying degrees of enthusiasm, and, in our turn, exert upon others.

Certain implications of this pervasive condition become clearer if we look at specific examples of deviant behaviour. Here is one dramatic instance of an unexpected breach in daily routine: 'My husband said, "Excuse me, I'm going to the loo". He never came back; he went to Spain with his girlfriend instead.'[4] When a husband or wife suddenly disappears from an apparently settled home, and can reasonably be presumed alive, those left behind may go to some trouble to retrieve the situation by locating the absentee and persuading him or her to return.[5] At least two important issues are at stake. Firstly, in common with many victims of more serious crime,[6] those left behind very often feel exposed to adverse public comment and consequently shamed by the action of one of their members. Whatever the motives of the one who has disappeared, his or her actions have inevitably disturbed the smooth running of a social unit which, in contemporary Western culture, is considered a buttress of wider society. Secondly, this action can lead to the uneasy suspicion that the missing person had never completely identified with hearth and home and now seeks a more acceptable alternative elsewhere. Simply because it is not possible to become a missing person unless someone misses you, the actual act of going missing is a complex social process which involves some conscious appraisal of the relationship between self and others. It can be seen as a process of disengagement which indicates the missing person's desire to change, however temporarily, an existing situation and assume a changed identity. For those who disappear permanently, as Lenore Weitzman discovered in the States, disengagement is the first stage in the creation of a new outward personality.[7]

These social dynamics were exposed to considerable publicity in the recent case of British Cabinet Minister John Stonehouse. After his disappearance and subsequent discovery in Australia, Stonehouse described his flight from London and abandonment of home and duty as an attempt to create a new identity for himself in totally different surroundings.[8] At his trial Stonehouse's psychiatrist stated that his client had tried to destroy the Stonehouse personality by disengaging himself from an array of domestic, political, and commercial associations and cultivating an alternative set of relations thousands of miles away.[9]

Individuals disappear, of course, from a wide variety of situations and in response to a wide variety of pressures. Nevertheless a common thread can be detected running through these several acts. The official designation of anyone as a missing person depends, as I remarked earlier, upon the existence of others whose fortunes are sufficiently tied up with those of the absentee for them to wish to establish some sort of control over him in the future. If search and rescue procedures fail, and a family member has to all intents and purposes disengaged himself totally, the situation can come to resemble the state of bereavement: it must be followed by a period of painful adjustment to enforced changes in social status and identity. For a small group of people the smooth 'working' of society, to use a core Goffman term, has been disrupted and someone will have to repair the damage.

Goffman's sociology takes us to the heart of the fluid interchange between deviance and normality. His perspective on orderly social interaction is one which allows for the continuous possibility of disorder and breakdown. According to his analysis, one source of tension in our social relations is that we are never completely absorbed into the situations in which we live and move and have our being:

> Sociologists have always had a vested interest in pointing to the ways in which the individual is formed by groups, identifies with groups, and wilts away unless he obtains emotional support from groups. But when we closely observe what goes on in a social role, a spate of sociable interaction, a social establishment – or any other unit of organisation – embracement of the unit is not all that we see. We always find the individual employing methods to keep some distance, some elbow room, between himself and that with which others assume he should be identified. (1961c, p. 229)

One of Goffman's central achievements is to show how the careful observation of processes of interaction, especially between people who come together in face-to-face encounters, can reveal the capacity of individuals to manipulate the very situations in which their identities are grounded and made evident to others. His analysis of social stigmatisation, in the book *Stigma*, throws into sharp relief some of the ways existing arrangements make it possible, and indeed often necessary, for individuals to divide up their loyalties and engage in the arts of impression management to conceal the fact. If we turn to the criminal offence of blackmail we can obtain some idea of the close working relationship between deviance and normality this context demands.

The kind of blackmail to which I refer is that defined by Goffman (1963, p. 96) as 'full', or 'classic' blackmail where the blackmailer obtains payment by 'threatening to disclose facts about the individual's past or present which could utterly discredit his currently sustained identity'. In a recent British case a middle-aged schoolteacher demanded £500 from his best friend after he learned that his friend had made love to his wife on two or three occasions. The threat was to tell the blackmail victim's wife that her husband, a respected church elder and freemason, had been unfaithful. The victim had sufficient confidence to inform his wife, and later the police, but there is evidence that many others who engage in secret deviant acts are much more willing to pay to sustain a respectable image of themselves. Even when unsuccessful, blackmail shows the price that rewarding and supportive relations with others can cost.

The extent to which we are admitted to desired forms of interaction is conditioned on a social level; not so much by who we 'really' are but by the kind of information and misinformation available to others in face-to-face interaction and through other channels of communication. Any degree of 'normality' to which we can lay claim is dependent on this information we make available to others or they can discover. It is therefore not necessary to be an adulterer, a homosexual, a thief, or to be directly responsible for any kind of deviation, to have one's reputation threatened and one's identity impugned.[10] Some years ago a sensational British Sunday newspaper printed the story of a young housewife in the Midlands who reacted to gossip in the neighbourhood about her sexual life by publishing a statement disclaiming any acts of intimacy with the tradesmen who visited her home.[11] Shortly afterwards the same newspaper included a letter from an 'Angry Wife' complaining that she had noticed, since she and her husband had separated on the grounds of his adultery, that the neighbours were avoiding her.[12]

In cases of reputational blackmail the victim pays the blackmailer to keep quiet because he fears the consequences of an adverse interpretation he believes others will make of the information which may fall into their hands. The victim's subjective assessment of his own situation is an important determinant of his willingness to yield to the blackmailer's demands. Men and women have been known to have paid blackmail to prevent the circulation of allegations which had no basis in fact and many have paid to conceal single errors which took place years before. One person was recently blackmailed by his illegitimate daughter who had been conceived during the last war and had only lately discovered the identity of her father. The crux of the matter is that the blackmailer acts as a potential publicity agent for the double life and it is for this reason that blackmail has become aptly known as 'moral murder'.[13] Finding an R.A.F. officer guilty of threatening to accuse a woman doctor of abortion, the judge spelled out the moral consequences of the crime: 'You must know that this sort of conduct might have had the most appalling results on this woman. The complete destruction of her soul might have followed from what you did or helped to do'.[14]

Public identity is thus a product of the use others make of the information put at their disposal. In this sense the self, says

Goffman, occurs within a complex of personal and other relationships. It:

> is not a property of the person to whom it is attributed, but dwells rather in the pattern of social control that is exerted in connection with the person by himself and those around him. (1961c, p. 194)

For Goffman all interaction is a moral enterprise involving the attribution of human character. The ability of the individual to distance himself from relationships which outwardly engage him, and so to deviate somewhat from the prescribed norm, is counterbalanced by the possibility that any information concerning such deviation may be added to his biography and used in evidence against him. The blackmail victim fears his guilty secret will make him less acceptable in the eyes of others and spoil his life; this fear that private details can be used to construct a deviant biography is not, of course, confined to blackmail victims and those who break the law.

In 1972 the British Government's Committee on Privacy, under the chairmanship of Kenneth Younger, published the Report of its investigation of 'intrusions into privacy by private persons and organisations, or by companies'. In the attempt to find a satisfactory definition of privacy and to determine which aspects required official protection the Committee took evidence from a large number of commercial, governmental, and professional agencies, and also commissioned a 'Survey of Public Attitudes' through the Home Office. The information gathered led the Committee to conclude:

> that the main concern about what is termed invasion of privacy involves the treatment of personal information. The 'information' which we have been urged to protect is that in which a person should be regarded as having something in the nature of proprietary interest, either, in most cases because it relates personally to him or because he has been entrusted with it by the person to whom it relates, as in the case of a doctor, tutor, employer or friend of the family. If the information is passed to another recipient who is also acceptable, then that recipient in turn can be said to be entrusted with it.[15]

In other words, most of those who expressed anxiety about the invasion of privacy were worried about problems of information control.

The moot question is: what kinds of information do people wish to keep to themselves and for what reasons do they wish to retain personal control? The two are linked together. On the morning after the Younger Report appeared, *The Guardian* put the whole issue into an editorial nutshell:

> Do you mind if other people find out about your bank balance, your salary or earnings, and any regular payments that you are making? Or about your health record and recent illnesses; about whether you get on well with your wife or husband; or about whom you do business with, and your political affiliations? You may think that all these are your private concern. So they are. But they are the kind of things that detective agencies and credit rating agencies can and will find out about you. They may be of use to your business competitors, litigants against you, personal antagonists, and even curious employers. They are also the kind of things that banks, insurance officers, and government departments sometimes inadvertently help them to discover.[16]

If we follow this approach we can see that in common with known blackmail victims, protestors against the invasion of privacy are ultimately concerned about the construction others may choose to place upon specific items of information which are taken from them. The rapid expansion of computerised data storage and retrieval systems reflects on the function of information in our lives. Publicity in the media concerning leakages of confidential information tends to provoke the sort of outcry which a few years ago followed allegations in *The Guardian* about the ease with which inquiry agents could get their hands on information held by government departments,[17] and the discovery of crime files, credit files and hire purchase arrears files on assorted communal rubbish tips.[18]

In their study of the social impact of technological changes in data processing Malcolm Warner and Michael Stone stress there is no such thing as a neutral or objective record of 'the facts' in any situation.[19] Once various items of information about a person have been collected they can be fed into a vast memory bank which has the gift of total recall. This innovation gives many more people access to records of events in the past which may, in the words of the

Younger Report, pose 'the threat of damage to the individual'. The Committee found:

> that the computer's facility to store, link, manipulate, and provide access to information gave rise to suspicions that complete personal profiles on a great number of people could be compiled; that information could be used for a purpose for which it was not initially collected; that some information could be inaccurate; that it facilitated access to confidential information by many people scattered over a wide area; that its powers of correlation were so superior to traditional methods that it made practicable what had hitherto been impracticable; and that it encouraged the growth of an entirely new scale of information-gathering and of organisations to do it.[20]

The point I wish to make is that we don't need to be the victims of blackmail to appreciate that it is through the personal control of information that we are able to manipulate the impression others have of us and sometimes to conceal behaviour we expect them to find unacceptable. 'Privacy', says the American writer Jerry M. Rosenberg, 'is the right of the individual to decide for himself how much of his life – his thoughts, emotions and the facts that are personal to him – he will share with others'.[21] From the study of missing persons we also learn that individuals can refuse to share themselves completely even in intimate situations where close interaction might be expected to preclude deception and the projection of misleading information. In contemporary society, as Goffman's meticulous observations repeatedly show, individuals are engaged in the manipulation – albeit sometimes unconsciously – of personal information in both public and private life.[22] Nowhere are these facts of life more noticeable than in the lives of those found guilty of a criminal offence.

Like attitudes towards any other kind of prohibited behaviour, community attitudes to crime are varied and complex. Although in this country, our knowledge of how ex-offenders are treated when they are released is less than complete,[23] we do know that the possession of a criminal record can have far-reaching influence on personal identity.[24] In our system of criminal justice the sentence is designed to isolate the defendant from the rest of society which, at that moment at least, is symbolically ranged in judgement against him. Obviously the offender may resent his punishment, and can protest his innocence, but it is difficult for him to ignore the fact that it also represents one stage in the acquisition of a deviant label with which he will somehow have to come to terms. In the following example one offender describes the memory of his first court appearance some years ago when, at the age of sixteen, he was convicted for stealing a radio from a guest's bedroom in the hotel where he worked:

> The much worse part of it was when they read out the details about me in court. I knew I was illegitimate of course, I'd always been aware of that since I was little; it'd gradually dawned on me while I was at the home that like a lot of other boys there I had a mother who wasn't married, and I didn't have a father. What I hadn't realised though, until that day when I heard it in court, was that my father had been my mother's brother; I wasn't just a bastard, I was the result of an incestuous union too. [He then goes on to tell how, on the basis of what he assumed was a socially correct interpretation of a single item of information, he reconstructed his own identity and awareness of self] You can tell you're illegitimate; it's not a very nice thing to say, but on the whole it's not something you can get over probably, it's not that unusual. But the other thing . . . you do have a terrible feeling that no matter what happens you couldn't ever be normal having been born like that. It's a feeling somehow of shame, that there's something different about you and there's no way round it, you are what you are and nothing's ever going to change it . . . I've never for instance in my whole life considered that it would be safe ever to have children myself in case I were to pass this . . . hereditary taint on to them. I do not believe I could ever be the father of a normal child, and I know this feeling will always remain in my mind whatever anyone says. It's the only thing so far that I still haven't been able to bring myself to tell my wife.[25]

Any private assessment of his own character by someone who has been up against the law is derived from the knowledge that it is possible for him to be transformed by the reactions of others from someone who has actually committed a crime into someone who is, at least in their eyes, a deviant individual and therefore to be excluded from unreserved acceptance. If we take into account the situation of the large number of adults who appeared before the juvenile courts and have since settled down to become hard-working and respectable citizens, or those who have committed a single crime perhaps when under considerable pressure, we obtain further confirmation of the unease the possession of a criminal record can induce. In 1972 a Committee chaired by Lord Gardiner drew attention to the problems facing people who had not been reconvicted for a number of years. Recorded evidence of their past offences, it was recommended, should in the future be inadmissible in the courts and its use should be prohibited in other walks of life. The Committee came to this conclusion after discovering several well-documented instances of a past criminal record discrediting men and women who had spent, 'ten, twenty or thirty years doing everything they can to live down their past and rehabilitate themselves'. It was estimated that as many as one million people in England and Wales had a criminal record but had been free of convictions for at least ten years. Whether or not all of these lived in fear of exposure, their rehabilitation could be said to be complete until society no longer held their past crimes against them. The existence of an accessible criminal record in the Criminal Record Office, at the court which convicted them, and, 'perhaps in the files of a local or national newspaper which reported the proceedings', meant that at any time in the future 'malice or chance may put an end to their rehabilitation, and expose them to endless unemployment and misery'. Matters could be even more difficult for a successful business or professional person:

> His friends may try to persuade him to take an active part in public affairs, but he cannot afford to take the risk, lest a political opponent, or a newspaper, might discover about his past and use it to discredit him. In that kind of situation, the possibility of blackmail may also add its weight to the grave distortion of the life which he might otherwise lead.[26]

As I observed earlier, an individual's assessment of the social value of his own moral character comes not only from his actual experience of stigmatisation but also from his expectations that others will react adversely towards him. In his careful analysis of the effects of the stigma of male homosexuality, Ken Plummer has noted:

> it is not an argument of interactionism that specific people have to actually react towards a deviant for 'labelling' to be successful: it

is often sufficient for the individual to simply react towards himself. 'Self-indication' and 'self-reaction', then, may be just as analytically important as societal reactions.[27]

When self-stigmatisation occurs the individual distances himself from his own actions, sits in judgement upon them, and is found guilty. Under painful self-criticism of this sort he may feel tormented by guilt and consequently impelled to confess his deviance and seek forgiveness. Confessions illustrate that men and women often feel unacceptable in someone's eyes; but also that they are not necessarily barred for all time from the road back to society. At the same time, rehabilitation can be a long and painful process and to regain acceptance it is often necessary both to apologise for the disruption the deviant act has caused and, even more importantly, disown the deviant self. Confessions of this kind are a form of apology which involves the individual separating himself into two parts: the part that is guilty of the offence and the part that dissociates itself from it and swears allegiance to the norms that have been violated.[28]

The following interesting example of a public apology is taken from the trial of a man found guilty of attempting to blackmail 'Dr X' in 1936. 'My act', he said in the dock:

> was one of madness, in a fit of desperation, due to debts and my inability to obtain capital for my invention. Further my home was in jeopardy. I do not know 'Dr X', neither do I know anything against him whatsoever, and in all sincerity I seek his pardon and offer him my most humble apology for the great wrong I have done him. I deeply regret my action, which has brought nothing but sorrow, pain and extreme embarassment to my people, and I fully realise the seriousness of it now. I plead, therefore, for the mercy of this court, of 'Dr X' in a manner apart from pleading the First Offender's Act. Further, I give my word never to offend either the law or my people ever again . . . I am pleading guilty, but without malicious intent.[29]

Of course, it is easy to doubt the sincerity of those who have been caught out and only apologise in the dock, but it is less easy, in spite of occasional evidence of wrongful convictions,[30] to doubt their technical responsibility for the offence. When someone who is not a suspect confesses to a serious crime like murder we are more predisposed to believe he is playing a deeper identity game. In English law 'confession' is usually taken to mean the acknowledge-ment of fault or offence to others through the formal declaration of injury. On a different level confessions have in Western culture long been seen as a special kind of motivational account which gives otherwise unobtainable insight into the confessant's personality. In this sense the ideal type of confession is the voluntary statement provided by an authentic law-breaker who gives himself up and so helps solve a crime.[31]

On July 6th 1971, a middle aged man walked into the office of the *Manchester Evening News* and calmly confessed that nineteen years before he had killed a prostitute in Liverpool. He described how he had gone, after drinking heavily, with her to some waste ground:

> Just as we got there I gave her a pound, a one pound note, then I turned her on the wall. While I was doing it she had her hands in my pockets after my money. I remember standing back and pushing her from me. I said, 'you lousy bitch'. I then grabbed a half brick and started raining blows on her head. She fell down. I hit her three or four times. I don't know how often. I was so full of drink I didn't know what happened to her . . . I then realised I had hurt her, but when I felt the blood I panicked. I took my pound note back . . . I ran to my kip house and on the way the rain started.[32]

The power of the penitent confession to relieve the burden of guilt and symbolically restore the confessant to the ranks of normal citizens was nicely revealed at the trial which followed. Counsel for the defence made an effective plea for leniency. His client, he stated, had 'nurtured this dark secret, kept it to himself, and was unable to obtain relief by discussing it with another human being'; and the defendant himself described how his life since the murder had been tormented by the recurring image of the battered face of his victim. The judge left the court for ten minutes, and returned to pass a sentence of twelve months' imprisonment: 'To me you are obviously a man of conscience . . . I don't care what offences you committed in the past.' Indeed, he was only passing the sentence at all because, 'I think ultimately you will be more happy having served a period of imprisonment for this death': a view which was later confirmed by the prisoner: 'I am', he wrote to his wife, 'at peace at last.'[33]

In a darker period of our penal history, when the law relied heavily on the death penalty for murder, confession had the power to restore the dignity of the offender even as he stood on the gallows. An examination of the ideology of confessions with its concepts of expiation, forgiveness, and redemption reminds us that British penal policy never advocated the total and irreversible social exclusion of the ordinary criminal. Confession, which has for centuries played a central role in the criminal prosecution of homicide, reflects a religious and secular concern to restore the offender's status as a fellow member of the human race. In this sense confession can be seen as a mode of human communication designed to bridge the gap between the convict and the community and thus to restore him to normal. Even when the crime for which a person has been convicted is particularly horrifying, as was true in the case of William Pritchard, the last man to be publicly hanged in Glasgow, the formal phraseology of the confession reflects a bid to restore the human dignity of the criminal:

> I, Edward William Pritchard, in the full possession of all my senses, and understanding the awful position in which I am placed, do make a free and full confession that the sentence pronounced upon me is just; that I am guilty of the death of my mother-in-law, Mrs Taylor, and of my wife, Mary Jane Pritchard; and that I can assign no motive for the conduct which actuated me, beyond a species of 'terrible madness' and the use of 'ardent spirits'.[34]

In admitting his responsibility the offender may thus judge himself and reaffirm the validity of the rules and the right of society to exact a penalty. His willingness to comply with whatever punishment awaits him is one more buttress to the social order of which he acknowledges he is part. William Pritchard paid the supreme penalty in 1865 in front of a crowd which had previously been exposed to sermons delivered by six ministers, one of whom had travelled all the way from Dublin.

Goffman, the complete sociologist, ('I personally hold society to be first in every way', 1974, p. 13), has a clear appreciation of the social processes within which our fear of deviance is enmeshed. He understands our dependence upon continuity and meaning, and throughout his work refers to the reassurance 'easy involvement' with others provides. He is fully alive therefore to the ever-present risk of breakdown which can throw any kind of situation into disarray. In whatever situation an individual finds himself, two vulnerabilities exist: impersonal risks such as fire, contagion and other sorts of natural disaster; and 'social risks' which are (1977, p. 327), 'those seen as a product of a malefactor's intention' and at the extreme end of the scale include assault, robbery, sexual molestation, and kidnapping. Members of society respond to social risks in terms of the law, physical and verbal counter-attack, disapproval and moral condemnation. However mundane the situation, and however peripheral the deviation may appear in the scale of disruptive behaviour, when a rule has been visibly broken some judgement is passed on whoever is deemed responsible and a penalty exacted. Preoccupation with deviance and control is not confined to the 'law-and-order' brigade but a fundamental condition of social membership.

There are important similarities in our responses to everyday 'situational improprieties', and serious criminal offences. Discourtesies shown to the Queen during a protest against the cost of her visit to Stirling University prompted a signed apology from the leaders of the Council of the Students' Association which still maintained the validity of the protest. Further indication of the bearing of social propriety on moral character came from the mouth of a senior porter who had helped to clear a route for the Queen through the vociferous group. She came out of it, he reported, best of all: 'She never flinched or blinked an eye, even when she seemed in danger of being crushed. She was just as a Queen should be – absolutely regal'.[35]

Allegiance to the rules of etiquette has wide implications. It is from such loyalty, such unwillingness to exhibit bad manners, that others gain an impression of basic normality, and making a good impression is extremely important for ourselves and for the society of which we are a part. As Goffman says:

> Whatever an individual does and however he appears, he knowingly and unknowingly makes information available concerning the attributes that might be imputed to him and hence the categories in which he might be placed. (1961a, p. 90)

As in the case of student protestors, imputations of deviant identity are often made after display of bad manners has caused confusion. Bad manners are often unexpected, often unfitting from the point of view of those offended, and sometimes often unfitting from the point of view of those offended, and sometimes downright provocative as in the following examples collected by me: 'While I was waiting to get served in a fish shop a woman came in with a little boy who was crying. I said, "What's up sonny?" He looked at me and said, "Shut your big mouth" '; 'Talking of people being rude, you should see the number of V-signs I get as a lollipop lady on a busy road'; 'I tried several pairs of shoes on in a shop and told the assistant I didn't like any of them. She replied, "I could tell you were going to waste our time as soon as you walked in" '. Good manners are part of the expected structure of normality; they vouchsafe to us that the world is not in the grip of anarchistic individuals and about to plunge out of control. If our reactions to situational improprieties have much in common with our reactions to serious criminal offences, are there any socially significant differences between them?

Goffman notes that in matters of face-to-face interaction the offence and therefore the guilt attached to it may be so small that the main concern is not so much to separate out the offender and punish him publicly as in a court of law, but to keep social traffic on the move. The remedy here is a ritual rather than a substantive one. As he puts it:

> The traditional view of social control seems to divide the world into three distinct parts: in one the crime is committed, in the second the infraction is brought to trial, and in the third (should the actor be found guilty) the punishment is inflicted. (1971, p. 107)

This comparatively clear division into separate spheres of action involving the intrusion of official personnel is often reported in socio-legal studies.[36] The distinction between the public realm of crime and punishment, and the private one, is that in the latter, especially in the field of micro-interaction, to quote Goffman again (1971, p. 107).

> The scene of the crime, the halls of judgement, and the place of detention are all housed in the same cubicle; furthermore the complete cycle of crime, apprehension, trial and punishment, and return to society can run its course in two gestures and a glance. Justice is summary.

Goffman's work reminds those who believe that sociologists of crime and deviance ignore the victims, and are only interested in justifying the offender, that it is only by paying attention to the conceptions of normality revered in a particular society that we get any insight into the individual identities of known deviants. We need to realise, too, that behind apparent agreement as to what constitutes a serious crime there are in practice various interpretations of ostensibly binding social rules. One can believe 'honesty is the best policy' without losing sight of the fact that there are situations in which it simply does not pay. Interpersonal violence, the destruction of property, interference with individual rights, and theft *are* some of the hard facts of modern life as they have been throughout the history of man, but there is little evidence that apparently similar acts of exploitation and disruption have the same meaning at all times and for all people. We live in a complex society and there is still the need, in spite of over one hundred years of criminology, to map out what Goffman calls the 'various behavioural subcultures' (1961c, p. 317).

Because it often appears to be a flamboyant attack on 'public property', urban vandalism is often described in stereotypical terms which ignore the variety of motives behind it.[37] Geoff Mungham has recently researched a large Welsh council estate with a reputation for toughness where, 'local vandals have created their own town tapestry on telephone kiosks and shopfronts'.[38] In this area, he discovered, contrary to the moral censure of external officials, no one actually living on the estate seemed, 'much concerned about this sort of destruction'. Local residents tended not to miss vandalised phone boxes since they all knew someone with a private phone who would help in times of trouble. Attitudes towards the shopkeepers whose premises suffered were more ambivalent:

> shopkeepers, it is widely felt, rook people anyway, and so deserve all they get. This ambivalence is rooted in the monopolies enjoyed by local shops. The response to their being vandalised reflects simultaneously held ideas about dependence and exploitation. Violent behaviour co-exists with, and is an expression of, this complex moral calculus.[39]

If we take an overall perspective on society – step back as it were from the everyday situations which force themselves on our immediate attention – we see it divided, rather like the self, into different territories. As Goffman describes it in *Frame Analysis*,

within these territories members struggle to make sense of what is
going on, and to define the relationship of their familiar everyday
lives to the wider world. In Paul Willis's fine study of twelve non-
academic working class 'lads' in their last year at secondary school
in the Midlands, we see how situational improprieties in the
classroom, and more serious delinquencies outside, represent a bid
on their part to inject meaning into life.[40]

To the school and the authorities these boys are a source of
irritation: a social problem. They stand in sharp contrast to the
pupils who subscribe to the aims of the school and generally conform
to its discipline. For the 'lads', school is senseless and unreal; entirely
unconnected to the real world of hard manual work outside.
Classroom disruption, interpersonal violence, illegal drinking, theft
and vandalism are ways of expressing their distance from the school
and identifying with the alternative standards of the adults with
whom they expect to spend their working lives. Their localised
opposition to authority represents a claim to an alternative identity
visibly reflected in a carefully cultivated appearance: 'longish well-
groomed hair, platform-type shoes, wide-collared shirt turned over
waisted coat or denim jerkin, plus the still obligatory flared
trousers'. (Willis), p. 151. These visible signs of disidentification
with the school promotes amongst their more conformist class-
mates, 'occasional fear, uneasy jealousy and general anxiety lest
they be caught in the same disciplinarian net, and frustration that
"the lads" prevent the smooth flow of education'. (Willis), p. 151.

Despite their capacity to cause trouble, the 'lads' cannot ignore
that they are encircled by the school and authority which has the
power to enforce some recognition of the norms it holds sacred. At
the end of term when one school leaver had been detected suffering
from the effects of a lunch-time visit to the pub, the headmaster
wrote indignantly to his father:

'your son had obviously been drinking, and his subsequent
behaviour was generally unco-operative, insolent, and almost
belligerent. He seemed bent on justifying his behaviour and went
as far as describing the school as being like Colditz'. [The culprit,
who wanted to secure his school leaving certificate so he could get
a job, replied with a formal apology:] 'I would like you to accept
my sincere apologies . . . the school itself has nothing to resemble
"Colditz" in any way whatsoever . . . I realise what I have done,
which might I add I find stupid now, but at the time not so stupid,

so I am now prepared to face the consequence which you see fit'.[41]

We are now back to the splitting of the self; to the ability of the individual to have a foot in several camps, particularly in our 'plural' society. Goffman's contribution to the analysis of micro-interaction, which has done so much to strengthen our understanding of the complexities underlying the social construction of individual identity, does not imply, as some critics have suggested, any rejection of history, macro-structures, or the divisive force of inequality. His belief that whatever cultural and structural pressures determine our lives are often experienced only in and through interaction with others recommends that social deviance is not always located in remoter company than our own; but is endemic to the organisation of everyday life in which we are all, with varying degrees of skill and success, participants.

EDITIONS OF GOFFMAN'S WORK USED IN THIS CHAPTER

(The dates are taken from the bibliography provided in the *Editor's Introduction*; the pagination for quotations cited in this chapter from the editions shown below).

(1961)   *Encounters: Two Studies in the Sociology of Interaction*, (Harmondsworth; Penguin).

(1961a)   'Role Distance', in Goffman (1961).

(1961c)   *Asylums: Essays on the Social Situation of Mental Patients and Other Inmates*, (Harmondsworth, Penguin).

(1963)   *Stigma: Notes on the Management of Spoiled Identity*, (Harmondsworth; Penguin).

(1971)   *Relations in Public: Microstudies of the Public Order*, (London; Allen Lane/The Penguin Press).

(1974)   *Frame Analysis: An Essay on the Organisation of Experience*, (Harmondsworth; Peregrine).

98   *The View from Goffman*

(1977)   'The Arrangement Between the Sexes', *Theory and Society*,
         Volume 4, No. 3, pp. 301–331.

CHAPTER ENDNOTES

1. Richard Sennett, *The Fall of Public Man*, (Cambridge; Cambridge University Press, 1977) p. 35.

2. See, in particular, Goffman, 1961a.

3. Anon., *Go Ask Alice*, (London; Eyre Methuen, 1972) p. 21.

4. *News of The World*, (22nd October, 1972).

5. M. Hepworth and M. Featherstone, 'Persons Believed Missing: A Search for a Sociological Interpretation', pp. 163–208, in P. Rock and M. McIntosh (eds), *Deviance and Social Control*, (London; Tavistock, 1974).

6. Susan Brownmiller, *Against Our Will: Men, Women and Rape*, (New York; Secker and Warburg, 1975).

7. L. J. Weitzman, *Social Suicide: A Study of Missing Persons*, Unpublished Ph.D, (Columbia University, New York, 1973).

8. John Stonehouse, *Death of an Idealist*, (London; W. H. Allen, 1975).

9. John Stonehouse, *My Trial*, (London; Star Books, 1976).

10. M. Hepworth, *Blackmail: Publicity and Secrecy in Everyday Life*, (London; Routledge and Kegan Paul, 1975).

11. *News of The World*, (12th October, 1969).

12. *News of The World*, (26th October, 1969).

13. M. Hepworth, op. cit.

14. M. Hepworth, 'Deviants in Disguise: Blackmail and Social Acceptance', pp. 192–218, in S. Cohen (ed), *Images of Deviance*, (Harmondsworth; Penguin, 1971) p. 216.

15. *Report of The Committee on Privacy*, (London; H.M.S.O., Cmnd. 5072, 1972) p. 19, para. 64.

16. *The Guardian*, (13th July, 1972).

17. *The Guardian*, (10th November, 1971).

18. *News of The World*, (19th December, 1971); *The Guardian*, (22nd August, 1970), (2nd July, 1971); and, (22nd December, 1971).

19. M. Warner and M. Stone, *The Data Bank Society: Organisations, Computers, and Social Freedom*, (London; Allen and Unwin, 1970).

20. *Report of The Committee on Privacy*, op. cit., pp. 179–180, para. 581.

21. J. M. Rosenberg, *The Death of Privacy*, (New York; Random House, 1969) p. 139.

22. See, in particular, Goffman, 1959 and 1974.

23. J. P. Martin and D. Webster, *The Social Consequences of Conviction*, (London; Heinemann Books, 1971).

24. R. A. Stebbins, *Commitment to Deviance*, (New York; Greenwood Press, 1971).

25. T. Parker, *The Twisting Lane: Some Sex Offenders*, (London; Panther, 1970) pp. 146, 159–160.

26. Justice, *Living it Down: The Problem of Old Conviction* Howard League for Penal Reform, together with, National Association for the Care and Resettlement of Offenders, (London; Stevens, 1972) pp. 6–7, para. 13.

27. K. Plummer, *Sexual Stigma: An Interactionist Account*, (London; Routledge and Kegan Paul, 1975) p. 21.

28. See, in particular, Goffman, 1971.

29. *The Times*, (11th November, 1936).

30. R. Brandon and C. Davies, *Wrongful Imprisonment: Mistaken Convictions and Their Consequences*, (London; Allen and Unwin, 1973).

31. See, M. Hepworth and B. S. Turner, 'Confessions to Murder, Critical Notes on The Sociology of Motivation', *British Journal of Law and Society*, Volume 1, No. 1, (1974) pp. 31–49.

32. P. Gillman, 'Murder on His Mind', *The Sunday Times* (Magazine Section), (2nd January, 1972).

33. Ibid.

34. W. Roughhead (ed), *The Trial of Dr. Pritchard*, (Edinburgh; William Hodge, 1906) p. 152.

35. *The Guardian*, (14th October, 1972).

36. A. K. Bottomley, *Decisions in The Penal Process*, (London; Martin Robertson, 1973).

37. S. Cohen, 'Who are the Vandals?', *New Society*, (12th December, 1968) pp. 872–878.

38. G. Mungham, 'The Sociology of Violence', *New Society*, (13th October, 1977) pp. 60–63.

39. Ibid., p. 62.

40. P. Willis, *Learning to Labour: How Working Class Kids Get Working Class Jobs*, (London; Saxon House, 1977).

41. Ibid., p. 28.

4: Goffman on Power, Hierarchy, and Status

By Mary F. Rogers

Among the most commonly overlooked set of insights offered by Erving Goffman is his commentary, comprised of both explicit and implicit elements, on the interrelationship among power, hierarchy, and status in everyday life. In fact, Goffman has been subject to criticism for his apparent failure to treat these sorts of stratification-related phenomena. To date the most detailed critique of Goffman along these lines is Alvin Gouldner's analysis.[1]

While Gouldner offers a multifaceted critique of Goffman, three interrelated themes therein are particularly relevant here. Gouldner maintains, first of all, that Goffman's perspective implies actors who are disengaged from social structures. He argues that Goffman's is:

> a social theory that dwells on the episodic and sees life only as it is lived in a narrow interpersonal circumference, ahistorical and noninstitutional, an existence beyond history and society.[2]

Thus Gouldner holds that Goffman's perspective is fundamentally lacking in attention to the historically conditioned institutional matrix within which everyday life occurs. Secondly, Gouldner argues that Goffman's dramaturgical model has no 'metaphysics of hierarchy'. According to Gouldner, that deficiency yields ambiguities such that Goffman might be read as being against existing hierarchies *or* as accommodating himself to current hierarchical arrangements by avoiding a treatment of them.[3] Gouldner tends to interpret Goffman in the latter manner, rather consistently criticising him for failing to confront the matter of hierarchy.[4] A final and closely related theme concerns Goffman's inattention to power.

Gouldner maintains that even in his micro-level focus Goffman fails to indicate how power affects individual's abilities to present selves effectively.[5] In sum, Gouldner attacks Goffman for defaulting with respect to some fundamental, pervasive dimensions of social reality, most particularly the stratification-related phenomena of power and hierarchy and their institutionalised manifestations.

Yet Goffman's default is more apparent than real. A careful study of his work reveals a series of significant, though sometimes implicit, insights concerning power, hierarchy, and an additional stratification-related phenomenon, social status. My principal purpose in this chapter is to examine and interrelate those elements of Goffman's work. In the process I hope to show that both the substance of and the spirit underlying those elements point to fundamental shortcomings in Gouldner's criticism as well as to some generally unrecognised profundity in Goffman's analyses.

Goffman is not regarded as a power theorist nor does he appear to consider himself a scholar of power, yet his dramaturgical perspective does contain significant, albeit implicit, insights into power and the related phenomena of influence and control. Goffman's scheme interrelating these three phenomena is intergrated with some fundemental insights on his part regarding social structure and its hierarchical elements.

In his major works Goffman has referred explicitly to the phenomenon of social structure or social order. While he has not *preoccupied* himself with social order, Goffman has indicated quite pointedly that a social-structural matrix sets the limits to which 'face' and status claims can be ongoingly stabilised. That matrix, Goffman suggests, variably extends or circumscribes opportunities for the autonomy and self-determination he deems necessary for the easeful, satisfactory maintenance of 'face' and self-respect.

Hierarchy is, of course, a universal feature of social structures. Goffman focuses on that feature by elucidating the manner in which the hierarchical structure of formal organisations tends often, particularly for members of lower organisational strata, to so severely limit effective opportunities for autonomy that proper demeanor becomes a problematic, if not humiliating, undertaking. In addition, he points to the systematic confusion between adjustment and conformity which tends to emerge in both the formally and informally organised realms of the mundane world. In Goffman's view both the formal-organisational denials of autonomy and the commonplace ambiguity regarding adjustment and conformity sometimes generate attempts at the maintenance of face through deviation from organisational and/or situational prescriptions regarding deference and demeanor. Specifically, Goffman suggests that 'secondary adjustments' and 'situational improprieties' may function as face-savers for individuals, whatever the functions they might serve at the group and societal levels.

Finally, Goffman's sensitivity to hierarchy and its basic consequences manifests itself in his references to the differential distribution of risk and opportunity, considered both objectively and subjectively. The manner in which Goffman discusses these phenomena expresses his awareness of the potency with which hierarchical structures, formal and informal, shape individuals' effective opportunities for maintaining desirable amounts of self-respect and social acceptability. It is significant, too, that Goffman refers to what is commonly called 'false consciousness' as a consequence of the social distribution of information. Moreover, he points to the possibly misguided but understandable efforts of individuals to achieve through 'false consciousness' a security which is systematically denied them by the social structure they thereby serve to perpetuate.

Thus Goffman's work is significantly provocative with respect to the matters of power, hierarchy, and status. Goffman himself has not claimed to offer analyses which elucidate those phenomena. Rather the thoroughness of his analyses suggests the broad manner in which the routinised behaviour of everyday life corresponds to and reflects the broader social patterns which intermesh to constitute a social structure. Goffman is to be credited, it seems, for the richness of the insights he offers into aspects of social reality which do not represent his focal concerns. To fault him for neglecting power and hierarchy seems, then, fundamentally misguided. To lay convincing grounds for that general position is the broad purpose of this essay.

POWER, INFLUENCE, AND CONTROL[6]

Throughout Goffman's works a persistent theme is that people display varying degrees of intentionality in affecting other individuals. That general theme undergirds Goffman's implicit approach to both power and influence and at the same time provides a basis for understanding how he comes to imply so much about those phenomena in his descriptions of everyday interaction.

Goffman points out that individuals can be wholly calculating in seeking desired responses from others; they can also be calculating but relatively unaware of it (1959, p. 6), a kind of middle ground on an intentionality-unintentionality continuum. At the unintentional extreme is the individual 'completely taken in by his own act' (1959, p. 17), whose motives operate naturally in the course of 'being himself' or 'being involved' (1974, p. 346).

For Goffman intentionality involves a conscious awareness on the part of the actor which might be called 'design' (1959, p. 4; 1963, pp. 14, 69); the intentional stands in contrast to the 'unwitting' (1959, p. 22) and the 'unmeant' (1959, p. 52). Goffman's usage of 'intentional' typically denotes not only awareness of preferred outcomes but also the calculated selection of certain modes of behaviour as *means* of achieving those outcomes. Thus glances, gestures, verbal statements, and positionings, which constitute the 'ultimate behavioral materials', can be used intendedly (de-signedly) or unintendedly (without calculation) (1967, p. 1). Clearly Goffman's usage of 'intentional' focuses on *interactional* goals, such as information control, impression management, and remedial results. Within his framework, then, intentionality involves conscious goal-oriented activity which is rooted in the proclivities of actors to assess each other and their capacities to manipulate the objects of such assessments. Sensitive to the fact that people can both knowingly and unknowingly make impressions (1961, p. 102), Goffman tends consistently to distinguish interaction in which people act better than they know how from interaction in which people consciously attempt to capitalise on their knowledge of how well they can indeed act (1959, p. 74).

As suggested earlier, Goffman's frequent references to intentionality provide a key to the manner in which he implicitly distinguishes power and influence from other phenomena which fundamentally affect the content and style of social interaction. In this regard Goffman's explication of 'strategic interaction' is relevant. *Strategic interaction* is a type of 'mutual impingement' in which, 'each party must make a move and where every possible move carries fateful implications for all parties' (1969, p. 127). Inasmuch as it involves 'calculative, gamelike aspects' (1969, p. x), strategic interaction is a specific *type* of interaction, namely a type characterised by full-fledged intentionality. That Goffman introduces a specific term with reference to such interaction suggests that he does *not* regard intentionality as a necessary nor pervasive feature of social interaction. Rather, it seems that from Goffman's perspective social life may be viewed as consisting broadly of strategic and nonstrategic interaction. The latter type of interaction rests on the routinisations by which people deal with the consequentiality of their interrelationships through 'continuous corrective control' (1974, p. 22). Strategic interaction emerges, 'when action is unexpectedly blocked or deflected and special compensatory effort is required' (1974, p. 22). Under those conditions motive and intent assume a felt significance which tends to undermine the taken-for-grantedness of everyday routinisations (1974, p. 22). The turn toward intentionality and 'compensatory effort' marks a move toward interaction which renders power relevant and influence likely; i.e., one's resources and their intentional invocation and/or activation become crucial when interaction is strategic.

Goffman's work thus reflects a fundamental but largely implicit distinction between the effects of interaction itself and the effects of power and influence. Specifically, Goffman does point to the inadvertent, unintended ways in which people affect one another's behaviour. Such effects, he implies, flow from the nature of routine interaction itself. It might be inferred that Goffman attends quite frequently to *interactional effects*, the short- or long-term changes in an individual's (or group's) behaviour which result from copresence itself rather than from behaviour intendedly directed at him by others. The behavioural effects of intentionality itself lie, then, in another realm. I shall show below that this realm is one having to do with power, influence, and control. In brief, intentionality serves implicitly in Goffman's works to specify a conceptual boundary separating power and closely related phenomena from other phenomena which are commonplace in social interaction.

POWER

Goffman's treatment of power is almost entirely implicit. In general, he treats power in terms of resources, focusing foremostly on people's differential *capacities* to affect others' behaviour.[7]

Goffman indicates that retaliatory responses to others' actions require authority and resources (1967, p. 222). Resources are capacities, which one 'can draw upon in his adaptations to the situation' (1969, p. 121). In his treatment of 'realised resources' as 'locally realisable events and roles' (1961, p. 28), Goffman suggests that the situation itself partially sets the parameters of one's power. That situational factors can be critical does not, though, diminish the significance of 'resource continuity'. 'The resources we use in a particular scene necessarily have some continuity, an existence before the scene occurs and an existence that continues after the scene is over' (1974, p. 299). At a rudimentary level, then, Goffman indicates that one's power in a given situation is a function of both individual-based and situation-based factors, which I have elsewhere described as instrumental and infra-resources.[8]

In terms of *instrumental resources* Goffman mentions position and various attributes which enable an individual to engage in bargaining (1959, p. 85). He also considers skills, largely interpersonal ones, which contribute to one's power. These include 'character', composure, 'presence of mind', and related characteristics which can be activated under 'perceivedly fateful circumstances' (1967, pp. 216ff.). Knowledge is also an important resource, (1961c, pp. 211–12). Goffman's concern with information control, misrepresentation, strategic secrets (1959, p. 142), and information states (1969, p. 121; 1974, pp. 133–4, 448) shows a continuing focus on the instrumental ways in which information can augment one's power.

In a central way Goffman also treats the situational and perceptual aspects of power. His attention to *infra-resources* focuses largely on perceptions, information, and access. Goffman is sensitive to the power-relevance of people's subjective assessments. He points out, for example, that a person may be:

unaware that something at hand is being determined. Or he may feel that the situation is problematic when in fact the matter at hand has already been determined and what he is really facing is revealment or disclosure. Or, finally, he may be fully oriented to what is actually happening. (1967, p. 153)

Such perceptions, which tend to augment or diminish one's power, are a function of both the information available to an actor and the past experiences he or she has had with a given other (1974, p. 299). Thus incomplete or distorted information can reduce the effective utility of one's instrumental resources as can the 'reputation' of a given other. In both cases the individual's perceptions are affected so as to render him or her less powerful in a given situation than those who have similar amounts and kinds of instrumental resources but also have infra-resources like accurate information and insights into the *current* likelihood that a given other will engage in influence successfully.

Goffman pointedly emphasises the importance of access as an infra-resource. He notes a close, though incomplete, correspondence among role played, information possessed and accessible regions (1959, p. 145). Rules of exclusion function to project insiders from intrusion (1963a, p. 145). Frequently such rules also create 'evidential boundaries'; i.e., barriers to perception (1974, p. 215). While Goffman typically treats the matter of access vis-a-vis his treatment of front and back regions and in-group and out-group alignments, he most emphatically indicates the relevance of access as an infra-resource in his remark that, 'he must be there in the flesh if the moment is to be his at all' (1967, p. 166). In other words, lack of effective access to given people or situations can severely curtail one's power relative to those who do have access.

Goffman does not provide an explicit definition of power. Yet he does use the term consistently to imply the capacity or potential to act effectively in social situations. *Qualitatively*, power involves potential intentionality. *Quantitatively* and relatively, it consists of instrumental and infra-resources. While Goffman has used illustrative data from other cultures and classes, by and large he has focused on an Anglo, middle-class, masculine world and is sensitive to that focus. (See: 1959, pp. 239, 244; 1961c, pp. x, 177, 179; 1963a, pp. 5, 132, 166–167; 1967, pp. 47–48, 113, 149; and 1971, pp. xiv–xv, 34, 41, 93). The frequency with which Goffman qualifies his observations suggests his awareness that within given subpopulations of a society or in other societies, different sorts of skills and circumstances might constitute resources. Thus Goffman implies that his concepts *as explicated* may not be widely applicable beyond the boundaries of the social world he has chosen as a focus.[9]

INFLUENCE

Influence is an interactional phenomenon to Goffman. As in the case of power, he provides no explicit definition; his use of the term implies its meaning. Goffman refers, for example, to influencing others through information management (1969, p. 13), suggesting that certain types of behaviour constitute influence insofar as they generate a change in others' behaviour. Goffman also incorporates the term influence in defining 'interaction' as, 'the reciprocal influence of individuals upon one another's actions when in one another's immediate physical presence' (1959, p. 15). That definition suggests Goffman's sensitivity to the phenomenon of interactional effects referred to earlier. Clearly Goffman favours, along with many other analysts, restriction of the term interaction to those social instances which clearly generate behavioral effects. Yet 'interaction' is often used with reference to, 'everything one might want to distinguish' (1974, p. 127). Implicit in Goffman's work is an apparent conviction that it is fruitful to distinguish interaction as a generic category of social behaviour from influence (or strategic interaction) which represents but one type of such behaviour. Specifically, interaction might be characterised as involving significant reciprocity, a relative absence of intentionality, and an ongoing modification of behaviour which is distributed rather evenly among participants. Conceived as a type of interaction, influence involves relative one-sidedness, intentionality, and behavioural modification which is concentrated among the targets of influence. That influence is a type of interaction is implied by the fact that influences must actively cooperate in order for influence to be successful (1974, p. 112). Thus influence is ultimately bilateral, although it can be treated as effectively unilateral relative to other types of interaction.

Goffman's implicit conception of influence is suggested by his explication of 'strategic interaction'. That conceptualisation is quite similar to numerous scholars' definitions of influence.[10] Scholars of influence typically treat various strategies of influence and Goffman, too, exhibits that sort of preoccupation. In general, he emphasises two broad types of influence strategies, namely communication management and sanctioning.

Actors can manage impressions created and maintained about the self through fabrication (1969, p. 13); i.e., intentional efforts to generate false beliefs in others about what is going on (1974, p. 83). Fabrication is an encompassing strategy of influence, including a variety of communication techniques which are available for specific purposes (1974, pp. 83–107). Among these techniques are innuendo, strategic ambiguity, crucial omissions, lies, and impersonations (1959, pp. 62, 64). Moreover, communication can be hinted at and thus easily denied (1967, p. 30). Goffman also discusses modes of concealment and covering as well as strategies of revealment (1969, pp. 18ff.). Finally, he observes that the body itself can be used communicatively in influence strategies (e.g., 'body gloss' 1971, p. 128), and that settings and equipment can be employed in the interests of rendering communication more influential (e.g., the 'front' 1959, p. 22).

Sanctioning receives less attention in Goffman's writings. He does, however, note the significance of rewards and punishments as strategies of influence (1961c, pp. 80, 178–179). His concern with 'situational proprieties' (1963a, p. 243) leads to consideration of an important but commonly neglected mode of negative sanctioning when he observes that such improprieties can be used to express 'interpersonal defiance' (1963a, p. 228), as well as to draw individuals into conflict (1967, p. 249). Such behaviour is simply communicative when expressions thus given result primarily in a registering of discontent or resentment. However, when another's moral claims are thereby undermined, resulting in embarrassment, negative sanctioning is involved. This type of influence strategy, then, cuts across the two broad types of strategies described.

CONTROL

Goffman uses the term 'control' (or 'social control') in two distinct ways, both as a process and as an effect. He refers to the 'process of social control' in terms of regulatory processes, sometimes involving sanctions, which reinforce institutional and/or situational norms (1961c, p. 38). In addition, he distinguishes formal from informal processes of social control (1971, p. 347). Processes of control can involve, 'tricky ways of sympathetically taking the other into consideration as someone who assesses the environment and might profitably be led into a wrong assessment' (1969, p. 17). The 'trickiness', sometimes intrinsic to processes of control, implies intentionality is also involved in 'containment'; i.e., 'taking others in' (1974, p. 83).

Goffman also refers to control as an effect, as when one has control of or control over perceptions. Control of people *results* from shaping their definitions of a situation (1959, pp. 3–4), or determining what they perceive (1959, p. 67). Frequently, such control results from labelling, as when inmates of total institutions are given 'all-embracing identifications' (1961c, pp. 84–85), or when stigmatised persons are so thoroughly categorised that their possibilities for autonomy are severely circumscribed (1963, p. 139). Ill-fame (1963, p. 70), negative labels, stereotypes, and ideologies constitute mechanisms generating control. Consistent with this usage of the term, Goffman points out that, 'we must start with the idea that a particular definition is *in charge of the situation*, and that as long as this control is not overtly threatened or blatantly rejected, much counter-activity will be possible' (1961, p. 133). Control, then, can be *in effect* and need not involve intentionally undertaken processes.

Goffman's conceptions of self control (1971, p. 121), and 'cooperator' also point to control as an ongoing state of affairs; indeed 'personal control' is critical to Goffman (1971, p. 346). Rules are effective because they are deemed appropriate and compliance with them allows people to conceive of themselves in favourable ways (1971, p. 98). Moreover, people tend 'voluntarily' to avoid those places where they are not welcome, saving face by venturing nothing (1967, p. 43). The 'cooperator', the 'normal', 'programmed', or 'built-in member' (1961c, p. 189), is, then, a controlled member of a social system, whatever the motives for his conformity.[11]

Goffman's two distinct conceptions of control represent a serious weakness in his conceptual scheme regarding power, influence, and control. That Goffman has used the same term with reference to qualitatively different phenomena is a problem. Perhaps more problematic, though, is his marked failure to specify precisely what each conception of control is designed to encompass. Conceived as a process, control seems hardly, if at all, distinguishable from influence. That the control processes which regulate behaviour sometimes focus on situational as well as institutional norms, that they may be informal as well as formal, and covert ('tricky') as well as overt clearly suggest that all control processes involve influence. Goffman's use of 'control' in the processual sense suggests that in some instances he may be trying to demarcate a subset of influence processes which are significantly formal and overt and focused on institutional norms; i.e., impersonal influence. His work, though, renders that judgment only a speculation since the conceptual ambiguities and inconsistencies regarding control are indeed real, tending to militate against the derivation of any precise idea as to why he uses control in this sense at all.

Conceived as an effect or ongoing state of affairs, control is similarly problematic. The controlled (and self-controlled) individual seems to be little more than the socialised individual whose secondary socialisation is ongoing as s/he participates in a given sociocultural system (with its available labels, ideologies, predominant beliefs, etc.) and interacts with some of its members (who

label, manipulate, and otherwise enact the cultural elements relevant to the situation at hand and/or their own identities). As an effect, then, control appears to represent the internalised content of primary socialisation *plus* overlays on that content which result from ongoing membership, participation, and interaction within a given social system. From this perspective, control is to some degree a 'condition of interaction' as well as an effect of past interaction, including influence. Thus the effect termed 'control' encompasses a complex configuration of phenomena, tending to render Goffman's conceptualisation seriously lacking in theoretical utility.

Nonetheless it is in his treatment of control as a routinised, ongoing effect that Goffman moves toward a transcendence of most conceptualisations of power. Most power scholars deal nearly exclusively with power, strategies of influence, and/or decision-making processes, constructing frameworks which fail to account explicitly for the day-to-day, routine conformity which generally corresponds to the preferences of the most powerful, influential members of a social system. In his treatment of control Goffman provides not only conceptual grounds for attending to that phenomenon but also bases for identifying the relevance of labelling, belief systems, and the like to power. Most importantly, he establishes grounds for treating the circumscription of in-tentionality in social life. Specifically, his insights point to the ways in which those with power can exploit dominant belief and value systems to maximise their preferred outcomes without engaging in influence as frequently or pointedly as would otherwise be the case.

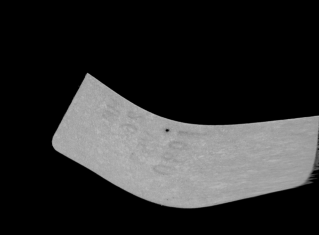

SUMMARY

In sum, Goffman conceives of power as a potential or capacity comprised of resources, importantly including infra-resources. The intended activation or invocation of one's resources is influence, an interactional phenomenon. Conformity to a given person's or group's preferences in the absence of direct influence is the empirical referent of control. Goffman elaborates this basic con-ceptualisation through attention to (1) key resources in middle-class American society (e.g., access and information); (2) specific st-rategies of influence (e.g. misrepresentation, sanctioning); and (3) those phenomena which tend to generate behaviour conducive to the interests of the powerful vis-a-vis their effects on perceptions and beliefs (e.g., labels, ideologies). Thus within his dramaturgical framework Goffman offers a rather far-reaching, intentionality-based commentary on power and related phenomena. In fact, his work suggests that the Sociology of Power is perhaps most rudimentarily the Sociology of Intentionality. That possibility would seem to merit serious consideration.

SOCIAL ORDER AND THE MATTER OF FACE

The framework within which Goffman's insights on power are embedded also encompasses a commentary on the centrality of hierarchy and status to an understanding of self-presentation and closely related phenomena. To understand that commentary on hierarchy and status requires not only a sensitivity to Goffman's implicit treatment of power but also an appreciation of his conceptions of social order and face, matters which I shall briefly discuss at this point.

In Goffman's view a *social order* consists of, 'variously motivated and variously functioning patterns of actual behaviour' (1971, p. x). Social order is a consequence of any set of moral norms which regulate the pursuit of objectives (1963a, p. 8). Thus a social order consists of patterns of behaviour which derive from a variety of motives and serve a variety of functions but which always bear some fundamental relationship to norms or ground rules which have an essentially moral quality. Every type of social order involves, then, a transformation of mere behaviour into conduct (1963a, p. 8). People do not simply 'behave' toward one another; rather they 'conduct' themselves according to restrictive and enabling norms which regulate their routine dealings with one another (1971, p. x). Conduct can be broadly regarded as a patterned adaptation to such ground rules, not simple conformity to, nor deviation from, them.

Central to the patterns of behaviour which constitute a social order is the phenomenon of claims (1971, p. 28). Every social order is based on the principle that any individual with certain social characteristics can morally expect to be valued and treated in an 'appropriate' manner (1959, p. 13). The unequal distribution of characteristics considered socially important and/or relevant is thus paralleled by an unequal distribution of the right to expect *deference* in a given situation and often trans-situationally. The degrees and modes of deference exhibited toward those sharing similar (amounts of) social characteristics points to the general location of such people in the 'hierarchy of society' (1967, p. 82). That hierarchy shapes situated interaction, then, by tending to determine the allocation of privileges and duties among copresent actors (1961, pp. 29, 31).

Since human beings rely so heavily on signs and symbols, quite minor things can be expressive of claims to deference (1967, p. 33). As claims-expressive behaviour, demeanour bears a necessary, though statistical, relationship to the amounts and types of deference individuals typically receive. *Demeanour* is, 'that element of the individual's ceremonial behaviour typically conveyed through deportment, dress, and bearing, which serves to express to those in his immediate presence that he is a person of certain desirable and undesirable qualities' (1967, p. 77). It consists not only of conduct but also of one's *personal front*, the items of expressive equipment identified with an individual and expected to accompany him wherever he goes (1959, p. 24). The overall 'social front' an individual presents through conduct and personal front is the basis on which others make assumptions about his or her moral standards and social worth (1974, p. 110). From a micro-level viewpoint, then, social status is ongoingly created and re-created through the interplay of types of conduct called deference and demeanour and their symbolic and ritual elements.

While many analysts indicate that an individual's social status is never fully nor absolutely *established*, Goffman provides a detailed commentary on that principle and its implications for everyday life. He emphasizes that while some status claims can be determined to be valid or invalid (e.g., the claim to be a law graduate), most such claims can be confirmed only *more or less* (e.g., the claim to be a music lover) (1959, p. 60). Specifically, he says:

> To *be* a given kind of person . . . is not merely to possess the required attributes, but also to sustain the standards of conduct and appearance that one's social grouping attaches thereto. . . . A status, a position, a social place is not a material thing, to be possessed and then displayed; it is a pattern of appropriate conduct, coherent, embellished, and well articulated. (1959, p. 75)

Thus among the 'dramaturgic elements' of the human situation are, 'Shared staging problems; concern for the way things appear; warranted and unwarranted feelings of shame; ambivalence about oneself and one's audience' (1959, p. 239). Every social situation encompasses, in other words, 'effectively projected claims to an acceptable self and the confirmation of like claims on the part of others' (1967, p. 105). In everyday conversation, for example, questions and statements can be regarded as sorts of status claims (1971, p. 162). Moreover, the interpersonal rituals of everyday life encompass a set of 'ratificatory rituals' whereby an individual's claims to an altered and desired status are accepted and confirmed by copresent others (1971, p. 67). Ritual and conduct interplay, then, with 'embodied expressive signs' (1963a, p. 34), in the ongoing construction of social status through the presentation of and responses to status claims.

Lest the foregoing seem like the contours of a 'parlour-game of oneupmanship',[12] the matter of self must be incorporated at this point. 'Face' is the critical concept here. Closely related to demeanour and social status, 'face' is, 'the *positive* social value a person effectively claims for himself by the line others assume he has taken during a particular contact' (1967, p. 5, emphasis added). 'Face is an image of self delineated in terms of approved social attributes – albeit an image others may share' (1967, p. 5): it is an encompassing idea about self which the individual, 'protects and defends and invest his feelings in . . . and ideas are vulnerable not to facts and things but to communications' (1967, p. 43). Demeanour and deference are, then, modes of conduct vitally important to the individual in terms of the potential they carry for intersubjective validation of his ideas about the fundamental worthiness of self. Indeed the main principle of the ritual order sustaining those conducts may be face rather than justice (1967, p. 44).

Since it concerns the very experience of self, face is centrally and continuously important to the individual. In fact, face-saving is a principle motive for conformity to interactional codes (1967, p. 12). Its social function is the ongoing mobilisation of individuals as 'self-regulating' participants in social life. Such mobilisation is generally successful in part because people learn universally, 'to have feelings attached to self and a self expressed through face' (1967, p. 44).

Therefore status claims, however petty they may seem, are expressive of a vital impulse having to do with self. Whatever triviality those claims might be judged as manifesting is, of course, learned and ongoingly reinforced within a given individual's circles of routinely copresent others. Goffman's analyses of self-presentation, impression management, and status claims (or, face, face-work, and face-saving), offer far more than a laying bare of what Gouldner has called, 'the elaborate strategies by which men ingeniously contrive to persuade others to buy a certain definition of the situation.'[13] These analyses by Goffman point generally to something much more profound than contrived attempts at persuasion.[14] In fact, Goffman's work turns largely on the principle that each human life can be viewed as a *moral career*, involving a regular sequence of changes in the person's self and his criteria for judging himself and others (1961c, p. 128). The moral career is two-sided. Internally it involves image of self and felt identity; externally it involves social location, style of life, and, 'is part of a publicly accessible institutional complex' (1961c, p. 127). Goffman's treatment of internal-external dynamic of moral careers leads directly to the matter of hierarchy as well as the phenomena of conformity and face-maintenance.

HIERARCHY, CONFORMITY, AND FACE-MAINTENANCE

MORAL CAREERS: AGENCY AND SELFHOOD

Goffman emphasises that spheres of self-determination are necessary in order for an individual to exhibit proper deference and act with proper demeanour (1967, p. 92). Since both types of conduct offer a commentary (intended or not) on the self (and thus shape the individual's moral career), the individual must be in some sense an *agent* with reference to each; the two phenomena cannot be conceived as having been created or imposed from outside the person who manifests them. A sense of self-determination is also crucial to the experience of being a full-fledged person (1971, p. 61), as is a degree of felt control over one's 'fixed territories' (1971, p. 288). In some highly fundamental respects, then, a sense of agency and self-determination is crucial to the maintenance of proper demeanour and deference and to the satisfying construction of one's moral career. So vital is this complex interrelationship that under conditions of extreme constraint the individual, 'is automatically forced from the circle of the proper' (1967, p. 93).

Under less extreme conditions the maintenance of a sense of self-determination can be nonetheless problematic. Documented elements of one's biography, for example, clearly limit the ways in which an individual can choose to present himself or herself (1961, p. 61). More importantly for present purposes, the individual's range of choices regarding manner of self-presentation, 'derives from the place of his kind in the social strucure' (1963, p. 112). Thus degree of felt and actual self-determination is more or less considerable and more or less satisfactory as a function of biographical and social-structural factors. In a similar vein it might be said that the modes in which given *types* of people can effectively attempt to maintain face are considerably shaped by the social structures in which their dealings with one another routinely occur. In sum, social structures set the effective parameters on individuals' degrees of felt self-determination and on their range of effectively available modes of maintaining face; self-image and social structure are complexly and dynamically intertwined as the notion of moral career so aptly suggests.

Social structure (or social order) is also a crucial determinant of another prerequisite of face-maintenance, namely privacy. Social life rests on an assumption that there will be some places where privacy is relatively insured (1974, p. 163); i.e., where demeanour and deference will not be potentially problematic. Privacy is not only a function of situation but also of conduct. Specifically, the way an individual can provide the least information about himself or herself (and thus maintain an important measure of privacy) is to 'fit in' by acting as people of that type are supposed to act (1963a, p. 35). Since 'fitting in' is *the* rule of interaction (1963a, p. 11), deviation from it is cause for special attention, which can often result in the revelation of more information about the individual and his or her motives than would otherwise be the case. Thus social order, the patterns of behaviour referred to earlier, generates a pressure toward conformity which derives in part from the need and/or desire for privacy as well as the desire to maintain face.

Goffman's work points, then, to the crucial significance of social structure with reference to both face and the felt self-determination necessary to its maintenance. Moreover, he is clearly sensitive to the unequal distribution of opportunities for face-maintenance as well as the ways in which social-structural factors render problematic the sense of self-determination through pressures toward conformity. These general notions can be specified more precisely by examining Goffman's perspective on organisations and hierarchy.

ORGANISATIONS AND HIERARCHY

Goffman's commentary on formal organisations and the effects of their hierarchical structures on conduct, face, degree of self-determination, and privacy best illustrates, or at least implies, his insights and focal concerns regarding the phenomenon of hierarchy.[15] In broad terms Goffman emphasises that, 'institutional arrangements . . . delienate the personal prerogatives of a member' (1961c, p. 47). More pointedly, he indicates that formal organisations involve an allocation of character and being just as thoroughly as they involve a distribution of duties and rewards (1961c, p. 111). Moreover, the mechanisms by which such allocations are accomplished include not only the propagation of organisational ideolgies but also the actions of organisational superordinates toward their subordinates which express a conception of them (1961c, p. 185).

From Goffman's viewpoint, then, the hierarchical structure of formal organisations has profound implications. The strata comprising an organisational hierarchy are collectivities of people whose characters, officially available modes of self-presentation, and rights to deference are largely specified by their stratum membership. In fact, formal organisations *stage* differences among constructed categories of people, defining those categories in terms of purportedly actual differences in social worth and moral character (1961c, p. 111). Over time membership in a given organisational stratum thus affects individuals' perceptions of their selves as well as of others in the organisation (ibid.). Moreover, members of a given stratum in an organisation tend to share a common fate, particularly so when the status of stratum members is relatively uniform, and to that extent they tend to develop a common character (1961c, p. 129).

Goffman's perspective points persistently to the fact that while both the opportunities and outcomes of members are shaped rather determinatively by their locations in the hierarchy, the perceptions and judgments which emerge as elements of the social order (the variously motivated and variously functioning patterns of actual behaviour) of an organisation are *socially* constructed and maintained. Thus while the 'reality' of superiority and inferiority and of worthiness and lack thereof is a deep, encompassing one which reaches well into the selves residing to some (often significant) degree in the organisation, it is at root a staged production. The social construction of such a profoundly consequential reality is a major theme in Goffman's treatment of hierarchy and organisation, a theme which leads him to conclude that even judgments about the 'pathological' are often lay, political, and ethnocentric rather than scientific in nature (1961c, pp. 363–364).

Yet the actors portrayed in Goffman's analyses are not 'cultural dopes'; i.e., the individual is not conceived as a, 'man-in-the-sociologists's-society who produces the stable features of society by acting in compliance with preestablished and legitimate alternatives of action that the common culture provides.'[16] Goffman instead emphasises that within every social establishment participants can be found to:

> decline in some way to accept the official view of what they should be putting into and getting out of the organisation and, behind this, of what sort of self and work they are to accept for themselves. (1961c, p. 304)

Thus even though chance-taking (sticking one's neck out) tends to be 'organised out' of the daily routines associated with job and home (1967, pp. 194–95), individuals nevertheless adopt within those routines relatively non-risky methods of maintaining distance between themselves and that with which they are supposed to be identified (1961c, p. 319). Various 'lines of adaptation', then, are developed in response to the internal-external dialectic of individuals' moral careers. In sum, from Goffman's vantage point hierarchy does not routinely nor narrowly oppress *per se*; rather it relativises the matters of human dignity and self-determination so as to render problematic for most people most of the time the maintenance of face.

ADJUSTMENT AND CONFORMITY

Notwithstanding the facts that people are not 'cultural dopesters', and that hierarchy problematises some profoundly central elements of individual existence, hierarchies do perpetuate themselves. And that perpetuation need not and usually does not rest on rather continuous invocation and/or activation of the power of the superordinates of those hierarchies. Rather people tend to be significantly *controlled* within hierarchies. The earlier discussion of control indicated how Goffman has elucidated the general ways in

which a state of affairs can be maintained which clearly favours the
more powerful without their having to engage in influence
repeatedly and pointedly. Among the modes by which such control,
as an ongoing state of affairs, can be maintained is the inculcation
and routine reinforcement of a commonplace confusion between
adjustment and conformity. This sort of confusion is among the
modes by which hierarchies can be perpetuated; i.e., by which
people can come to routinely cooperate in the social orders which
circumscribe their opportunities for felt dignity and self-
determination, even while refusing to cooperate thoroughly.

In general, people today as fully as their predecessors must bear
the 'cross of personal character' when in the presence of others
(1971, p. 187). Interpersonal rituals link people together by
providing bases for, 'ordering events accommodatively' (1971, p.
164). In everyday life deviation from commonplace ground rules
can thus be regarded and experienced as disruptive and unfair, on
the one hand, and expressive of questionable character and/or
moral inferiority, on the other hand. While the existential conditions of modern and pre-modern people share this similarity,
modern peoples commonly experience circumstances which render
them more vulnerable to confusing adjustment and conformity. In
particular, there is a fairly popularised 'good-adjustment theory'
(1963, pp. 108–23), which ideologically sensitises people not only
to the necessity of adjustment but also to the need for accommodating themselves to those elements of social order which are among the
sources of their 'adjustment problems' in the first place. In addition,
people today are routinely involved in role-segregation.
Consequently,

> however the individual presents himself on any occasion before
> any audience, there will be other places, times, and audiences
> when he quite properly conducts himself in a manner that would
> discredit this first performance were his other conduct to be
> vividly brought to light. (1974, pp. 168–9)

Under such conditions 'adjustment' unsurprisingly becomes an
issue for many participants in social life just as 'character' seems
always to have been an issue for human being sharing a social order
which is rooted in ultimately moral ground rules. These general
conditions, then, constitute a peculiarly modern set of pressures
toward conformity even as the opportunities for increased in-

dividuality seem historically to have expanded.

It might also be argued that formal organizations with their finely graduated hierarchies represent pervasive systems of control, perhaps as thoroughgoing for the average individual today as clan and community were historically. Within formal organisations conformity to expectations in the 'prescribed spirit' (adjustment) represents acceptance of an identity as 'a particular kind of person who dwells in a particular kind of world' (1961c, p. 186). In other words, official definitions of proper conduct across a wide range of behaviours, 'expand a mere participation contract into a definition of the participant's nature or social being' (1961c, p. 179). Thus can, 'we begin to see the self-defining implications of even the minor give-and-take in organisations' (1961c, p. 181). Formalised hierarchies tend to generate a systematic, (and quite useful!), confusion between obedience to others and the individual's own personal adjustment (1961c, p. 385). Like rules in general, the official prescriptions and definitions tend to be effective in part because within the organisational context compliance not only brings rewards (however meagre or generous) but also allows individuals to assess positively who and what they are (1971, p. 98).

Broadly considered, then, 'adjustment' or 'being adjusted' has tended to become a major component of 'face' in modern life with adjustment and conformity tending to become systematically and pervasively confused. And all the while those who conform also maintain their distance from the niches prescribed for them, for face is to be maintained as much by the span between self and hierarchy as by conformity to whatever the official line prescribes for people of a given kind (stratum). To this extent the internal and external aspects of moral careers appear to stand frequently, if not necessarily, in a dialectical relationship to one another.

SECONDARY ADJUSTMENTS AND SITUATIONAL IMPROPRIETIES

In direct response to formalised hierarchies people often engage in *secondary* adjustments as fundamental modes of distancing themselves from organisational roles and the selves implied therein (1961c, p. 189). A *secondary adjustment* is:

> any habitual arrangement by which a member of an organisation employs unauthorised means, or obtains unauthorised ends, or both, thus getting around the organisation's assumptions as to

what he should do and get and hence what he should be. (1961c, p. 189)

Secondary adjustments thus involve the creation of 'participation statuses' (1974, p. 224), which are not officially recognised and in fact depart from what is officially available to organisational members. Goffman refers to two major kinds of secondary adjustments. *Disruptive* ones rest on participants' intentions to abandon the organisation or to radically change it; *contained* ones involve fitting into the existing structure of the organisation (1961c, p. 199). While Goffman chooses to focus on the latter, he notes that such adjustments can serve to deflect efforts away from disruption (1961c, pp. 199–200), and hence away from possible change.

Inasmuch as secondary adjustments represent responses foremostly to hierarchical arrangements it would be expected that their frequency and form vary among strata within an organisation (1961c, p. 201). Specifically, if stratum membership significantly shapes people's face-related prerogatives, then it seems reasonable to suppose that members of those strata in which face is organisationally rendered the most problematic would be likelier to distance themselves from the organisation through secondary adjustments. Goffman points out that:

Persons at the bottom of large organisations typically operate in drab backgrounds, against which higher-placed members realise their internal incentives, enjoying the satisfaction of receiving visible indulgences that others do not. (1961c, p. 201)

Not only are people occupying such a position likely to use secondary adjustments but so also are those 'higher-placed' members whose positions entitle them to special secondary adjustments of the 'expense account' variety (1961a, pp. 201–2). Thus those organisational members who have considerable power and those who have very little appear to share a tendency toward secondary adjustments, although the latter grouping seem likelier to make use of both disruptive and contained types.

Secondary adjustments can, then, elucidate the distribution of power within a hierarchy. Those with considerable, often massive, amounts of power can use their status, information, privacy, authority, and other resources to enjoy perquisites above and beyond those which are officially specified as part of their privilege

within the organisation. Those whose power is severely circumscribed within that same hierarchy often have so few and such small
amounts of relevant resources that their most efficient activation lies
in the form of secondary adjustments. Secondary adjustments *can*,
though need not, communicate that the practitioner, 'has some
selfhood and personal autonomy beyond the grasp of the organization' (1961c, p. 314). Thus members of strata with very little
power may not be able to influence those higher in the hierarchy to
recognise their selfhood; i.e., their dignity, their adulthood, and the
like. The same power, though, may be activated in order to carry
out secondary adjustments. And indeed some such adjustments may
serve only and 'self-preservingly' to express what perhaps can be
effectively expressed in no other way, namely a, 'rejection of one's
rejectors' (1961c, p. 315). In fact, within some organisations
members of the lowest stratum may find their condition, 'so
degrading, so unjust, and so inhuman that the only self-respecting
response' (1963, p. 225), is some sort of secondary adjustment.

Situational improprieties represent a different sort of response to
the kinds of 'problems of self' which routinely arise for members of
the lower strata in organisational hierarchies, yet they seem often to
arise from the same sorts of face-related motivations and to express
the same sort of self-preserving distance from the organisation and
its definitions. Among the variety of motivations which can give rise
to 'misconduct' in a situation is the desire to express resentment
toward a social establishment or institution (1963, p. 223).
Situational improprieties can be used, then, to do, 'something about
one's relation to an official in the situation' (1963, p. 228). Thus
such improprieties can be foremostly acts of interpersonal defiance
(1963, p. 228). Paradoxically, though, such acts often bespeak a
deep concern about the establishment (1963, p. 226), again
suggesting a dialectic between the internal and external aspects of
individuals' moral careers.

In response to hierarchy and the minimal power it provides them,
members of low strata, then, tend still to assert their selves in face-
maintenance attempts. That the officially created and sustained
differences among strata are rather thoroughly *constructed and staged*
has an 'unofficial' parallel comprised foremostly of secondary
adjustments and situational improprieties. Those modes of behaviour might be regarded as counter-constructions and counter-
stagings which, if nothing else, express for their practitioners selves
that exist apart from and faces that can be maintained in spite of the

hierarchy which threatens both in fundamental ways. Thus the 'dramaturgical character' (1961c, p. 110), of the unequal distribution of character and personal prerogatives within a hierarchy, though staged, has profound and far-reaching consequences. An earlier point bears reiteration here; extreme constraint automatically forces individuals from the realm of the proper (1967, p. 93). Such pressures to depart from propriety represent an extreme but not infrequent consequence of the kinds and degrees of control formalised hierarchies often generate with respect particularly to their lowest-ranking members.

RISK, OPPORTUNITY, AND FALSE CONSCIOUSNESS

Goffman has indicated that chance-taking tends to be 'organised out' of the routines of everyday life (1967, p. 195); what risks and chance-taking remain tend largely to be nonvoluntary. In any event whatever risks and opportunities inhere in daily life occur together and the individual's perception of each may but does not necessarily coincide with the actual distribution of possibilities (1967, pp. 151–52). Generally, individuals and groups have different base-lines for assessing risk and opportunity (1967, p. 157). Crucial to the determination of such base-lines are surely *information states*; i.e., the knowledge individuals or groups have as to why events have occurred, what is currently happening, who the relevant actors are and what is tending to motivate them, and what the outcome is likely to be (1974, pp. 133–34). Insofar as the distribution of information states among individuals and groups is patterned, that pattern would seem at least crudely reflective of the distribution of *senses* of opportunity and risk. The crucial relevance of information states accounts in part for the commonness with which an, 'individual may never become aware of the risk and opportunity that in fact existed, or may become alive to the gamble he was making only after the play is over'(1967, p. 161).

Equally crucial to the determination of base-lines for assessing risks and opportunities are organisational arrangements. The hierarchical distribution of power and prerogatives within organisations parallels the distribution of information, as the earlier discussion of power implied. Thus not only do risks and opportunities vary with stratum membership but so also do the information states necessary for accurately perceiving those realities. While mobility within an organisational hierarchy affects an individual's ability to calculate risks, in part because it affects one's information state, movement up and down within a hierarchy is not typical, at least not in terms of relatively long-distance movement. Clearcut, consistent insights into the linkages between risk/opportunity and institutional arrangements are to that extent not commonplace. In Goffman's terms:

> Appreciation of risks to his self-conception is part of everyone's moral experience, but *an appreciation that a given risk level is itself merely a social arrangement is a rarer kind of experience*, and one that seems to help disenchant the person who undergoes it. (1961c, p. 167, emphasis added)

To the extent that they are commonly denied that route (and others) to disenchantment with institutional arrangements, people often and understandably not only misperceive their effective opportunities and risks but also lean toward individualistic rather than structural 'explanations' in accounting for their own and others' outcomes. (In other terms, 'face' is ongoingly problematic in part because of commonplace failures to recognise that structural as well as individual factors determine opportunity and risk.) Goffman thus points to social-structural factors as well as the social distribution of information as determinative of 'risk levels'. Moreover, he is explicitly aware of the uncommonness with which people recognise the social sources of risk and opportunity.

Unsurprisingly, then, Goffman remarks a number of times about a phenomenon which Marxists would call 'false consciousness'. For example, Goffman indicates that, 'conventional persons often maintain the rules consistently enough to remain unaware of the situational obligations their conduct sustains' (1963a, p. 226). Habitual conventionality can circumscribe awareness of the very expectations which might militate against one's own group's interests as well as diminish the likelihood of perceiving that one's behaviour in fact serves to sustain those expectations. Within Goffman's framework 'false consciousness' is considered insofar as Goffman does treat the commonplace inability of people to recognise: (1) the social-structural sources or risk and opportunity; (2) the obligations which channel their behaviour; and, (3) the ways in which their own behaviour sustains those obligations, all of which nonrecognition can contribute to the maintenance of conditions which are not in the interests of those serving thusly to perpetuate such conditions.[17] Yet Goffman points out that 'interests' have a special status in human affairs. The fact that individuals can and often do share interests provides a basis for collective action (1969, p. 46), but individuals typically have more than one interest (1969, p. 47). And here face as a central, ongoing concern of individuals is highly relevant, for it is a common (perhaps universal) interest which can conflict with interests in change, deviance, protest, equal opportunity, and other alternatives which might circumscribe the sorts of relative nonrecognition cited above. Thus face-maintenance can, like the 'cross of personal character', actively preoccupy most people most of the time at the cost of important insights into the structural factors which shape their experiences and outcomes. More specifically, concern with face often prevents the very kinds of mis-conduct which would constitute the most effective antidotes to false consciousness.

Concern with face impels people, then, to cooperate in perpetuating the very structures which allocate character and being so as to cheat some individuals of their fair share of both and to render most others anxious about the validation of the fair share they currently have. Among the stigmatised, for example, concern with face sometimes leads to a 'self-betraying kind of stratification' (1963, p. 107), in which the more or less socially rejected engage in the creation of invidious distinctions among themselves. More generally, he comments:

> Whatever his position in society, the person insulates himself by blindnesses, half-truths, illusions, and rationalisations. He makes an 'adjustment' by convincing himself with the tactful support of his intimate circle, that is is what he wants to be. . . . And as for society, if the person is willing to be subject to informal social control – if he is willing to find out from hints and glances and tactful cues what his place is, and keep it – then there will be no objection to his furnishing this place at his own discretion, with all the comfort, elegance, and nobility his wit can muster for him. . . . Social life is an . . . orderly thing because the person voluntarily stays away from the places and topics and times where he is not wanted and where he might be disparaged for going. He cooperates to save his face, finding that there is much to be gained from venturing nothing. (1967, p. 43)

Thus do the notions of false consciousness, control, 'adjustment', and face interplay within Goffman's framework. In the simplest terms Goffman recognizes that for most people:

> there are many good reasons to take comfort in . . . uneventfulness and seek it out, voluntarily foregoing practical gambles along with risk and opportunity. . . .The question is one of security. (1967, p. 174)

The question is also, as Goffman's work often implies, one of power.

DISCUSSION

A BROADER VIEW

Before reexamining Gouldner's critique of Goffman, I shall discuss Goffman's stratification-related insights in a broader theoretical context than has been adopted thus far. Considered in this broader context, the implicit linkages between Goffman's ideas and those of other analysts become clearer as does the richness of Goffman's insights. Specifically, within a more general context it appears that to a significant degree Goffman details the micro-level specifics of what a number of analysts writing in the 1950's preceived as emergent trends among the new middle classes.

As was indicated earlier, Goffman describes a world which is preeminently Anglo, masculine, and middle-class. Goffman thus focuses on the white-collar world, a segment of our society which reveals much of what is characteristic of 20th century American life.[18] Moreover, the world of the new middle classes consists, as much of Goffman's work implies, of:

> a loose collection of occupational strata, probably more anxiety-ridden than the rest of the culture, dominated by the drive to distinguish themselves from the working class, uncohesive, held together by no common bond except the fact they are caught in a kind of Purgatory between the Hell of the poor and the Heaven of the rich and powerful.[19]

That world is further characterised by a visible 'democratisation' of behaviour patterns with a concomitant erosion of visible status differences.[20] The lines dividing status groupings have become significantly blurred,[21] and symbolic minutiae have become proportionately more emphasised.[22] The psychology of the new middle classes thus tends to be the 'psychology of status striving' with people's status claims increasingly expressed by appearance, as the label white-collar implies.[23] Historically the drift has been away from the injunction to know one's station and toward the question 'Do I belong?'.[24] Status insecurity and a 'virtual status panic' have become to that extent increasingly commonplace.[25]

C. Wright Mills offered a penetrating analysis of the major historical and structural changes generative of the behavioural and psychological traits of the new middle classes. He notes with particular emphasis three sorts of major changes, including contemporary modes of bureaucratisation, the nature of most white-collar job skills, and the urban character of the new middle classes. First of all, the work environment of the new middle classes is typically a 'mere fragment' of a large bureaucracy,[26] which at one and the same time raises a hierarchy and levels out personnel.[27] Moreover, the white-collar hierarchy, while not purely bureaucratic,[28] does involve minute gradations of rank and fragmentation of skills to a degree that status distinctions within the hierarchy militate against status solidarity, tending rather to promote increased status competition.[29] Yet the status competition generated within the white-collar hierarchies commonly achieves little for white-collar workers except frustration which often expresses itself off the job in the form of more intense status striving.[30] Secondly, white-collar jobs increasingly involve skills with persons rather than things, services rather than goods being sold.[31] In some sense the employer of such workers buys their social personalities, creating a 'personality market' involving the commercial exchange of, 'those traits which affect one's *impressions* upon others'.[32] Finally, the white-collarite is disproportionately represented among metropolitan residents. And:

> The metropolitan man's biography is often unknown, his past apparent only to very limited groups, so the basis of his status is often hidden and ambivalent, revealed only in the fast-changing *appearances* of his mobile, anonymous existence.[33]

Mills considered the interplay of those conditions as generative of a type of person who instrumentalises his own personality and appearance through the practice of 'selling himself'.[34] Mills also indicated that these tendencies spill over into off-the-job spheres, tending to create, 'a public-relations aspect to private relations of all sorts, including even relations with oneself'.[35] 'Adjustment' under such conditions tends to become an ongoing problem, increasingly manifested by an adjustment-oriented person who:

> simply want to merge into his social landscape, to offer as little exposed and vulnerable surface as possible. . . ., to take his place in the scheme of society with a minimum of effort and an economy of psychic hurt.[36]

The new middle classes, then, occupy a social terrain which is both ambiguous and demanding status-wise. Several decades ago Mills and others pointed to the likely psychological and interactional consequences of that terrain. Goffman has effectively, it seems, detailed the form and content of a great deal of the everyday social behaviour of people who occupy the amorphous class position which Mills described from a macro-level viewpoint. Sensitive to the class biases of his analyses and to the dangers of characterising more remote social processes on the basis of close-at-hand, rather immediately observable ones, Goffman points out, though, that:

> we must be very cautious in any effort to characterize our own society as a whole with respect to dramaturgical practices. (1959, p. 245)

In addition, he indicates that the dramaturgical perspective is but *one* of five perspectives which are useful in elucidating the nature of social orders. (1959, p. 240ff.). Each perspective, 'can be employed as the end-point of analysis, as a final ways of ordering the facts' (1959, p. 240), and the facts emphasised within each perspective are also relevant to the matters of principal concern within the other perspectives (1959, pp. 240–1). Thus Goffman's use of the dramaturgical perspective offers insights which are also relevant to the technical, political, structural, and cultural perspectives on social life. In general, Goffman seems to have developed a framework perhaps particularly applicable to the study of the new middle classes and yet not lacking utility with reference to an understanding of contemporary American life generally, a framework distinctive in its emphases and yet not lacking fruitfulness with reference to complementing other sociological perspectives.

GOULDNER'S CRITIQUE

Given the foregoing discussion of Goffman's ideas as they relate to, imply about, and address the matters of power, hierarchy, and status, a reexamination of Gouldner's critique yields mixed results. First of all, it seems fairly clear that Goffman does not describe actors as if they were unattached to an institutional structure, even though he does not attend to any specific type(s) of institution in great detail. Goffman's strategy is rather to indicate the determinative and general influences of social orders, including public order, and 'social establishments' on behaviour in everyday life. On the other hand, Gouldner's contentions about the ahistorical character of Goffman's analyses seem generally valid. Goffman does, however, deal with micro-level historical factors, particularly biography and past experiences with given others, as conditioning both the behaviour and effective options of individuals. While the ahistorical character of his analyses is perhaps understandable given his micro-level focus, it is nonetheless the case that that character may limit the overall richness of his work and probably serves to aggravate the difficulties inherent in deriving macro-level insights from his micro-level analyses.

Secondly, Gouldner's insistence that Goffman offers no 'metaphysics of hierarchy' seems significantly inappropriate. Goffman has paid considerable and explicit attention to the hierarchial arrangements which crucially differentiate individuals' prerogatives regarding face as well as their amounts of power, antonomy, and privacy. In addition, he has stressed the fundamentally dramaturgical nature of such differentiations, thereby providing grounds for a processual approach to hierarchies as they shape everyday life. To fault him for failing to offer a 'metaphysics of hierarchy' is to overlook significantly the degree to which such a metaphysics in fact informs considerable portions of Goffman's analyses.

Finally, it seems rather clear that Goffman does imply a great deal not only about power but also about influence and that he explicitly treats the fundamental nature and effects of control. Perhaps Gouldner's criticism of Goffman in this regard reflects presuppositions as to how power, hierarchy, and related matters should both be conceptualised and analysed. In any event Gouldner seems to have criticised Goffman more than a bit too harshly, perhaps even too carelessly, given the degree to which

Goffman does concern himself with the very matters Gouldner regards as rather thoroughly neglected in his work.

In conclusion, it might be suggested that one of the difficulties in fully appreciating the insights which Goffman offers into American society (or at least major segments of it), is not only his rather strictly micro-level focus but also his rather consistent concern with the *conditions* of interaction and social order as well as their *situated* aspects. Specifically, Goffman treats phenomena such as self, face, moral career, self-control, and other fundamental phenomena in a manner which points to their status as universal conditions of social order as well as social interaction.[37] Interspersed with those efforts is a concern with interaction and order as socioculturally situated phenomena; this concern is clear, for example, in his treatments of psychiatric definitions of the 'pathological', formal organisations, and institutionalised gambling. That Goffman intermeshes these two sorts of principal preoccupations seems potentially fruitful with respect to sociological theory; it seems, though, potentially confusing for those who attempt to cull insights from his analyses.

Let me conclude on a note which concerns the relevance of Goffman's ideas to an understanding of contemporary American life. It strikes me that major portions of Goffman's works, namely the portions in which the ideas summarised here are discussed, parallel in an interesting manner a recent work by Sennett and Cobb.[38] Like Sennett and Cobb, Goffman is pointedly concerned with 'problems of self', foremostly problems related to positive self-image, dignity, autonomy, and felt control over the fundaments of one's life. Unlike them, he has portrayed the white-collar rather than the blue-collar experience of and typical responses to those problems. Perhaps as Sennet and Cobb and Goffman suggest, the differences generated by hierarchies are, after all, principally dramaturgical ones which are politically maintained. In any case beneath the symbolic trappings blue- and white-collar Americans seem to confront similar existential problems emanating from the maldistribution of power in American society.

EDITIONS OF GOFFMAN'S WORK USED IN THIS CHAPTER

(The dates are taken from the bibliography provided in the *Editor's Introduction*; the pagination for quotations cited in this chapter from the editions shown below).

(1959)   *The Presentation of Self in Everyday Life* (Garden City, New York; Doubleday Anchor).

(1961)   *Encounters: Two Studies in the Sociology of Interaction,* (Harmondsworth; Penguin Books).

(1961c)   *Asylums: Essays on the Social Situation of Mental Patients and Other Inmates,* (Garden City, New York; Doubleday Anchor).

(1963)   *Stigma: Notes on the Management of Spoiled Identity,* (Harmondsworth, Penguin Books).

(1963a)   *Behaviour in Public Places: Notes on the Social Organisation of Gatherings,* (New York, Free Press of Glencoe).

(1967)   *Interaction Ritual: Essays on Face-to-Face Behaviour,* (Garden City, New York; Doubleday Anchor).

(1969)   *Strategic Interaction,* (Oxford; Basil Blackwell).

(1971)   *Relations in Public: Microstudies of the Public Order,* (New York; Harper and Row).

(1974)   *Frame Analysis: An Essay on the Organisation of Experience,* (New York; Harper and Row).

CHAPTER ENDNOTES

1. Alvin W. Gouldner, *The Coming Crisis of Western Sociology,* (New York; Avon Books, 1970) pp. 378–90.

2. Ibid., p. 379; related criticisms have been advanced by Harold Garfinkel, *Studies in Ethnomethodology,* (Englewood Cliffs; Prentice-Hall, 1967) p. 174; and by J. R. Young and Garth Massey, 'The Dramaturgical Society: A Macro Analytic Approach to Dramaturgical Analysis', Unpublished paper, (The Red Feather Institute, Colorado State University, n.d.).

3. Gouldner, 1970, op. cit., p. 379.

4. Alvin W. Gouldner, *For Sociology,* (New York, Basic Books, 1973) p. 347.

5. Gouldner, 1970, op. cit., p. 487.

6. In this section, I draw heavily on my article, 'Goffman on Power', *The American Sociologist*, Volume 12, (April, 1977) pp 88–95.

7. Goffman refers, for example, to the 'power to enforce' (1974, p. 446); 'power to cause' (1963a, p. 40); and the 'power to give the show away or disrupt it' (1959, p. 82; 1974, pp. 119–120). It can be inferred from this that power is a capacity or potential which may or may not be used.

8. Mary F. Rogers, 'Instrumental and Infra-Resources: The Bases of Power', *American Journal of Sociology*, Volume 79, (May, 1974) pp. 1418–33. Briefly put, instrumental resources are the *means* of influence, those attributes, circumstances, and possessions which can be activated or invoked to reward, punish, and/or persuade others. Infra-resources, on the other hand, are those attributes, circumstances, and/or possessions which *relative to a given situation* must be had before one's relevant instrumental resources can be activated or invoked.

9. This awareness suggests Goffman's affinity for a systemic orientation to the study of power. See, Rogers, 1974, op. cit., pp. 1421–3, for a discussion of that orientation.

10. See, for example, Dorwin Cartwright, 'Influence, Leadership, Control', pp. 1–47, in James G. March (ed) *Studies in Social Power*, (Ann Arbor; University of Michigan Press, 1965) p. 4; Terry N. Clark, 'The Concept of Power', pp. 1–47, in Terry N. Clark (ed) *Community Structure and Decision-Making*, (San Francisco; Chandler, 1968) p. 47; William Gamson, *Power and Discontent*, (Homewood, Illinois; Dorsey, 1968) p. 60; Andrew S. McFarland, *Power and Leadership in Pluralist Systems*, (Stanford; Stanford University Press, 1969) p. 6; Talcott Parsons, 'On the Concept of Political Power', pp. 251–284, in Roderick Bell, David V. Edwards, and R. Harrison Wagner, (eds) *Political Power*, (New York; Free Press, 1969) p. 226; William H. Riker, 'Some Ambiguities in the Notion of Power', pp. 110–19, in Bell Edwards, and Wagner, (eds), op. cit., p. 117; and, Herbert A. Simon, 'The Nature of Authority', pp. 123–127, in William A. Glaser and David L. Sills (eds) *The Government of Associations*, (Totowa, New Jersey; Bedminster Press, 1966) p. 123.

11. Goffman (1963a, p. 226) acknowledges that habit may underlie conformity with consistent conventionality tending to undermine awareness of the rules of conduct which habit sustains.

12. See John O'Neill, *Sociology as a Skin Trade*, (New York; Harper and Row, 1972) p. 216.

13. Gouldner, 1970, op. cit., p. 384.

14. Sensitive to that profundity, Ernest Becker, in *Escape from Evil*, (New York; Free Press, 1975) pp. 15, 13, acknowledges that, 'many people have scoffed at Goffman's delineation of the everyday modern rituals of face-work and status forcing', and yet Becker maintains that Goffman has shown with, 'consumate art how people impart to one another the daily sense that each needs, not with rivalry and boasting, but rather with elaborate rules for protecting their insides against social damage and deflation.'

15. While this commentary focuses on 'total institutions', it is important to bear in mind that Goffman (1961c, p. 5) contends that, 'none of the elements I will describe seems peculiar to total institutions'. What differentiates total institutions from other formal organisations is the *degree*, often extreme, to which they manifest the characteristics Goffman elucidates.

16. Harold Garfinkel, 'Studies of the Routine Grounds of Everyday Activities', pp. 1–30, in David Sudnow, (ed) *Studies in Social Interaction*, (New York; Free Press, 1972) p. 24.

17. Goffman has pointed to the general meaning of 'false consciousness' as the failure of people to recognise their own interests and at the same time indicates his own intentions as an analyst with respect to that phenomena. He has recently said, 'he who would combat false consciousness and awaken people to their interests has much to do, because the sleep is very deep. And I do not intend to provide a lullaby but merely to sneak in and watch the way people snore.' (1974, p. 14)

18. See, C. Wright Mills, *White Collar*, (New York; Oxford University Press, 1956).

19. Max Lerner, *America as a Civilisation*, Volume II, *Culture and Personality*, (New York; Clarion Books, Simon and Schuster, 1957) p. 488.

20. Kurt B. Meyer, 'The Changing Shape of the American Class Structure', pp. 62–69, in Holger R. Stub (ed), *Status Communities in Modern Society*, (Hinsdale, Illinois; Dryden Books, 1972) pp. 66–7.

21. See, Lerner, 1957, op. cit., p. 471; and Meyer, 1972, ibid.

22. Meyer, 1972, op. cit., p. 67.

23. Mills, 1956, op. cit., p. 241.

24. Lerner, 1957, op. cit., p. 535.

25. Hans Gerth and C. Wright Mills, *Character and Social Structure*, (New York; Harcourt, Brace and World, 1953) p. 321; and Lerner, 1957, op. cit., p. 475.

26. Mills, 1956, op. cit., p. 461.

27. Ibid., p. 209.

28. Ibid., p. 210.

29. Ibid., p. 254.

30. Ibid., p. 255.

31. Ibid., p. 182.

32. Ibid., p. 182, emphasis added.

33. Ibid., p. 252, emphasis added.

34. Ibid., pp. 182, 184.

35. Ibid., p. 187.

36. Lerner, 1957, op. cit., p 656.

37. Goffman is explicit in this regard with reference to the matter of face. He says, 'ordinarily, maintenance of face is a condition of interaction, not its objective'. (1967, p. 12)

38. Richard Sennett and Jonathan Cobb, *The Hidden Injuries of Class*, (New York; Vintage Books, 1973).

5: The Class Position of Goffman's Sociology: Social Origins of an American Structuralism

By George Gonos

All social theory is class-based. Any theoretical system or problematic expresses the imaginary relation of a class or class-fragment to the real relations of production that characterise a social formation in a particular historical conjuncture. The sociology it produces contains, in a form stamped by its class position and more or less transfigured or obscure, a semblance of the structures and processes constituted by each of the levels of the social formation – the economic system, the political system, and the cultural-ideological system – and of the personality system of its agent ('theorist'), each of which exercises some determination on the theoretical system.[1] As an imaginary construction, a theoretical system enjoys a certain degree of autonomy from its material base such that it can reflect earlier or anticipated later stages in the history of the social formation.[2]

The class position of a theoretical system is not the expression of a static, 'objective' place in a social formation, but a product of the continual opposition and struggle between classes and their mutual transformations over time; that is, it is to be located in the *dynamics* of class structure. Thus, the sources of inspiration and deep sentiments of social theory have typically to do with the incipient rising and falling destinies of classes or fragments, their short- and long-term victories and defeats, and the residues of present overt and covert, real and imaginary forms of class struggle in the minds of theoretical agents.

This chapter analyses the class position of the theoretical system contained in the sociology of Erving Goffman.[3] It is an attempt to explore the relationship between the class position of this sociology and key elements of its theoretical system or, more generally, the manner in which class position is a determinant in the production of a problematic. The rationale for such an analysis is twofold. It lies, first, in the enhanced knowledge of the theoretical system that results from an examination of the material relations that underlie its production. Second, it allows an initial assessment to be made of the affinities to certain ideologies and openness to alliances or courses of action that its carriers might demonstrate in emerging historical situations. This is a beginning programme for a sociological analysis of a theoretical system. It does not necessarily yield immediate conclusions regarding the 'truth value' of the theoretical system, yet the potential role of this system in an overall social-scientific strategy should undoubtedly be made clearer as a result.

Only Alvin Gouldner has, to date, presented an analysis pointing to the salient social and historical factors conditioning Goffman's sociology, and attempting to identify its class position.[4] Of particular relevance to this paper is his conclusion regarding the latter issue. According to Gouldner, Goffman's:

> dramaturgical view of social life resonates the sentiments and assumptions of the new middle class: of the 'swinger' in the service-producing sector of the economy, of the status-conscious white-collar worker, professional, bureaucratic functionary, and of the educated middle class, rather than of the propertied groups.

> The sociology of Erving Goffman is, in my view, a complexly articulated theoretical expression that resonates the new experience of the educated middle class. This new experience has generated new conceptions of what is 'real' in the social world, along with a new structure of sentiments and domain assumptions that are dissonant with the kind of utilitarianism once traditional to the middle class.[5]

There is much that is valuable in Gouldner's short analysis of Goffman's sociology, but this paper will take issue with his conclusion regarding its class position, that is, the proposition that it is a sociology of the 'new middle class'. The accelerated expansion in the ranks of white collar employees of corporate and government organisations was certainly a development of great importance in the formation of Goffman's sociology; this sociology does indeed reflect the social changes and new experience brought about by the giant corporation. But rather than constituting an expression of the class position of its employees, it represents a critical reaction to the life-style and ideology of these new middle classes. Its own class position, it will be shown, is that of the 'lumpen-bourgeoisie', that is, of the traditional or 'old' middle class of small independent entrepreneurs in the practically demolished state it had been brought to by 1950 when the construction of Goffman's theoretical system was begun.

In determining the class position of a theoretical system, a moderately accurate initial reading of the sociological works in question is an obvious requirement. On this count one must fault the majority of Goffman's readers to date. Their typically abstract interpretations, made independently of an analysis of the relation of the theoretical system to other levels of the social formation, have been grossly affected by their strong covert biases in theoretical directions inconsistent with those of Goffman's sociology. What has been produced is a set of commentaries almost astounding in its inability to apprehend the most fundamental aspects of Goffman's problematic.[6] It may be well, then, before embarking on the main argument of this make some preliminary remarks on the character of Goffman's theoretical system.

The body of Goffman's sociology may be characterised as a pertinacious effort to defeat humanism in the sanctuary of perhaps its most endeared and protected subject, everyday face-to-face relations. The object of this sociology is constituted by the structures that govern these relations. They are isolated by breaking synchronically into the continuous stream of observable activity and are taken, in the last analysis, to be natural objects, and are studied as such. These structures are of two fairly distinct orders. In its studies of 'interaction', Goffman's sociology attempts to lay bare the most elementary or natural structures of face-to-face social life, those which are found in all societies at all times, though 'pitched and combined' in different ways (1955, p. 45). In its studies of 'frames', it analyses higher order, culturally arbitrary structures of collective activity and the modes of experience generated by them. A 'frame' represents a complex transformation (or 'keying') of natural structures (1974, pp. 40–7). Society, Goffman's sociology tells us, is a 'framework of frames'.

A more substantive rendering of this theoretical system will be given in a later section, after its social origins have been explored. Here it is begun merely to place in question the common reading of Goffman's sociology as a version of contemporary 'humanistic' sociology or interactionism. Thus, to pick on Gouldner, as it is his analysis of the class position of this system which is in question, it can be rather flatly indicated that he is mistaken in suggesting that, 'Goffman's image of social life is not of firm, well-bounded structures', but rather focuses on the 'episodic', the 'fluid', transient encounter'; that, in Goffman's sociology, activity appears 'disengaged from social structures'; that here 'sturdy social structures drift away into the background'.[7] A moderately accurate reading of Goffman's sociology does not produce evidence for these remarks. Nor does it lend credence to the common type about the link between the systems of Goffman and Mead,[8] but rather suggests the workings of theoretical systems in many ways opposed. Such misreading can hardly lay the basis for a valid assessment of class position. This said, we must now explore how the actual theoretical principles of Goffman's sociology, which in short constitute a version of structuralism, represent the theoretical advancements of a very particular class position in the post World War II period in America.

GOFFMAN'S SOCIOLOGY AND THE NEW MIDDLE CLASS

The years following the close of World War II produced at least one branch of American sociology that was discontinuous with that of the pre-war era. In it is reflected an uneasiness or disillusionment with what the rapid growth of the American economy and the 'modernisation' of American society had brought, in some contrast to what had been projected. Counter-trends had called into question the previously assumed rationality of urbanisation and the expected further democratisation of political life as natural evolutionary processes. But the development that perhaps had most to do with the changed face and character of American society, and disturbed certain analysts, was the apparent reversal of the process of industrialisation and the signalling rise of the white collar employees in commerce, advertising, marketing and sales, management, civil service, banking and insurance, accounting, the media, research, public relations, and the professions.[9] 'The situation of the new middle class', C. Wright Mills wrote, 'may be seen as symptom and symbol of modern society as a whole.'[10]

In such key period works as those of Riesman, Mills, and Whyte,[11] one finds a striking confluence of concern, focused around the social and political character of this newly expanded class. Each agonised over whether the kind of work that had been created by the rationalisation of the corporation was consistent with the individualism and competitiveness that were assumed to be the foundation of American society. All contended, with varying degrees of conviction and alarm, that it was not. Their examination of the work and leisure lives of the new middle classes produced a picture of menacing social forces that had become greater than individual actors, of behaviour as routinised and trivial, and of consumption as manipulated by the contrived images of the media. The new society and its typical character-type was placed against the backround of an image of 'self balanced' 19th century 'competitive' capitalism and its character-type. At issue was the demise of liberal society.

The early works of Goffman's sociology were produced at the same time as these. Their purpose was altogether different however – not to picture a troubling new society or to raise historical or moral questions regarding the survival of the old one, but to construct a science of face-to-face interaction. Nonetheless, the common concerns of the period inevitably penetrated into, even propelled, this effort so that Goffman's early sociology can clearly be seen as dealing with the same issues (in transposed form) as the works mentioned. It will become clear as well that it took a somewhat different stand on them.

The importance in the formation of Goffman's sociology of the prevalent image presented by the new middle class person can be gauged by the fact that one prominent (perhaps the 'normal') character-type found within it (and there labelled 'middle class') fits so well the descriptions of Mills' 'Little Man', Riesman's 'other directed' man, and Whyte's 'organisation man'. Indeed, as the results of Boltanski's empirical analysis show,[12] the occupations of the new middle classes are over-represented in the examples employed in Goffman's *The Presentation of Self in Everyday Life*. But there are characters (perhaps the leading ones) of other classes also depicted in Goffman's sociology and, as will be shown in the next section, it is the perspective of a certain class of these others that the sociology represents, and from which the picture of the new middle class is drawn. First, though, it is important to assess the actual influence of the presence of the new middle class of Goffman's sociology, not in its provision of a class perspective, but in the manner that its situation supplies central themes and concerns.

We can turn to Gouldner for a general statement:

> Dramaturgy [Goffman's sociology] marks the transition from an older economy centered on production to a new one centered on mass marketing and promotion, including the marketing of the self . . . In this new 'tertiary economy' with its proliferating services, men are indeed increasingly producing 'performances' rather than things. Moreover, both the performances and products they produce are often only marginally differentiated; they can be individuated from one another only by their looks. In this new economy, then, sheer appearance is especially important.[13]

Anyone familiar with Goffman's sociology recognises the pertinance of the trends noted by Gouldner to its essential character. Here, it will be necessary to unravel the strands of this analysis and make specific the links between the material processes refered to, especially work relations, and the themes and concepts contained in Goffman's sociology.

The distinctive character of the work of the new middle classes was made a point of by those social commentators writing at the time Goffman's theoretical production was begun. This work entailed, as Mills simply put it, a 'shift from skills with things to skills with persons'.[14] 'The one thing they [the new middle classes] do not do', he added, 'is live by making things'.[15] Goffman's sociology called it 'people-work', and extended the notion to that work in organisations where people were not just the objects but also the products:

> This *people-work* is not quite like personnel work or the work of those involved in service relationships; the staff, after all, have objects and products to work upon, but these objects and products are people. (1961c, p. 74)

Work, for the new middle classes, meant that sociability was part of the job.[16] Employees are trained, it was said, not in skills in the traditional sense, but in being certain kind of persons.[17] Poise, sangfroid, aplomb – terms that would gain currency in Goffman's sociology – came to have importance as qualities on the job. The white collar employee, as Mills put it, made a, 'sale of those traits which effect one's impressions on others',[18] so that, 'courtesy, helpfulness, and kindness, once intimate, are now part of the impersonal means of livelihood'.[19] 'The product now in demand', observed Riesman, 'is neither a staple nor a machine; it is a personality'.[20] Thus did Mills' phenomena of 'presentations', as distinct from 'reality', reveal itself in this situation and gain the recognition of social observers.

The work of the new middle class involved a high level of what Goffman's sociology (1957, p. 121) would call 'other consciousness'. In leisure activity as well, the 'typical character of the "new" middle class' was seen as 'other directed' by Riesman.[21] That is, one survived by, 'paying close attention to the signals from others', by maintaining, 'an exceptional sensitivity to the activities and wishes of others'.[22] Thus had Preedy entered upon every social scene, that obsequious character from fiction that served Goffman's sociology as the prototypical performer in its first full-length study (1959, pp. 4ff).

Two related themes repeatedly arose from considerations of the work of the new middle class: manipulation and the cold, apparently immoral, management of impressions. It was the giant corporation, with its increasing and evermore scientific marketing of marginally diversified goods and services, that was responsible for the creation of, for Mills, 'a new universe of management and manipulation'.[23] But it was its new middle class agent, responsible for making these commodities appear to have definite use-value, who became its 'symbol' and embodiment. In Mills' words: 'the forms of power that are wielded, all up and down the line, shift from explicit authority to manipulation'.[24] It was this manipulation that became a natural part of the 'world' of Goffman's sociology.

The largest share of the work of manipulation is done when an audience is presented a partial view; thus the importance of 'barriers to perception' (1959, pp. 106ff), and unequal 'information states' (1974, pp. 133ff) in the portrayal of interaction in Goffman's sociology. That these are natural to the work-situation of the new middle class is attested to by the frequency with which the 'secret' (that which is hidden from one status group by another) arises as a theme in discussions of this situation, as opposed to the openness that is understood to be characteristic of relations among manual labourers.[25] In Poulantzas' words:

> The various petty-bourgeois agents each possess, in relation to those subordinate to them, a fragment of the fantastic secret of knowledge that legitimises the delegated authority [they] exercise.[26]

The relevant citation from Riesman, in respect to the American new middle class, sounds like a part of Goffman's sociology.

> The other-directed person gives up the one face policy . . . for a multi-face policy that he sets in secrecy and varies with each class of encounters.[27]

Taking up the issue at one point in a characteristically formalistic manner, Goffman's sociology (1959, pp. 141–4) analysed the different 'types of secrets'.

As for 'impression management', Goffman's sociology wished to show that its necessity was built into the structure of unproductive labour. In its various occupations, one faces the 'problem of dramatising one's work' (Goffman, 1959, p. 32) because, as this sociology thought of it, the instrumental acts themselves are not well adapted to a vivid conveyance of the qualities and attributes claimed by the employee. He continues:

> The work that must be done by those who fill certain statuses is often so poorly designed as an expression of a desired meaning, that if the incumbent would dramatise the character of his role, he must divert an appreciable amount of his energy to do so.

Thus, 'individuals find themselves with the dilemma of expression *versus* action' (1959, p. 33). Special effort must be made so that the invisible aspect of the labour of the new middle class, which Braverman refers to as the 'magical feat' of the expansion of unproductive capital, be made to appear tangible.[28] 'Individuals are concerned', Goffman's sociology proclaimed, 'not with the moral issue of realising . . . standards, but with the amoral issue of engineering a convincing impression'. (1959, p. 251)

The consideration of the rise of the new middle class split post-war American sociology, as it had split theorists of earlier eras of capitalism in which it was relevant, into two opposing camps, depending on whether the development was seen as generally one of 'embourgeoisement', or 'proletarianisation'. It is to the latter camp that Goffman's sociology belongs. From this perspective, two assumptions of bourgeois society are placed in question: (1) that the work of the new middle class agents requires real skill, and (2) that it is skill or actual ability to which social success is linked. Thus, Braverman's study of work in the 20th century attempts to refute the functionalist 'thesis of upgrading' that assumes an increasing level of skill to be necessary to most kinds of work and to demonstrate the pervasiveness of the process of the 'dequalification' of labour, not least for that of the new middle classes. The idea that the work of the new middle class, especially, requires some mystification seems central to the structuralist problematic.[29] Its contention in this regard is that the knowledge or skill necessary to new middle class occupations is not what it is made out to be; that it is not skill in the traditional sense but proper discipline and personal style that is involved. These 'skills' are devalued as being 'natural' to those of particular class background and relevant only within the context of capitalist relations of production. In any case, they are less tangible, less easily proven, and more easily affected than traditional skills. Paper certification, of course, is always potentially forged.

Such a scepticism regarding the work of the new middle class was voiced at the time of the production of Goffman's early sociology by the commentators we have considered. Mills noted that 'personality often replaces skill as a requirement: a personable appearance is emphasised as being more important in success and advancement than experience or skill or intelligence'.[30] Riesman similarly suggested that in 'other directed' society, social mobility 'depends less on what one is and what one does than on what others think of one'.[31]

Goffman's sociology too rejected the assumption that success, at least in the established middle class occupations, was related to talent, skill or initiative. Rather, it was made a matter of proper symbolisation.[32] For example, he reminds us that:

> we tend to justify our class gains in terms of 'Cultural' values which everyone in a given society presumably respects—in our society, for example, education, skill, and talent. As a result, those who offer public proof that they possess the pet values of their

society cannot be openly refused the status which their symbols permit them to demand. (1951, p. 297)

Goffman's sociology stresses position as the source of authority and legitimacy, not personal attributes. It noted slightly later, for instance, how:

> executives often project an air of competency and general grasp of the situation, blinding themselves and others to the fact that they hold their jobs partly because they look like executives, not because they can work like executives. (1959, p. 47)

Thus it could be suggested that, 'One of the richest sources of data on the presentation of idealised performances is the literature on social mobility'. (1959, p. 36)

The problem being alluded to here – that is, the problem of qualifications, or the legitimacy of performances – is central to Goffman's sociology and, in the early works, its starting point. The material base for this problem is suggested by the enormity of the deception involved when, beginning with the 1950 US Census, the middle category of 'service workers' was introduced, as apart from unskilled operatives and labourers, implying a skill increment that was in fact not present in its work.[33] What Goffman's sociology reports on is the everyday reproduction of this official statistical manoeuvre in the flesh of face-to-face encounters. The official deception was an objective indicator of trends that had served, in the words of Goffman's sociology, 'to weaken in our minds the moral connection between legitimate authorisation to play a part and the capacity to play it'. (1959, p. 59) Thus, the underlying concern of the first publication of Goffman's sociology is 'the fact that a symbol of status is not always a very good test of status' (1951, p. 295). 'It is always possible', he continued, 'that symbols may come to be employed in a "fraudulent" way, i.e. to signify a status which the claimant does not possess'. (1951, p. 296). The issue of what Goffman's sociology later called 'misrepresentation' (1959, pp. 58ff) is here opened. Its second publication took up the same problem, 'persons conducting themselves as though they were entitled to the rights of a particular status and then having to face up to the fact that they do not possess the qualification for the status'. (1952, p. 455)

A final issue in understanding the formation of Goffman's

sociology is pointed to by the manner in which our commentators
saw the strategy and tactics of the corporation, its 'machineries of
promotion and advertising',[34] as having been displaced into the
interpersonal world, including the seemingly 'private' lives, of its
new middle class agents. Mills continues:

> What began as the public and commercial relations of business
> have become deeply personal: There is a public-relations aspect
> to private relations of all sorts, including even relations with
> oneself.

> In the new society, selling is a pervasive activity, unlimited in
> scope and ruthless in its choice of technique and manner. The
> salesman's world has now become everybody's world, and, in
> some part, everybody has become a salesman. The enlarged
> market has become at once more impersonal and more
> intimate . . . The market now reaches into every institution and
> every relation. The bargaining manner, the huckstering animus,
> the memorised theology of pep, the commercialised evaluation of
> personal traits – they are all around us; in public and in private
> there is the tang and feel of salesmanship.[35]

From the normal relations of new middle class agents in a corporate
context follows the normal presumption of dishonesty in their
everyday interaction.[37] In Goffman's words,:

> As members of an audience it is natural for us to feel that the
> impression the performer seeks to give may be true or false,
> genuine or spurious, valid or 'phony'.

> it seems that there is no interaction in which the participants do
> not take an appreciable chance of being slightly embarassed or a
> slight chance of being deeply humiliated. (1959, pp. 58, 243)

In fact, taking the matter one important step further than had the
other commentators, Goffman's theoretical system specified that, in
truth, there is no such thing, not even in intimate settings, as an
authentic performance (see e.g., 1959, pp. 70–6); that the terms
'authenticity' and 'misrepresentation' are only pragmatic ways of
seeing (1951, p. 297). This is what corporate practices and the
relations among the new middle class agents had revealed.

The world of the new middle classes, as Arno Mayer has said, is one where 'the mixture of illusion and reality tend to be weighted in favour of the former.'[38] As we have seen, it was their world – though actually created by monopoly capital, the 'men at the top' – that provided the basic insight for Goffman's sociology, that of the natural 'discrepancy between appearances and overall reality' (1959, p. 44), and the assumption that it was the former that naturally dominated the latter. But as for the new middle class agents themselves, Goffman's sociology gleefully contends that they live in an illusory world, holding to, 'the ideology of honest performers, providing strength tot the show they put on, but a poor analysis of it' (1959, p. 70). What the rise of the new middle class provided for Goffman's sociology, as it had for the work of Riesman, Mills and Whyte was the soil for reflection and, ultimately, *critique* of this class position from what were in some ways more old-fashioned bouregeois values; and in the case of Goffman, at least, for the construction of an alternative problematic, a transformation of some of the most fundamental conceptual schemes in American sociology, for he is not the sentimental sort.

THE CLASS POSITION OF GOFFMAN'S SOCIOLOGY

Not often noted is the fact that Goffman's sociology has always been an extremely class conscious one. Throughout it demonstrates a preoccupation with symbols of class status and relations between those of different rank. Especially in its early works, factors of class and status figure as primary determinants in the social interactions portrayed. Goffman's sociology defines social classes as 'discrete or discontinuous levels of prestige and privilege' (1951, p. 296).There are no examples offered of actual social mobility. A substitute is provided for it by the 'circulation of symbols', that is, the appropriation of the symbols of one (upper) class by some individuals from a lower one (1951, p. 303).

In its first publication, Goffman's sociology rather abstrusely observed:

Social classes as well as individual members are constantly rising and falling in terms of relative wealth, power, and prestige . . . [W]e find that sources of high status which were once unchallenged become exhausted or find themselves in competition with new and different sources of status. It is therefore common for a whole class of persons to find themselves with symbols and expectations which their economic and political position can no longer support. A symbol of status cannot retain for ever its acquired role of confirming status. A time is reached when social decline accelerates with a spiral effect: members of a declining class are forced to rely more and more upon symbols that do not involve a current outlay, while at the same time their association with these symbols lowers the value of these signs in the eyes of others. (1951, pp. 302–3)

In analysing the class position of Goffman's sociology, and the determinations this exercised on its theoretical system, the 'rising and falling' classes (or fragments) in question are the 'new' and the 'old' middle classes. The decline and virtual dissolution of the 'old' middle class – its once independent entrepreneurs drawn into employee status – and its groping for new symbols of status to replace lost ones, is as important a factor in the formation of Goffman's sociology as the simultaneous expansion of the 'new' middle class that threatened it. Yet, neither of these class fragments can be said to have provided this sociology with its class position; rather, it found its calling in the balance of events. Goffman's sociology took up the position of the 'lumpen-bourgeoisie'.

Mills defined the lumpen-bourgeoisie as the remains of that class of small, independent entrepreneurs that had been left by the rise of corporate capital, and which was now completely dominated by it. Mills outlines the decline in its financial and moral well-being, and draws a vivid characterological portrait of the wretchedness of the lumpen-bourgeois in his attempt to retain an integrity that was no longer possible.[39]

Goffman's sociology is sympathetic to the idea of independent entrepreneurship, even in these times; but it is favourable only to that of a special kind. That is, it is a sociology of the lumpen-bourgeoisie only if one employs a more complete sense of the term than Mills did, one that recognizes that its routine business operations are, by natural proclivity, illegal ones. From the start, Goffman's sociology takes up an interest in the 'routine methods of circumvention' of 'restrictive' authorities (1951, p. 302), and views society from the perspective offered by its 'underworld'. It derives its theoretical system from the practice of 'planned illegal exploitation' (1952, p. 451). The reliance on illegal methodology represents, of course, a flagrant deviation from middle class morality. As will be seen, such an orientation has crucial implications for a social-scientific theoretical system.

It is the perspective available to those of specific 'careers' that serves to concretise the lumpen-bourgeois position of Goffman's sociology. The ideal manifestation of this position is found in the con man, the independent lumpen-bourgeois businessman whose game is the extortion of his 'mark'. From this position, other 'careers' where a similar outlook and methodology prevail are identified for sympathetic treatment. Chief among these has been the mental patient, the poor 'mark' of society or, more specifically, of 'society's cooler', the psychotherapist (1952, p. 461), who has simply 'outmanœuvred' him (1961c, p. 306). In its studies of a variety of these 'sympathetic characters', Goffman's sociology focuses, not on lumpen-bourgeois, but rather on lumpen-proletarian (in its term, 'lower class') 'careers'. But the same perspective, that of illicit practice, is involved.

Again consulting Boltanski's analysis, we find that figures of the lumpen-proletariat provide for a substantial percentage (11.5) of all mentions in Goffman's *The Presentation of Self in Everyday Life*.[40] The virtual absence of the working class (less than 2%) is notable. Not subject to the same contemptuous treatment as the new middle class (which provides a great number of the negative examples), the working class seems barely to exist. Its practice yields no lessons for Goffman's sociology. Only the illicit practice of the lumpen-classes does. Such a 'sympathetic character' as the mental patient does not, of course, 'work the system' for a material livelihood as does the con man, but rather for the personal integrity that both understand only illicit practice can afford. The two are in league with one another, then, in terms of their use of illicit methodology to make out and in the dignified character they share when comparing themselves with their self-perceived class enemies, professionals and corporate executives, i.e., the organisation men.

An examination of the situation constructed in *Asylums* (1961c) reveals a fairly good symbolic representation of the class analysis contained in Goffman's sociology. Our theoretical agent (Goffman) takes up (with probable reluctance but, happily, for illegitimate reasons) a position on the 'lowest level' of the hospital staff. From this position is produced a sympathetic treatment of the 'lower class' inmates and a relentless attack on their servicing 'professionals' who, in their salaried organisational roles, have lost their autonomy, integrity, and real service potential. *Asylums* derives what are perhaps the strongest sentiments anywhere in Goffman's sociology from the tightly contained and continuous face-to-face confrontation of these classes within the walls of the 'total institution'. The predicament of the lumpen-proletarian inmate there, 'stripped' of his means of livelihood, and 'self', reflects that of the lumpen-bourgeois in what Goffman's analysis indicates is a Total (i.e., Corporate) Society. The point of view taken in the hospital is one provided by its 'underlife', that web of illicit undercover activities constructed for utilising, 'available artifacts in a manner and for an end not officially intended' (1961c, p. 207). It is a study of the illegitimate appropriation of material goods and symbolising equipment necessary for maintaining an otherwise denied status. To find confederates here the lumpen-bourgeois is pleased and amused.

The con man of Goffman's sociology is a small entrepreneurial hold-out from the process that would make of him an example of Whyte's 'organisation man' in the new relations of production. Rather than 'take the vows of organisation life',[41] and make himself fit for corporate capitalism, he continues to exist outside these relations and, in the manner of the lumpen-classes, is parasitic upon them. His real property expropriated, the con man owns his own 'means of production' in the form of the 'tools' of poise and impression management. The con man is repulsed by the dull life and 'middling prestige' (Mills) of the new middle class, and hopelessly attracted to the bourgeoisie, wishing to appropriate symbols of its wealth and live in its style. Fraud and extortion are the con man's means to emulate the bourgeoisie and retain a personal integrity the new middle class person lacks. The early interest of Goffman's sociology in the structure and limits of 'misrepresentation' was taken up, it must now be said, with an eye to the opportunities it afforded.

In Goffman's sociology, only the con man and the sympathetic characters in other lumpen-class positions are able conscientiously to demonstrate *in practice* crucial aspects of the morality of the old middle class, which it says are only paid 'lip service' by the new middle class employee. We see that it is only through illegal activity that the little man can retain, in corporate capitalism, such old bourgeois qualities as independence, flair, ingenuity, individual initiative, thrift, and competitiveness. Such interpretations as Gouldner's therefore become untenable:

Goffman's dramaturgy is an obituary for the old bourgeois virtues and a celebration of the new ones.

Dramaturgy thus premises a disenchantment with the older utilitarian culture. It uses the new utilitarian culture as a standpoint for an implicit critique of the old.[42]

Indeed, one could say that it is closer to being the other way around.

Far from being a 'celebration' of the new middle class, Goffman's sociology represents an assault on it from the standpoint of the lumpen-bourgeois. For him, there is only contempt for the ex-independent businessman, now a dependent proletarianised employee, equally exploited by capital as the wage-earner, and probably more prone to easy manipulation by mere images and the media. Thus, the critical sentiments of Goffman's sociology are directed, like Mills' in *White Collar*, at those middle class persons who 'work for someone else, on someone else's property'.[43] The criticism almost reaches the pitch of a character attack, one line of which focuses on what is seen as the routinised, eventless existence of the new middle classes, the fact that, as Mills said, 'their career proceeds according to its rules and within its graded channels'.[44] Goffman's sociology characterises the life of what it refers to as the 'middle classes' as devoid of 'action', and attempts to ground this idea in scientific concepts. 'Action' is a concept taken from its lumpen-class subjects, and refers to activity that is consequential (subjectively, at least) and 'problematic', i.e. undetermined in outcome (1967, pp. 149–94). Thus, 'gambling is the prototype of action' (ibid., p. 186).

It is the attempt of the 'middle classes' to 'minimise the eventfulness of their lives', employing what Goffman's sociology labels the 'Calvinistic solution of life' – 'an incremental orientation to long-range goals expressed through acts that have a very small additive long-term consequence' (ibid., p. 175). The middle class person is:

> likely to avoid . . . chance-taking and squirm out of occasions he has not avoided. In our society, after all, moments are to be lived through, not lived. (ibid., p. 260)

He can only 'expect to enjoy the rises laid out within a respectable profession'.[45] And Goffman tells us: 'The less uncertain his life, the more society can make use of him.' (1967, p. 174)

Goffman's sociology thus creates a division of the world akin to that between 'beat' and 'square', and places itself on the side of those of 'action', no matter how trivial its instances; form, in this sociology, is the main thing. It is through 'action', risk, the gamble – i.e., personal investment – that the lumpen-bourgeois or lumpen-proletarian gains his self-respect, demonstrates his superior character (1967, p. 268), and upholds lost portions of the old middle class code. A list of occupations in which 'action' is a part shows a dearth of those within corporate capitalism; these are, for the most part exotic or police jobs (1967, p. 172–4).[46] One's best bet in this regard seems to be, according to Goffman:

> criminal life, especially the non-racketeering varieties, which yields considerable opportunity but continuously and freshly subjects the individual to gross contingencies . . . [It] requires constant orientation to unpredictable opportunities and a readiness to make quick decisions concerning the expected value of proposed schemes. (1967, p. 173)[47]

The contrast between middle class and lumpen-bourgeois orientations is neatly summarised as the, 'difference between holding a job down and pulling a job off.' (ibid., p. 166).

In the view of the lumpen-bourgeois, the middle class attempt to avoid action, like the Calvinistic forbidance of gambling, represent its naïve idealism. The truth, that Goffman's sociology teaches, is that one does not have the choice not to gamble, that all of life *is* a gamble. The study of gambling necessarily takes us 'from pots and prizes, neatly definable, to protracted payoffs . . . from circumscribed gambles to wider arenas of living' (1967, p. 160). Those who would try to 'keep their character up and their costs down' (ibid., p. 262) are misled; it is the professional gambler who perceives things correctly and who is a sympathetic character. Thus, Goffman's sociology seems to decree, as the epigraph to Mills' *White Collar* portended, that the time has come, 'when the man who did not gamble would lose all the time, even more surely than he who gambled'.[48] By this formula, it is the respectable new middle class person who is the loser.

In Goffman's sociology, the new middle class is viewed to have a generally ideological relation to its world. The treatment of it in this regard parallels that of Whyte, who characterised the new middle class as clinging to an outmoded Protestant Ethic when its existence was actually governed by a new collectivism, what he called the 'Social Ethic'. Goffman's sociology plays on the contradictions between the class situation of the new middle class agents as dependent employees and the individualism they espouse; and between their own manipulation as puppets of the corporation and their ideology of openness, trust and spontaneity.

In contrast, it is the lumpen-bourgeois – the con man – who, in Goffman's sociology, has a keen realistic understanding of the new corporatism; who recognises the difference and actual relation between what is outwardly communicated and the reality of the game. The con man, free of the inhibiting illusions of the new middle class, can scientifically utilise the techniques of manipulation and impression management (i.e., the techniques of the 'big bourgeoisie' itself) in operating its business. Taking his cue from corporate practice, the con man once and for all rejects the purely 'moral connection' that typically ties appearances to essence. (This realisation of insights from corporate capitalism is why Goffman's sociology is not simply a critique of the 'new' society from the standpoint of the 'old' one.) Thus, the con's 'real crime', Goffman's sociology suggests, is that, 'he robs all of us of the belief that middle-class manners and appearance can be sustained only by middle-class people' (1959, p. 18fn.). Like the gambler, the con man's natural orientation is, 'in contrast to the middle class perspective that tends to define occupational position as something only deservedly acquired and deservedly lost' (1967, p. 193). Whereas the new middle class person is intimidated by the ideological force of the state's legal/illegal distinction (or timid and unscientific in his approach to minor infringements), the lumpen-bourgeois realises that the actual practice of capitalism has always meant the circumvention of the law.[49] The con man is the true capitalist.

This new middle class man serves as the 'mark' of Goffman's sociology, just as he is the usual 'mark' of the con. I say new middle class *man* because this mark is never, for example, the routinised office worker, i.e., from the 'feminised' sector of the so-called new middle class.[50] Rather, it is that intermediate employee who, in Braverman's words,[51] has 'bits of specialised knowledge and delegated authority', and 'a tenuous working independence' or, in the perspective of the con man, a small parcel of masculinity and the money to demonstrate it. This thin coat of masculinity is what, according to Goffman's sociology the con man plays on:

The mark's readiness to participate in a sure thing is based on more than avarice; it is based on a feeling that he will now be able to prove to himself that he is the sort of person who can 'turn a fast buck.' For many, this capacity for high finance comes near to being a sign of masculinity and a test of fulfilling the male role. (1952, p. 452)

The new middle class mark is extorted by a cool, manipulative street entrepreneur who invokes his tenuous independence and frail masculinity. The con reveals the truth about his mark and demonstrates his own superiority by employing himself a feminine methodology.[52]

In the perspective of Goffman's sociology, the con man is a much more respectable character than his mark. As the con argues:

the mark is a fool and not a full-fledged person, possessing an inclination towards illegal gain but not the decency to admit it or the capacity to succeed at it. (1952, p. 455)

In contrast to the true professionalism and competence of the con man, we are faced with the shallowness and hypocrisy of his new middle class counterpart. (Not only the con game, but also the lumpen-proletarian occupations of the sympathetic characters are viewed in Goffman's sociology as more fully 'careers' than the new middle class positions, 1961c, pp. 127ff.). More than popular conception allows, con men are here seen as highly civilised. The whole affair between con and mark is seen as more civilised, at least, than some of the, 'barbarous ceremonies in our society, such as criminal trials . . . that are expressly designed to prevent the mark from saving his face' (1952, p. 462). For the con man, it is good 'business policy' to save the mark's face, (as it is good policy for other sympathetic characters of the 'underlife' to leave the materials they work with in order, thus protecting their racket). Overall, the con man is dignified, polite, respectful and appreciative of human diversity, and properly disapproving of lower disruptive elements. And, he is more open and honest than his middle class counterpart, this being a natural prerequisite for those admittedly practicing outside the laws of the state and according to those of the 'brotherhood'. The con man, in Goffman's account:

is part of a brotherhood whose members make no pretense to one another of being 'legit.' A white-collar criminal, on the other hand, has no colleagues, although he may have an associate with whom he plans his crime and a wife to whom he confesses it. (1952, p. 451)

Goffman's sociology is constructed by viewing society in the perspective of the lumpen-bourgeois 'operator' (1952, p. 461). Much of its conceptual apparatus and terminology are directly appropriated from the mental apparatus and argot of the con man and the other sympathetic lumpen-class characters, right up to the notion of the 'frame' as a structure of containment and illusion. This mental apparatus is formed in the *practice* of these subjects, i.e., in 'working the system'. In Goffman's system, sociological knowledge of the 'rules' on which a social order is built is seen as available only to those who are in this specific working relation to them. Thus, we read that:

Their [inmate 'underlife' figures] conduct may be of great importance to the student if he wants to learn how the particular institution can be worked and how institutions in general might be worked. (1961c, pp. 299)

In order to work a system effectively, one must have an intimate knowledge of it. (1961c, pp. 211–2)

Thus, compared to their marks in what they know, con men are 'somewhat more God-like' (1974, p. 134). Contrariwise, it appears not to be in its own 'class interests' that the workings of the social order become too clear to those of the middle class (1951, p. 297). Wisely, then, Goffman's sociology takes the perspective of the 'underlife' figures and it is they, not academic social scientists, who are consulted for the final arbitration of theoretical matters. Their practice can demonstrate the liability of the academic's concepts, as when the observations of an undercover spy are cited to countervail the idealistic assumptions about 'intersubjectivity' made by Mead (1969, pp. 72–3). Goffman's works may be read as 'how to's', as Gouldner suggests, only because his sociology makes practice the criterion of knowledge.

In the lumpen-bourgeois perspective of the con man, one can discern the latent features of a full-blown theoretical system. When elevated to scientific status, in Goffman's sociology, this sytem is a structuralist one. Some of its key elements and oppositions – a suspiciousness of outward 'communication', a rejection of the notion of a subject's 'authenticity', an assumed discrepancy between appearance and reality, an orientation to the 'rules' of social order and an epistemology that dictates a particular relation to them – have already revealed themselves. A more complete rendering will be given it in the next section.

First, a comment should be made regarding the determination of the class position of this theoretical system. What has been demonstrated thus far with regard to Goffman's sociology is its appropriation of a lumpen-bourgeois perspective on society, one aspect of which is the sharp ridicule of the new middle class. It should be clear, however, that this does not in itself necessarily invalidate the proposition that this perspective 'resonates the sentiments and assumptions of the new middle class' for, as has been stressed, social theory does not necessarily reflect the immediate material situation of its carriers. It could be that the new middle class wishes in its theory to recall the world of independent entrepreneurship and fantasise an existence outside the law, or that it is especially prone to self-chastisement. It is in part for this reason that we need do more than 'read' theory; we need observe its 'behaviour' and the practice of its carriers. In doing so, what one finds regarding Goffman's sociology is that it is not the case that it has resonated with those 'readers' of 'new middle class' orientation. Neither does one find the 'educated middle classes', as Gouldner suggests, so 'sensitised to the irrationalities of the modern system of rewards', as to produce this affinity.[53] What one does find among these readers is, first, much resistance to a true understanding of it (its difficulties notwithstanding) and, second, when some dawning understanding is achieved, a great protest in the high tones of moralistic humanism.[54] While criticising Goffman's sociology for exalting 'sheer appearances', they stand with pride by the exalted essences of the new middle class, reiterating their belief in the spontaneity and innocence of this class, in the efficacy of its 'understanding' and good will, in its neutrality, and in its honest 'self'-expression. In locating the sociology that does in fact resonate with the sentiments of the new middle class we need look not to Goffman's sociology, but elsewhere – in the direction that the systematic misreading of Goffman's sociology takes us – to the ideology of the new middle class to which Riesman, Mills, Whyte and Goffman have all pointed.

THE 'INVERSION' OF SYMBOLIC INTERACTIONISM

Like the American social theorists of the early 1950s who have been discussed, those who are attributed with constructing a 'social psychology' in the early decades of the century were faced with a situation that had become 'increasingly corporate'.[55] We must, for a moment, consider their solution to the dilemma this posed for the old middle class ideology of individualism and competition. Simply put, the theoretical system constructed by those such as Cooley, Mead, and Dewey, to whom we refer, suggested the compatability of individualism with corporate expansion by stressing a natural harmony between 'self' and society. In their works, society did not appear as a coercive reality, outside the individual. A person's work, and his moral duty to the community, were seen as perfectly compatable with self-expressive tendencies. Through his role in building corporate society, the unique individual could fulfil his potential. The old stress on competitiveness was outmoded, for society, it was brought out, is a collective endeavour. Such ideas were the reason Whyte could later view these thinkers as having ushered in what he called the Social Ethic.[56]

The 'social psychology' developed by these theorists reflected their understanding of macro-social processes at the interpersonal, or situational, level. The continuity between self and society could be seen everywhere. Outward activities, or gestures, were interpreted as expressions of 'self'. Human relations, it followed, were characterised by a mutual transparency of social actors. Thus Cooley could invoke the image of the 'looking glass self': 'Each to each a looking glass/Reflects the other that doth pass'. Outer indications were an eye on the soul; appearances reflected an underlying essence.

Social interaction was said to consist of a dialectical communication of intentions through shared 'significant' symbols, made possible by the 'reflexive' quality of human consciousness. The basis of society lay in the penetrating 'intersubjectivity' that resulted. In Cooley's words:

Society is an interweaving and interworking of mental selves. I imagine your mind, and especially what your mind thinks about my mind, and what your mind thinks about what my mind things about your mind. I dress my mind before yours and expect that you will dress yours before mine.[57]

Through such a process, it was said, society is internalised in the individual, resulting in a moral consensus in which 'selves' are integrated at the level of consciousness. Social scientific methodology reflected this analysis. 'I conclude', wrote Cooley:

> that the imaginations which people have of one another are the solid facts of society, and that to observe and interpret these must be a chief aim of sociology . . . We have to imagine imaginations.[58]

It was to the heritage provided by this theoretical system that the various strands of what is now taken as 'humanistic' sociology laid claim, including those of phenomenological sociology and symbolic interactionism. It is often said, of course, that Goffman's sociology is another instance of this problematic. This section should make clear why this is a mistaken notion.

Studying American society in the early 1950s, Riesman, Mills and Whyte found much to be sceptical about in the theoretical synthesis that had been offered. In their observations we can see the potential foundation for a theoretical transformation they didn't accomplish. First, it seemed clear to them that one's 'self' was no longer very often expressed in one's work or social activity. Rather, the individual was seen as making 'presentations' dictated by the image desired by the corporation. One's 'self' had become, 'the instrument of an alien purpose'.[59] 'Sincerity', Mills noted, 'is detrimental to one's job'.[60] As the corporate ethic spread, 'common values and mutual trust' (i.e. intersubjectivity), it was recognised, could no longer be assumed, for 'one knows that manipulation is inherent in every contact'.[61] Secondly, social institutions were now seen as having a coercive reality apart from the human agents who occupied them. It wasn't so much the abilities of the man of position, but the position or place itself in which authority was now seen to inhere.[62] 'Today the man is the shadow of the firm', reported Riesman.[63] In accordance, vice and virtue were conceptually transferred from human agents to the seemingly autonomous system of 'organised irresponsibility' which had expropriated them.[64] It was a complex anonymous system of rules that governed the decisions and initiatives of its men.[65] The new hero being celebrated in society, Whyte suggested, was Society itself.[66]

Every assumption of the problematic of Dewey, Mead and Cooley – the intersubjectivity of social actors, the expression of 'self' in activity, the primacy of the individual and his role in constructing social reality – was placed in question by these observations. If they had not been contained in a moralistic framework, but rather taken as basic insights into the nature of society, one might have recognised in them the workings of a problematic we know as structuralism. But they were not. Riesman, Mills and Whyte took, as their perspective for a critique, the morality of the old middle class. Considering that there was no return and that they pointed to no alternative future, the conclusion to be drawn from their observations was bound to be an ambivalent one: 'are these defects to struggle against – or are they virtues in disguise?'[67]

By rejecting a moralistic approach in favour of a positive one, and by taking up the more materialistic position of the lumpen-bourgeoisie, Goffman's sociology fashioned from such observations a theoretical system that was a di⌣unct alternative to the one constructed by Cooley, Mead and Dewey. It entailed a return to social psychology. In this realm, it represents an 'inversion' of the symbolic interactionist problematic, as it had come to be called.[68] The opposition between the two systems, one structuralist, the other interactionist, can be seen in nearly all of their constituent elements. In what remains of this section, only certain of these can be touched on.

In Goffman's theoretical system, there is no natural continuity or harmony postulated between the individual and society; rather, each of these constitutes a system in its own right, and they are naturally antagonistic. A mode of authority different than that implied in the humanist model is suggested, one based not on a consensus of values, but on what Goffman's sociology calls a 'working consensus' involving a *compromise* of ideals. Here, the individual acts not on the basis of internalised norms or moral commitment, but because of the bargain that has been struck with him, and he will move for a better one. Put differently, social performances are understood as extorted from their agents. Though values are regularly paid lip service, conduct is not bound by morality but by possibilities. Behaviour is tactical and strategic by nature.

In Goffman's problematic, an agent's observable behaviours are not considered as indications of a 'self'. This relation between outward activity and 'self', we are instructed, is a variable effect, governed in any context by rules Goffman has recently called 'connectives' (1974, pp. 211ff, 479), which specify the appropriate manner in which character and agency are to be attributed to performers. Hence, the notion of 'authenticity' (or 'self-expression') is rejected. The idea of a 'sincere' or 'spontaneous' act is regarded as a fallacy, a part of the ideology of everyday life. In Goffman's problematic, no 'private sphere' is imagined where authenticity and openness prevail. The same analysis applies to, 'any concrete social establishment, be it domestic, industrial or commercial' (1959, p. xi). What actors interpret as authenticity is the result of small allowances tolerated by institutional arrangements such that a less than fully prescribed involvement in present activity, or 'role distance', may be expressed by dramatising another of one's equally social attachments (1961, pp. 85–152). What is sensed as intersubjectivity is the result not of sympathetic understanding, but of a careful following of the rules that pertain to relations between those of particular statuses, building a 'bridge' between them with certain emotional specifications (1957, pp. 116–17).

The 'self' is eliminated as a free subject and creator of the world. An 'institutional view of the self' as a social construct replaces it:

> The self . . . can be seen as something that resides in the arrangements prevailing in a social system for its members. The self in this sense is not a property of the person to whom it is attributed, but dwells rather in the pattern of social control that is exerted in connection with the person by himself and those around him. This special kind of institutional arrangement does not so much support the self as constitute it. (1961c, p. 168)

An earlier version is structurally similar:

> In our society the character one performs and one's self are somewhat equated, and this self-as-character is usually seen as something housed within the body of its possessor . . . In this report the performed self was seen as some kind of image . . . While this image is entertained *concerning* the individual, so that a self is imputed to him, this self itself does not derive from its possessor, but from the whole scene of his action, being generated by that attribute of local events which renders them interpretable by witnesses. A correctly staged and performed scene leads the audience to impute a self to a performed character, but this

imputation – this self – is a *product* of a scene that comes off, and is not a *cause* of it. The self, then, as a performed character, is not an organic thing that has a specific location, whose fundamental fate is to be born, to mature and to die; it is a dramatic effect arising diffusely from a scene that is presented. (1959, pp. 252–3)

In Goffman's problematic, then, 'impression management' and 'expression engineering' are not aberrant deceptive practices, i.e., pathologies, characteristic of certain kinds of interaction or particular to our society; they are descriptions of social life in nature. From such an analysis, it is clear that appearances, at least those aspects within the possible control of social agents, cannot be relied upon for a 'reading' of a scene. Thus, Goffman's problematic focuses attention not on 'communication', i.e., the intentional and symbolic level (as in Mead's framework), but rather on 'expression', i.e., the aspects of a performance or supporting scene that 'seem immune to fabrication and dissimulation' (1969, p. 58), such as 'unmeant gestures'. The spoken form of communication is considered especially untrustworthy: thus one cannot 'rely overly for data upon what the person says he thinks he imagines himself to be' (1961c, p. 127). Stated goals, values, etc. are always related to ideology, or are tactics in themselves.

Goffman's problematic postulates a discontinuity between science and everyday experience. The scientific apprehension of 'everyday life' requires a rigorous conceptual apparatus to be built. A scene is studied without resort to a subjective place within it. The selective perception or one sided view associated with the method of Verstehen and its focus on the intentions or imaginations of actors is rejected. Every element of a scene must be taken in and related back to the expressive totality. A natural science of human behaviour is espoused. This is not so different from animal behaviour that the methods and findings of ethology are not very useful. In Goffman's problematic there is a constant affirmation of the physical reality of the natural environment. The constraints on social life following from the fact that it is 'modeled' on, and embedded in, nature is seen in every social situation. The subjectivism characteristic of symbolic interactionism, in which primacy is given the definition of the situation, is repudiated.

If interaction was to Mead and Cooley a dialectic of communication, in Goffman's problematic it is a degenerative spiral of expression (see Goffman, 1969, pp. 58ff), a cycle of deception and concealment rather than inner understanding. Not intersubjectivity but opaqueness characterises human interaction; each agent gleans the other's behaviour for evidence of his next move. In short, there is a shift from symbolic interaction to 'strategic interaction'. While the former leads to a sociology of interpretation, the latter leads to one of prediction. This said, one is left with the problem of how, in Goffman's problematic, social order is accounted for. Some basis, other than value consensus or mutual understanding, must be postulated to limit the spiraling possibilities, i.e., the anomie, of amoral strategic interaction. Some limits, Goffman's sociology notes, are given in the natural structures and imperatives of human interaction. For the greater part, perhaps, they are provided by the 'frame'. This structure fixes interaction at a certain level and in a certain genre, providing rules regarding, for instance, how signs are to be 'interpreted', how outward indications are to be related to 'selves', and what 'experience' will accompany activity. These rules are ordinarily unconscious to agents and essentially non-negotiable. A frame thus defines a matrix of possible situations that can be generated.

Perhaps the purest example of a frame in Goffman's sociology is found in its continuing fancy with gambling. In this activity, of course, the possible outcomes of a 'play' and the probable occurence of each are fully calculable. What is pleasing, it seems, to Goffman's sociology is the contrast it presents between the abstractness of its rules, which are reducible to a mathematical formula, and the flush of experience and emotion generated when these rules are followed in collective activity. Note also that a professional gambler with an extraordinary knowledge of the rules and the unfolding multiple possibilities each play presents can beat the game, but in doing so leaves the rules intact.

Goffman's problematic thus promotes the study not of observable interaction or 'everyday life' as such, but its eternal structure and ideology; not of situations, but their frames. To gain knowledge of these structures, i.e., become conscious of their rules or laws, requires that a certain stance be taken up within the particular life-forms in which they take on their everyday appearances. Specifically, it requires that one cast off the ideological subservience to these life-forms that can conceive only of living in and by their particular rules, making obeyance an unquestioned certainty. To make an object of something more lasting and firm within them, one must resist the moral force behind them and take up a practice 'outside' the authority of their particular rules. Thus, as historical materialism by necessity draws on illegal practice with respect to the laws of the state in gaining knowledge of the laws of history, Goffman's structuralism by necessity draws on illegal practice with respect to the norms of 'civility' in gaining knowledge of the laws of interaction. A science of society whose object is structures or rules must be one in which the question of the legality or illegality of its practice is reduced to a mere question of tactics, or utility. An openness to, though not complete reliance on, illegal methodology must be maintained as one important means of exposure of the system of rules and its normal operation.[69] In regard to state law or social norms, science of this kind is wholly unprincipled, in essence a criminal activity. Goffman's structuralism intends to be such a science. As a theoretical system, it is the natural concomitant of a lumpen-bourgeois position or, more specifically, that illegal methodology specific to the career of the con man.

In contrast, the position and practice of the new middle class is not viable to a structuralist science of rules. By instinct it holds fast to legality and 'civility' as a mode of existence. The new middle class enmeshed in the ideology of the state and of 'everyday life', is rendered totally dependent on their life-forms. Thus, the rules governing these forms remain unconscious. The theoretical product of the new middle class is interpretive sociology, e.g., symbolic interactionism or phenomenological sociology, the study of variation in meaning.

We can understand theoretical systems in the post World War II conjuncture as intellectual products of different class fragments, each faced with the expansion of monopoly capital. Symbolic interactionism, reflecting the new middle class aspirations for promotion within the legal structures of the corporation, takes up the bias of expansion, that is, the bias of the bourgeoisie. Goffman's structuralism, reflecting the lumpen-bourgeois attempt to 'make-out' in somewhat degenerating categories of existence, takes up a stance generally antagonistic to many features of the 'new' society. In the former, we find the elements of a healthy picture: a radiant morality, a sense of upward mobility and forward progress, a self-expressiveness of social actors, a pluralism of multiple subcultures. In the latter, we find closed avenues and fixed boundaries; not an open negotiable order, but a 'secret' corporate one.

CONCLUSION: THE POLITICS OF GOFFMAN'S THEORETICAL SYSTEM

Humanistic sociology and Goffman's structuralism are both, in the broad sense, middle class ideologies. The differences between them derive, as we have seen, from the fact that they represent different fractions of this class. The politics of any middle class theoretical system reflect the contradictory position of that class: its deep ambivalence.[70] There is a manner in which one can read too much 'politics' into these theoretical systems, for they are by nature escapes from politics, and full of ambiguities on such matters. Ultimately, their political leanings can be determined only in class struggle, by the paths the fractions of the middle class follow with respect to the polarisation forced on them by the strategies of the proletariat and bourgeoisie. Thus, in reading this theory, it is the openness to certain external ideologies, and the potential for alliance of its agents with other classes, rather than its inherent politics, that may be debated. Recently, in Europe if not in America, structuralism (a revived theoretical interest in Durkheim) has served for some as the means for a flirtation with Marxism, i.e., an alignment with the working class. It is in light of this that, in conclusion, a couple of points pertinent to the 'politics' of Goffman's structuralism will be made.

The appropriation of the perspective of the con man means, in the first instance, an appropriation of his object. Sociologically, of greatest relevance to the con man are the rules of the face-to-face ceremonial order, for it is with respect to this order that his tactics are carried out. His knowledge of the structure of face-to-face 'worlds' may indeed be God-like, but it is strictly limited to this level of social phenomena. Likewise, the object of Goffman's sociology is constituted by the social structures that most immediately and directly regulate face-to-face relations. To the extent that his sociology inadequately conceptualises the whole of society, such an exclusivity of interest results in a kind of empiricism. If society is a 'frame-work of frames', as we are told, Goffman's structuralism should be criticised for never analysing and, indeed, making only the vaguest references to, the 'framework' that is presumed to exist. The 'frames' are thus 'radically decontextualised';[71] that is, each is studied in its own right without real examination of its own structural supports or its functions in a higher order system. Each separate 'frame analysis' suffers from the lack of both a precise location of its object and a knowledge, expressly called for by Goffman's structuralism (1961, pp. 33–4), of the 'transformation rules' that tie it to higher order structures. Knowledge of the highest order frame, the mode of production, is outside the scope of Goffman's theoretical system. In the flattened social formation it conceives, tactical and strategic objectives cannot be formulated except with respect to the most immediate social objects and, apparently, with only the most immediate material goals in mind.

Another natural aspect of the lumpen-bourgeois perspective is its penchant for order, i.e., the order of the status quo. It is only from a relatively stable social order that the lumpen-bourgeois, in a parasitic relation to it, can extort a livelihood. It is the present order that both defines his rewards and stabilises their value. Anarchism, of the kind attempting to disrupt the ceremonial order, or revolutionary activity, must be denounced by the lumpen-bourgeois as not in his immediate interests.[72] On this matter, one can refer in Goffman's sociology to the focus on and apparent preference for what it calls 'contained' as opposed to 'disruptive' kinds of illicit activities, those with 'the characteristic of fitting into existing institutional structures without introducing pressure for radical change' (1961c, pp. 199–200). While the lumpen-bourgeois may, 'hold the whole "legit" world in . . . contempt', (1959, p. 18fn), and routinely engage in illegal practices, his perspective does not entail a rejection of this 'world' or of bourgeois law, for these form the basis of his livelihood.

The theory and practice of the lumpen-bourgeois is oriented not to social change but to stable social structures. Symptomatic of this, Goffman's theoretical system does not contain a concept of motion or history. (In Mead's theoretical system, one is often reminded, the ideas of social *process* and of individual's changing society are foremost; but because it does not make possible a knowledge of concrete social structures, i.e., of the circumstances to which this activity is subject, these must remain idealistic notions.) Goffman's sociology is oriented, like its lumpen-class subjects, to cheap experience in leisure and to knowledge for business' sake of the structures relevant to immediate and individual gain. Its own briefly sustained realisations of the limitations of its vision due to its specific social and historical location (e.g., 1967, p. 263), in no way frees it from these limitations. 'Action', – at least in bourgeois culture' (ibid.), and no less in Goffman's sociology – specifies 'the single individual' as 'decision maker and executor, the relevant unit of organisation'. Its relevant events are those, 'that can be watched and portrayed in toto, from beginning to end at one sitting', ruling out 'the rise of capitalism or World War II' as examples (ibid.).

Goffman's theoretical system thus projects a lingering romanticism of the individual, of petty illegality, of 'action' that can fit into a 'breath of experience'. To render it viable to more historic interests, there is the need to employ its realistic categories to create the possibilities of gearing tactics and strategies to less immediate and individualistic goals, and of engaging in instrumental, not purely expressive, action capable of producing real structural change. Simultaneous with its local face-to-face components, conduct must be understood as taking place on the stage of history. It is thus mandatory to gain firm knowledge of those 'frames' that define the epochs of history, and upon which those of a lower order are dependent.

When viewed in an open and objective manner, it becomes clear that the theoretical system contained in Goffman's sociology represents a bolder and more unusual contribution to social science than is typically suspected. When viewed from a different class position than it represents, that of the working class, it is a theoretical system that itself displays a relative openness to a more complete science of human relationships and human history.

EDITIONS OF GOFFMAN'S WORK USED IN THIS CHAPTER

(The dates are taken from the bibliography provided in the *Editor's Introduction*; the pagination for quotations cited in this chapter from the editions shown below).

(1951)   'Symbols of Class Status', *British Journal of Sociology*, Volume II, (1951) pp. 294–304.

(1952)   'On Cooling the Mark Out: Some Aspects of Adaptation to Failure', *Psychiatry*, Volume 15, No. 4, (November, 1952) pp. 451–63.

(1955)   'On Face-Work: An Analysis of Ritual Elements in Social Interaction', in Goffman, (1967).

(1957)   'Alienation from Interaction', in Goffman, (1967).

(1959)   *The Presentation of Self in Everyday Life*, (Garden City, New York; Doubleday Anchor).

(1961)   *Encounters: Two Studies in the Sociology of Interaction*, (New York; Bobbs-Merrill).

(1961c) *Asylums: Essays on the Social Situation of Mental Patients and Other Inmates*, (Garden City, New York; Doubleday Anchor).

(1967)   *Interaction Ritual: Essays on Face-to-Face Behaviour*, (Garden City, New York; Doubleday Anchor).

(1969)   *Strategic Interaction*, (Philadelphia, University of Pennsylvania Press).

(1971)   *Relations in Public: Microstudies of the Public Order*, (New York; Harper and Row).

(1974)   *Frame Analysis: An Essay on the Orgnisation of Experience*, (New York; Harper and Row).

CHAPTER ENDNOTES

1. The place of the social formation in question in the system of international stratification also plays an important role in the determination of a theoretical system.

2. This paradigm for the study of theoretical systems is formulated from the structural approaches of Louis Althusser, *For Marx*, (New York; Vintage Books, 1970); and *Lenin and Philosophy and Other Essays*, (New York; Monthly Review Press, 1971); Talcott Parsons, *The System of Modern Societies*, (Englewood Cliffs, New Jersey; Prentice-Hall, 1971); ad Nicos Poulantzas, *Classes in Contemporary Capitalism*, (London; New Left Books, 1975).

3. In this analysis, the class situation of the theoretical agent himself, i.e., Goffman, and its relation to the theoretical production is not considered. The theoretical system might find elucidation in the study of this relation, as it might in multiple others, but it is not of necessary interest here. This is because of the way intellectual figures may, 'transcend their social origin and situations' [Arno J. Mayer, 'The Lower Middle Classes as Historical Problem', *Journal of Modern*

History, Volume 47, (1975) pp. 409–36, p. 430], such that we can refer to the relative autonomy of theoretical work from its material base, including the objective situation of its immediate producer. The terms, 'class situation', and 'class position' derive from Poulantzas, (1975) op. cit., pp. 14 ff. In the writing of this chapter, I wish to express gratitude for helpful discussions and support to Professor Robert Gutman, Suzanne Paquin, and Steven Vallas.

4. Alvin W. Gouldner, *The Coming Crisis of Western Sociology*, (New York; Avon Books, 1970) pp. 378–90.

5. Ibid., pp. 381, and 388–9.

6. A beginning attempt to introduce some theoretical clarity to this matter may be found in my article, ' "Situation" versus "Frame": The "Interactionist" and the "Structuralist" Analyses of Everyday Life', *American Sociological Review*, Volume 42, No. 6, (1977) pp. 854–67.

7. Gouldner, op. cit., pp. 379–80.

8. For example, ibid., p. 396.

9. As between the goods-producing and 'service' sectors, see Daniel Bell, *The Coming of Post-Industrial Society*, (New York; Basic Books, 1973):

> The great divide began in 1947, after World War II. At that time the employment was evenly balanced. From 1947 to 1968 there was a growth of about 60 percent in employment in services, while employment in the goods-producing industries increased less than 10 percent. (p. 130).

10. C. Wright Mills, *White Collar: The American Middle Classes*, (New York; Oxford University Press, 1951) p. xx.

11. David Riesman, *The Lonely Crowd: A study of the Changing American Character*, (New Haven, Connecticut; Yale University Press, 1950); Mills, op. cit.; and, William H. Whyte, *The Organisation Man*, (New York; Simon and Schuster, 1956).

12. Luc Boltanski, 'Erving Goffman et le temps du soupçon', *Information sur les Sciences Sociales*, Volume 12, No. 3, (1973) pp. 127–47, esp. pp. 143–4.

13. Gouldner, op. cit., p. 381.

14. Mills, op. cit., p. 182.

15. Ibid., p. 65.

16. See, Riesman, op. cit., p. 136; and Bell, op. cit., p. 163.

17. Mills, op. cit., chapter 8.

18. Ibid., p. 182.

19. Ibid., p. xvii.

20. Riesman, op. cit., p. 46, emphasis in original.

21. Ibid., p. 20.

22. Ibid., pp. 21, 22.

23. Mills, op. cit., p. xv.

24. Ibid., p. 106.

25. Bell, op. cit., p. 127; and Harry Braverman, *Labor and Monopoly Capital*, (New York: Monthly Review Press, 1974) p. 326.

26. Poulantzas, op. cit., p. 275.

27. Riesman, op. cit., p. 139; see, also, Mills, op. cit., p. 168.

28. Braverman, op. cit., p. 301.

29. See, Samuel Bowles and Herbert Gintis, *Schooling in Capitalist America*, (New York; Basic Books, 1976) Chapter 5; and Poulantzas, op. cit., pp. 258-9.

30. Mills, op. cit., p. 186.

31. Riesman, op. cit., p. 45.

32. See, Gouldner, op. cit., pp. 380, 389.

33. Braverman, op. cit., pp. 434-5.

34. Mills, op. cit., p. 165.

35. Ibid., p. 187.

36. Ibid., p. 161.

37. Bravermann, op. cit., pp. 302-3.

38. Mayer, op. cit., p. 428.

39. Mills, op. cit., pp. 28-33.

40. Boltanski, op. cit., pp. 143-4.

41. Whyte, op. cit., p. 3.

42. Gouldner, op. cit., pp. 383, 384.

43. Mills, op. cit., p. 71.

44. Ibid., p. 109.

45. Compare Goffman 1961c, p. 128 with Mills, op. cit., pp. 92-3.

46. Mills, op. cit., pp. 92-100, identifies another such occupation, one within the corporate firm but requiring quite different character from that of the 'ordinary white collar employee'. This, 'New Entrepreneur', as Mills calls him, is, except for his organisational affiliation, a character of sympathetic appeal to Goffman's sociology.

47. Daniel Bell, 'Crime as an American Way of Life: A Queer Ladder of Social Mobility', in *The End of Ideology*, (New York; Free Press, 1960), explains how, in the 1940s, organised crime, like capitalism itself, shifted its focus from production (industrial racketeering) to consumption, i.e., the direct exploitation of the citizen as consumer.

48. Of interest as part of the historical context to Goffman's sociology is the fact

that the shift to gambling was the most significant change in organised crime in the 1940's, according to Daniel Bell (1960, op. cit., p. 130). 'Interestingly enough', Goffman's sociology observes, 'we have become alive to action at a time when . . . we have sharply curtailed in civilian life the occurrence of fatefulness of the serious, heroic, and dutiful kind.' (1967, p. 193).

49. See, Bell, 1960, op. cit., p. 148.

50. Neither were these subaltern occupations the concern of Whyte, op. cit.

51. Braverman, op. cit., p. 406.

52. The low-burning feminism found throughout Goffman's sociology is related to this.

53. Gouldner, op. cit., p. 389.

54. See, for example, George Psathas, 'Goffman's Image of Man', *Humanity and Society*, Volume 1, No. 1, (1977) pp.84–94.

55. John Dewey, *Individualism Old and New*, (New York; Minton, 1929) p. 146.

56. Whyte, op. cit., pp. 20–2.

57. Cooley, quoted in Lewis A. Coser, *Masters in Sociological Thought*, (New York; Harcourt-Brace-Janovich; 1971) p. 306.

58. CharlesHorton Cooley, *Human Nature and the Social Order*, (New York; Schocken Books, 1964) p. 47.

59. Mills, op. cit., p. 184.

60. Ibid., pp. 183.

61. Ibid., p. 188.

62. Ibid., p. 109.

63. Riesman, op. cit., p. 139.

.64. Mills, op. cit., pp. 108–9.

65. Ibid., pp. 92–3.

66. Whyte, op. cit., pp.248ff.

67. Ibid., p. 6.

68. The concept of 'inversion' derives from Althusser (1971, op. cit., p. 169). It does not mean simply a 'standing on its head' of an established problematic. Rather, a 'reshuffle' of its terms is involved: certain notions disappear, others survive, and some new ones appear.

69. For a discussion of the question of legality or illegality of practice and its relation to theory, see Georg Lukacs, *History and Class Consciousness*, (Cambridge, Massachusetts; M.I.T. Press,, 1971).

70. On the political ambivalence of Goffman's sociology, see, Gouldner, op. cit., p. 379.

71. Suggested by Basil Bernstein in personal communication.

72. This issue is sporadically addressed in Goffman's *Relations in Public: Microstudies of the Public Order*, (1971) which, in important ways, is influenced by the threats that were posed to public order in the 1960's.

6: Erving Goffman and the Development of Modern Social Theory

By Randall Collins

As a writer, Erving Goffman operates on many different levels. The variety of interpretations he has received – no two of them alike – makes us suppose that his analyses, or his capacities for presenting himself, are endlessly varied and not to be categorised. Throughout his work he has toyed with the relativistic gambit of social reality-constructing, although usually in tandem with assertions about the bedrock of social rules and obligations. One is tempted to find the larger frame of endless alternation between these views more compelling than the Durkheimian determinism lodged within.

Is this multileveled complexity on the surface or in the depths? I would say we can capture the main features of Goffman's work under two headings: Goffman's popular side, and his scholarly side. The latter, taken as a whole, has been relatively constant; the work changes, but the principles of transmutation are clear enough. The popular side ought to be given less attention; the scholarly contributions of Goffman are so often overlooked that they deserve the centre of the stage. But to miss the popular side would be to miss a secret of Goffman's power, and to miss some key, if unconscious, insights that Goffman's work offers about the historical world we have just been passing through. In what follows, I will, firstly, briefly sketch Goffman's popular persona; secondly, analyse Goffman's scholarly methods and the theoretical traditions to which he contributes; and then, finally revert to the popular image for some reflections on role-distance, intellectuals' reflexivity, and the cultural revolutions of the twentieth century.

AS HERO-ANTHROPOLOGIST?

For those who like him, Goffman is a kind of hero-anthropologist, donning his pith helmet in the darkest reaches of our own society. He is the man who took the dare of finding out what it's *really* like to be treated as if you are crazy, by having himself committed to a mental hospital with only the secret connivance of the superintendent (well, *almost* – he actually posed as a recreational therapist and blended in with the group); who took a job as a Nevada casino dealer to study the fast action scene; who wrote an eyes-open study of the mutilated and stigmatised, feeling his way into the lives of those suffering what no one would want to have happen to anybody. And having proved his courage, his cool, and his stomach out in the wilds of everyday 'real life', he forces us to the line of self-consciousness about the taken-for-granted, at best uneasily-reflected-upon things we all do all the time.

Goffman's most popular territory, then: the things people don't talk about. Embarrassment, flustering and making a fool of oneself in company: Goffman catches it in his steely gaze. How the hostess behaved when the dog shat on the carpet during her tea party; how we behave toward closed doors, both from the front and from behind; how we put on a social face each morning in the bathroom mirror; how eyes meet and then look away while passing on the street; how making love may be the ultimate performance rather than the ultimate intimacy. Goffman sits back with his psychiatrist's aplomb, letting the patients throw ashtrays past his ear, observing their demeanour (and his own), watching all do deference to the demands of the situation. Reading Goffman, we know we are all uneasy passengers with averted eyes descending in our social elevator like a coffin being lowered into the grave. And we know Goffman knows it, too, when we read at the end of his essay, 'Where the Action Is' (1967a), that the Nevada slot machines give out little mutilated twitches of the self at the barren ends of the earth.

Goffman resonates with the public moods over the years. He treated games and strategies, con men and international espionage amid the nuclear shadows of the CIA-infested 1960s. He conveyed a sense of why people are wary of each other on the public street that went far beyond the violence of crime, protest, and ghetto uprising. And he leapfrogged to a deeper level of reflexivity upon the mind-blowing happenings of the psychedelic era.

Goffman at his best is the explorer of our social unconscious. He lets us know why it is unconscious – not because it is buried in our dreams or the dark recesses of the mind, but because it is right on the surface. In fact, it *is* the surface itself, a surface we need to look *through* to keep everything else in focus, and hence a surface that cannot bear much self-consciousness without dire results. Freud occupied a similar territory early in the century, when intellectuals began to point to each others' Freudian slips and claimed to know the unconscious meanings of everyday behaviour. Freud reached America most powerfully in the 1930s and 1940s, when Goffman was a student, and there is a sense in which Goffman is the next stage one level over, revealing the underside of everyday life but with the insights of sociology rather than psychology. The theories differ, but Goffman shares several of Freud's ambivalent appeals. Freud's dictum that in civilisation we are all neurotic becomes translated by Goffman into the social inevitability of artificial realities, and the deep and ever-present vulnerability of individuals to each other. And yet Goffman, too, opens the way to a therapy, the one-upmanship and black humour of the 1950s crystallising into a self-consciousness foreshadowing the honesty revolution that flared up at the turn of the 1970s.

Goffman's popular appeal, one might say, comes from his showiness and his topicality. Perhaps all the more so because on the surface of it, Goffman's works go out of the way to strike a calm, detached, and scholarly note. It is to this note we should first attend, for here are the treasures of mid-twentieth-century observational sociology, (and a good deal of twentieth-century intellectual life as well), sitting around half unobserved because most readers have been mesmerised by the popular themes to which they point. Goffman's self-expressed concerns are virtually the opposite of the image of hipster and iconoclast in which he is often placed. Yet when all is said and done upon Goffman's explicit scholarship, it will be worth while returning to the popular persona once more. The traditions to which Goffman contributed as a serious theorist, with a little historical development, themselves provide a lens through which to understand the significance of Goffman's popular appeal, and thus perhaps of the energy that drives his work.

OR, TRADITIONAL SCHOLAR?

Goffman's written self-presentation is the outcome of scholarly correctness. His language is cool and precise. His claims are modest.

He suggests his points rather than trumpeting them; he offers his perspective of dramaturgy or impression management as merely one of five alternative social perspectives, along with the technical, political, structural, and cultural (1959, p. 240). Yet his concerns are unyieldingly theoretical, and theoretical in the grand tradition: they always concern the central questions of the conditions of social order. However sensational the material, Goffman transforms it with a classically Durkheimian strategy. Mental hospitals and paranoid breakdowns are important because they tell us, by a process of experimental subtraction, what are the conditions for normal self and normal interaction. Con men and spies reveal the vulnerabilities and the resources upon which all shared realities are built; the theatre and the bizarre newspaper clipping tell us about fundamental human competencies which undergird mundane life.

These are not the canons of narrower academicism, to be sure, and Goffman has been attacked by the proponents of a studiously quantified and scientised sociology as impressionistic and unserious. Goffman never raises his voice in reply, in fact scarcely deigns to reply at all. The polemic of academic specialists is not part of Goffman's repertoire.

His writing is very pristine then, perhaps too much so for the proper packaging of his themes. Goffman organises his materials in careful analytical sequences, generating comprehensive taxonomies of his own making and leaving his mark across near-virgin territories of face-to-face sociology. Notice his array of coinages and concepts shaped to his own use:

Face-work, deference and demeanour, impression management and the presentation of self; frontstage and backstage, teams and team-work, discrepant roles; a typology of secrets: (dark, strategic, inside, entrusted, and free); moral careers, total institutions, and ways of making out in them; commitment, attachment, embracement, engagement, and role-distance; focused and unfocused interaction, face engagements, accessible engagements, situational proprieties and improprieties, and the tightness and looseness of situational rules; vehicular units and participation units; territories of the self: (personal space, use space), turns, information and conversational preserves; territorial violations; markers and tie-signs; supportive interchanges (access rituals) and remedial interchanges (accounts, apologies, body gloss); frames, keyings, fabrications, frame-breaking and out-of-frame activity.

And within these, further taxonomies of sub-types.

Yet oddly, even as many of these concepts pass into wider sociological use, Goffman himself abandons them with the publication of each book, going on to a new set of coinages for the next. This conceptual frontiersmanship is not the result of radical shifts in topic, for Goffman has been faithful to a set of themes throughout – face-to-face interaction, the creation and vulnerabilities of social belief, mental illness in relation to social normalcy. Nor can one say, taking the opposite tack, that Goffman is forced to manufacture new terminology to justify repeating the same old materials. For each of his works, carefully examined, reveals a new body of *empirical* materials that he brings to his themes.

His early 'interaction ritual' papers, the most predominantly theoretical of his works, draw loosely upon a variety of background observations, as befits pathbreaking analysis. *The Presentation of Self in Everyday Life* draws heavily upon the Chicago School's treasury of occupational studies, on linguistic studies of occupational argot, and upon Goffman's dissertation research in a Shetland Island community. *Asylums* covers the results of organisational sociology and insiders' accounts of total institutions, along with some of his field observations in St. Elizabeth's mental hospital (those observations concerning patients' vulnerabilities and defences in relation to the institution itself). *Behaviour in Public Places* uses another set of St. Elizabeth's materials, this time to demonstrate by the Durkheimian norm-violation technique the moral bases of public order; and balances this with primary sources on moral ideals themselves, analysing an extensive collection of etiquette books. *Encounters* broadens out to the more positive side of interaction, drawing upon observations of merry-go-rounds, horseback riders, and cocktail parties, with the essay, 'Where the Action Is' coming from participant observation as a casino dealer. *Relations in Public* has the benefit of a decade of micro-studies of everyday life, of conversation, people passing on the street, and the like, and Goffman can review a burgeoning field that had grown up around him. *Strategic Interaction* and *Frame Analysis* cull yet other sources of data – memoirs of spies, newspaper clippings of cons and put-ons, insiders' accounts of the theatre and the movies.

In short, Goffman's work is that of a theoretically oriented empiricist, be it an empiricist who has broken new grounds in our conception of empirical materials. He has steadily broadened and deepened his empirical bases, while maintaining a theoretical focus that should ensure cumulative development in explanatory power. For this very reason, the non-cumulative look of Goffman's work is puzzling, and some of the blame is due to his continual shifts in concepts. Goffman never re-uses earlier concepts in later works, manifesting a kind of role-distancing from his own previous work; and he very seldom refers to his earlier work in any respect. This one never gets from Goffman himself any overview of his own theory, and one is left to figure out for oneself if one is to expect any theoretical unity or only a string of self-contained virtuoso performances. The same organisational trait is found in each work separately. For although Goffman is a master of the upbeat ending, with a strong theoretical point jumping from the last paragraph – and often the last sentence – of every work, he does not pause to survey the ground that has been conquered. Every book, every paper, lays itself out smoothly before the reader in architectonic symmetry. But the order presented does not invoke the order of the theoretical traditions within which Goffman works. Goffman's systematic quality is a taxonomic frame within which his explanatory ideas show only their surface of immediate relevance, while obscuring their connection with the long-standing theoretical issues that make up the central questions of sociology.

For notwithstanding his other merits, in my opinion, Goffman's contributions are most striking as developments of the major theoretical ideas of the twentieth century. Such theoretical work is necessarily trans-individual. It plays up the formulations of famous masters, though these 'classics' are only the emblems of a larger intellectual community of the past whose debates they focused into a striking mnemonic. It situates contemporary empirical and theoretical work in terms of the major long-term questions of the field, and it provides for its own superceeding by implying a future in which still more adequate formulations will be found. As I will shortly demonstrate, Goffman is preeminently a team player in the intellectual world, and from the theoretical content of his work one would hardly expect him to slight the social basis of any activity (although he has never written on the sociology of the intellectual world per se). Nevertheless, Goffman does not situate his work as part of a historical development of theory. He does not exactly bury his roots: there are scattered references to Durkheim, Radcliffe-Brown, Simmel, Cooley, Freud, and occasional citations of the more nearly contemporaneous work of Parsons, Sartre, and Kenneth Burke, and in Goffman's later works, to Wittgenstein, Austin,

Schutz, and Garfinkel. The nature of the references and of Goffman's theoretical discussions (cryptic at best), though, makes it easy to miss the significance of what Goffman is doing. The citations do not differentiate between important and unimportant traditions, and hence make it easy to take Goffman for a processual reality-constructing symbolic interactionist, or whatever reading one wants to bring to him. Goffman's low-key theoretical note also tends to leave the centre of the stage for Goffman's own conceptual innovations, and were it not for Goffman's unwillingness to give any long life to his own coinages, one might wonder whether his stance is one of modesty or the reverse.

Intellectual progress being inherently collective, we need have no qualms about presenting Goffman's work in a different light than he himself does. We need have no modesty on his behalf; modesty is rarely an intellectual virtue in any case, and a straightforward overview of the theoretical themes in Goffman's work, and of the larger theoretical and empirical efforts in which it is historically situated, will show more continuity (and more progress) than he allows either himself or the intellectual field as a whole.

Goffman has gone through several theoretical phases, although it would be misleading to separate them too firmly. More accurately, he has had different strands of theoretical interest, somewhat overlapping in time. His early work is heavily within the tradition of Durkheimian social anthropology, with a slight admixture of symbolic interactionism. To be sure, Goffman's constant interest in the idea of the social self, in the early essays, in the title of *The Presentation of Self in Everyday Life*, and in *Asylums*, *Stigma*, and *Encounters*, together with a focus on face-to-face situations and a theme of social reality-construction, has given many observers the impression that Goffman is simply a follower of Mead and Cooley. The external facts seem to support this interpretation: Goffman's training at the University of Chicago in its symbolic interactionist heyday under Herbert Blumer, Louis Wirth, and Everett Hughes; his scattering of references to Cooley and to Kenneth Burke (whose symbolic-dramaturgical processualism was much in vogue at Chicago in Goffman's student days); and his heavy use of Chicago-based empirical studies. Yet Goffman equally scatters his pages with references to Durkheim and Radcliffe-Brown, to Simmel and Sartre, and to a host of less theoretical sources. Strikingly enough, one looks almost in vain for references to the classic symbolic interactionist, George Herbert Mead, or to his major contemporary exponent, Blumer. Explicit references count for relatively little in fixing Goffman's theoretical concerns; as we shall see, though, his early theoretical arguments are strongly Durkheimian, but applied in a new empirical direction to the microscopic materials of situational interaction in modern civilised life.

In the works of the 1960s, Goffman became increasingly oriented to an empirical exploration of this new realm. The Durkheimian concern for ritual tended to face into a reference to functional rules of social order, and the latter was pressed little further than to provide a rationale for an elaborate taxonomy of features of everyday life interaction. Yet even here the ritual model occasionally reappeared, as in the analysis of supportive and remedial interchanges in *Behaviour in Public Places*.

During this period as well, one can discern an interest in game theory. The economic bargaining aspect of this does not interest Goffman, still less its mathematical formalisation. But he does speak highly of the strategic nuclear arms race analyses of Thomas Schelling for separating the informational side of bargaining from the expressive side. Goffman pursues this theme in several works, especially *Strategic Interaction*, and his subsequent two books make use of the rich vein of empirical materials it uncovered for him regarding spies, gamblers, and con men. Here Goffman seems to have most nearly yielded to the temptation to be merely entertaining and topical, but an analytical message does come through. The earlier emphasis upon a functional coordination among social actors in upholding the fabric of social reality shifts over to a greater concern for the way in which this may be a conflictful situation among rival reality-constructors. At the end of this progression, we find the theme of multiple realities and the manœuvring that is possible to contain one constructed reality within another.

In his latest major work, Goffman turns explicitly to the issues of social epistemology and social phenomenology. The earlier concern for self and for ritual interaction are gone: the individual having been declared dissolved, in *Relations in Public*, into a myriad of concepts specific to different analytical tasks, rituals almost squeezed out of the picture by Goffman's new focus of attention. In *Frame Analysis*, Goffman directly confronts the ethnomethodologists (which is to say, as directly as he ever deals with other theorists, which is relatively little in terms of explicit and sustained discussion). The ethnomethodologists are the theoretically most radical and also empirically most thorough of sociologists working upon the social construction of realities (upon common sense practical reasoning, as they prefer to express it) and on the competencies and contingencies underlying this. Both theoretically and empirically, they challenged Goffman by pushing his themes and his researches onto more radical grounds. Goffman responds to them somewhat ambivalently, repudiating their more relativistic claims with counter-assertions of the rule-bound and externally constraining qualities of social life. Here he returns to some of his early Durkheimian themes. Yet at the same time, Goffman reemphasises the fragility and theatricality of social belief. Goffman does not resolve the issue, but he does advance it by giving an elegant device for dealing with it. His frame model gives us a strong analytical grip on perhaps the key problem uncovered by Garfinkel and stressed by his most radical followers: the potentially infinite regress of levels of analysis and hence of levels of reality itself.

Goffman's theoretical allegiances and associations, then, are mixed and somewhat shifting over time. His classic early work is heavily Durkheimian anthropology, with some mixture of themes from the symbolic interactionists, Kenneth Burke, and situational-processualism generally; later Goffman has toyed with the more conflictual and utilitarian themes of game theory, and grappled with the epistemological challenges of social phenomenology. In the following sections, I will deal with these three themes, examining Goffman's works but also the larger traditions within which they are situated. My aim throughout is to assess the progress of these fields as a whole and Goffman's contributions to them.

DURKHEIMIAN SOCIAL ANTHROPOLOGY

The central themes of most of Goffman's early works are Durkheimian. His early papers are collected under the title *Interaction Ritual*. The phrase is exceedingly apt and deserves wider currency (although Goffman, of course, himself neglects it, just as he neglects most of his coinages). For the core of Durkheimian approach, on the level of empirical field work, is to see people's behaviour through the lens of ritual and its group-sustaining functions, to look beneath the usual surface of practical business and see the real dynamics of the crowd and its moral ties beneath.

The article 'On Face-Work' is Goffman's first important statement. Its title lends some place to pin a symbolic interactionist connection on Goffman, but it is nevertheless subtitled, 'An Analysis of Ritual Elements in Social Interaction'. It very quickly states the key elements of Goffman's early social-anthropological model. How people come on in conversation and in their appearance, their 'line', is usually 'legitimate' and 'institutionalised'. Being legitimate means it is normative; one feels it is morally proper 'that this should be so' for one to act this way, and *also* for other people to help one sustain one's line. Being institutionalised means it is part of the cultural apparatus of society: people repeat certain lines over and over under some hidden social constraint to do so. Society and its collective conscience, then, is not a big balloon in the sky; it is a deep and complex moral arrangement in our everyday encounters, to help each other stage their personal realities. Reality-construction may be focused on individual selves, but it is carried out collectively; as Goffman states at the end of the paper, under the heading 'The Nature of the Ritual Order': 'the ritual order seems to be organised basically on accommodative lines' (1955, p.42).

The conclusion is worth quoting in full:

societies everywhere, if they are to be societies, must mobilise their members as self-regulating participants in social encounters. One way of mobilising the individual for this purpose is through ritual; he is taught to be perceptive, to have feeling attached to self and a self expressed through face, to have pride, honor, and dignity, to have considerateness, to have tact and a certain amount of poise. These are some of the elements of behaviour which must be built into the person if practical use is to be made of him as an interactant, and it is these elements that are referred to in part when one speaks of universal human nature.

Universal human nature is not a very human thing. By acquiring it, the person becomes a kind of construct, built up not from inner psychic propensities but from moral rules that are impressed upon him without. These rules, when followed, determine the evaluation he will make of himself and of his fellow-participants in the encounter, the distribution of his feelings, and the kinds of practices he will employ to maintain a specified and obligatory kind of ritual equilibrium. The general capacity to be bound by moral rules may well belong to the individual, but the particular set of rules which transforms him into a human being derives from requirements established in the ritual organisation of social encounters. (1955, pp. 44–5)

Goffman's other major early statement, 'The Nature of Deference and Demeanour', is even more explicitly Durkheimian. It begins:

> Under the influence of Durkheim and Radcliffe-Brown, some students of modern society have learned to look for the symbolic meaning of any given social practice and for the contribution of the practice to the integrity and solidarity of the group that employs it. However, in directing their attention away from the individual to the group, these students seem to have neglected a theme that is presented in Durkheim's chapter on the soul. There he suggests that the individual's personality can be seen as one apportionment of the collective *mana*, and that (as he implies in later chapters), the rites performed to representation of the social collectivity will sometimes be performed to the individual himself.[1] (1956a, p. 47)

And it concludes:

> In this paper I have suggested that Durkheimian notions about primitive religion can be translated into concepts of deference and demeanor, and that these concepts help us to grasp some aspects of urban secular living. The implication is that in one sense this secular world is not so irreligious as we might think. Many gods have been done away with, but the individual himself stubbornly remains as a deity of considerable importance. He walks with some dignity and is the recipient of many little offerings. He is jealous of the worship due him, yet, approached in the right spirit, he is ready to forgive those who may have offended him. Because of their status relative to his, some persons will find him contaminating while others will find they contaminate him, in either case finding that they must treat him with ritual care. Perhaps the individual is so viable a god because he can actually understand the ceremonial significance of the way he is treated, and quite on his own respond dramatically to what is proffered him. In contacts between such deities there is no need for middlemen; each of these gods is able to serve as his own priest. (1956a, p.95)

The Presentation of Self in Everyday Life is an elaboration of these two papers. It introduces the mechanics by which face-work is done and ritual deference paid to these little collectively supported realities called selves. The book takes us backstage amidst the stage props, and hence seems to have more iconoclastic tone than the earlier papers. But the theoretical model is much the same, although references to it are now buried rather more deeply. The dramaturgy of everyday life is explained, not as a Machiavellian conflict of opposing con men, but as a moral and functional process of creating order. Consider, for example, the following sections:

> any projected definition of the situation also has a distinctive moral character. It is this moral character of projections that will chiefly concern us in this report. Society is organised on the principle that an individual who possesses certain socil character-istics has a moral right to expect that others will value and treat him in an appropriate way. Connected with this principle is a second, namely that an individual who implicity or explicitly signifies that he has certain social characteristics ought in fact to be what he claims he is. In consequence, when an individual projects a definition of the situation and thereby makes an implicit or explicit claim to be a person of particular kind, he automatically exerts a moral demand upon the others, obliging them to value and treat him in the manner persons of his kind have a right to expect. (1959, p.13)

Later in the same book Goffman refers to the ritual distance given to the performer, and quotes Durkheim (the same passage he quoted in 'The Nature of Deference and Demeanour'): ' "The human personality is a sacred thing; one does not violate it nor infringe its bounds, while at the same time the greatest good is in communication with others." ' (1959, p. 69)

Goffman does add a twist of his own to this Durkheimian model of ritual social order. Society is upheld as a moral entity, not, as symbolic interactionism would have it, merely as a cognitive-informational process of defining situations. All social reality-constructing is constrained by shared moral obligations. Social reality, although constructed, is not constructed in free-flowing processes in which nothing is foreordained or anything can emerge from a new situation, as the followers of Thomas' dictum seem to believe. Yet for all this criticism of symbolic interaction, Goffman does take something from it: a sense of the potential fluidity and hence fragileness of social realities. Social life, under functional constraints for people to uphold consistent definitions of reality both for oneself and for each other, is nevertheless forced into a two-sidedness: a frontstage and a backstage. As Goffman states in very nearly the closing words of the book:

> We come now to the basic dialectic. In their capacity as performers, individuals will be concerned with maintaining the impression that they are living up to the many standards by which they and their products are judged. Because these standards are so numerous and so pervasive, the individuals who are performers dwell more than we might think in a moral world. But, *qua* performers, individuals are concerned not with the moral issue of realising these standards, but with the amoral issue of engineering a convincing impression that these standards are being realised. Our activity, then, is largely concerned with moral matters, but as performers we do not have a moral concern with them. As performers we are merchants of morality. Our day is given over to intimate contact with the goods we display and our minds are filled with intimate understandings of them; but it may well be that the more attention we give to these goods, then the more distant we feel from them and from those who are believing enough to buy them. To use a different imagery, the very obligation and profitability of appearing always in a steady moral light, of being a socialised character, forces one to be the sort of person who is practiced in the ways of the stage. (1959, p. 251)

Ultimately, then, we have a functional model, not a moral-cultural one. Unlike Parsons, Goffman does not find social order to be founded on *internalisation* of moral obligations; the obligations, rather, come because of the way we encounter pressures from each other in specific situations to help each other construct a consistent definition of reality. In order to live up to this *external* morality, one is forced to have a non-moral, manipulative self as well.

Goffman is no iconoclast. He does not take the side of the beleaguered individual against falsities of society, but condemns this outlook sarcastically as an effort 'to keep a part of the world safe from sociology' (1961c, p. 152). Goffman rather takes the standpoint of society as fundamental, for without it nothing else would exist. He brings a sophisticated awareness of the problems society has in protecting itself, and hence the pressures individuals undergo (and make for each other) in order to keep up the society that makes them what they are. Goffman's studies of deviance are made for the same purpose. Embarrassment and alienation from interaction are important in that they show the norm by its violation; and although there are continuous difficulties that make violations always possible, the fundamental importance of the norm creates pressures to bring violators back into line.

The nature of the 'norm', though, cannot be taken for granted, since the term is a gloss on a set of social processes that empirical analyses like those of Goffman have now opened up for us as issues to explore. Goffman's descriptive rhetoric does not always advance this search. 'Conversation', he says, 'has a life of its own and makes demands on its own behalf. It is a little social system with its own boundary-maintaining tendencies' (1957, p. 113). Here he echoes the social-system ideas popular in the late 1950s in Parsons, political science theorists, and others. In *Behaviour in Public Places*, Goffman claims that social order is based on a set of moral norms, alternately referred to as rules. And later, in *Frame Analysis*, despite a much more relativistic outlook on social reality, he asserts that, 'frameworks are not merely a matter of mind but correspond in some sense to the way in which an aspect of the activity itself is organised . . . Organisational premises are involved, and these are something cognition somehow arrives at, not something cognition creates or generates', (1974, p. 247). Reality is external, and is generally recognised by individuals consensually. For examples, Goffman falls back on formal games; one can always recognise when someone is playing checkers, whatever transformations of this setting might be added onto it.

Yet it may well be that we recognise games as something artificial, different from ordinary life, precisely because they have explicit rules, while ordinary social life does not. An observer may offer a description of interaction as a set of practices guided by rules, but the question remains: are these rules merely an observer's convenient summary of what goes on, or are they formulations that participants have explicitly in their heads and refer to in order to guide their actions? In fact, just how such social cognition is done is now open for study, in part because of Goffman's encouragement of this area of micro-research. But Goffman does not carry his research in this direction nor to this level of detail. Nor does he give a sustained argument for his perspective and against the alternatives. Despite the smoothness of his appeals, the question should be regarded as still open and still awaiting definitive proof.

In general, Goffman seems to overstate the necessity of a single, strong definition of reality. He seems to regard any retreat from this ideal state as scarcely tolerable to the social fabric, and speaks of 'the utter mayhem that would result were the individual to cease to be a gentleman' (1967a, p. 170). This is all the more suspicious when we see that Goffman draws his favorite examples of ritual interaction from the most polite social classes in a very settled period of history. How much order of a given kind may be found is much more of a variable than Goffman would have us belive, and hence his functional claims that such order is produced by inexorable necessity seem empirically very loose.

These problems are endemic to the Durkheimian tradition. Since this tradition includes, in my opinion, the major strengths, and the major weaknesses, of modern sociology in general, it is worth examining its intellectual history a little more broadly.

Durkheim provides the classic aha! experience of sociology. He broke through the common-sense surface view of society in a number of ways, showing that society is not merely a utilitarian order of practical business. Indeed, it can operate practically only because it is founded on a prior pre-contractual, pre-rational solidarity. He mounted a series of efforts to prove his point. He gave a logical argument to show that there must be an implicit contract to uphold any explicit contracts, and a historical-comparative argument that earlier societies are based on a strong and repressive collective morality. He concluded that the group is prior to the individual; the individual, as a relatively autonomous centre of identity and self-reflection, emerges only under particular conditions of social structure, notably a high division of labour. And he rounded this off by deducing that group solidarity gives meaning to life, and attempted to show this empirically by examining the conditions for its opposite – suicides which should occur where social bonds are lacking.

Durkheim's insights cut in several directions. On one side, he is a functionalist and an evolutionist, tending to reify society, or at least make its normative demands for order an overriding force. For society is the source of morality; there is no reference point beyond it. Order is both necessary as an ontological property of social existence and the fundamental moral category itself. Hence Durkheim and his followers tend to make no distinction between arguments as to what is good and analyses of the causes of particular forms of social order. This tendency is most notable in the macro-level followers of Durkheim, especially Talcott Parsons.

To put this point another way: functionalist Durkheimianism ignores stratification, at least insofar as recognising stratification as based upon any struggle for domination. This, I believe, is the essential weakness of the position. For stratification, and the various resources for conflict and domination that produce it, are the major explanatory tools that can actually be demonstrated empirically to explain the range of social variations and historical changes.

From another angle, the problem is methodological. A purely functional analysis is highly interpretive. It shows a pattern, argues that this must enable society to sustain itself, and then closes its books. Functional analysis is hard to take further because society as a whole is the basic entity under consideration. All forms of order fall under the same rubric, and to seek conditions for *which* form among them is called forth does not easily fall within its purview. To look for such internal comparisons implies that parts of society do not all operate together as a system, and that individuals and their resources may act as independent variables in their own right.

Functionalists seeking stronger empirical support by the method of empirical comparisons have had two options: (1) to compare societies in their totalities, usually by establishing evolutionary stages; (2) to compare deviance with normalcy. The evolutionary comparison, though, has caused difficulties because in fact historical societies have not followed neat evolutionary patterns. They have not followed the same sequences of change, nor maintained external independence from each other as separate, self-regulating systems. The historical record, in fact, tends to give much more support to the role of conflict, conquest, and domination, and their material means and spoils. The other alternative, to compare deviance with normalcy, runs into a similar problem: risking functional theory by empirical test, it tends to find that pressures for a fuller empirical account begin to point to elements of struggle and domination over who and what is considered deviant, and hence pushes again towards a more pluralistic and conflict-oriented analysis.

Durkheim, though, opened up possibilities for analysis in several directions. Alongside a macro, totalistic, and functional approach, he also developed a very powerful micro approach. Working against the background of the French crowd-psychologists of his day, Durkheim was able to focus on society as actual interaction of human bodies in particular places, and to see that all such interactions have two levels: the cognitive, symbolic level of manifest consciousness; and the emotional, 'moral' level in which common feelings are developed and strengthened by cognitive focus and emotional contagion.

From this come some of Durkheim's most striking insights. One of his most paradoxical formulations, that crime contributes to social solidarity, is based on the insight that punishment of deviants is a ritual occasion that bolsters the norm by creating ceremonial solidarity around it in the very act of punishing its transgressor.

Later, Durkheim showed that religion is fundamentally a set of ceremonial actions, assembling the group, heightening its emotions, and focusing its members on symbols of their common belongingness. Thus Durkheim's most striking formulation: that god is society, and that the type of society determines the type of sacredness it recognises. And since ceremonies generating and regenerating our sense of the sacred and the profane underlie all possibilities of mundane social cooperation, in effect society is a religious phenomenon.

These analyses, to be sure, can be taken in a purely abstract, macro-functional sense, and this is the way they have generally been taken. Durkheim's analysis of crime has been applied by Kai Erikson, for example, but only in the macro sense of arguing that every society, as a totality, must produce a given rate of deviance.[2] But taken in a strictly micro sense, the analysis cuts in a very different direction. If a punishment ceremony creates social solidarity, then we might expect, from the perspective of a struggle for domination, that individuals and groups would attempt to make use of such ceremonies to create solidarity that bolsters their own preferred positions and undermines those of their opponents. Similarly, religious rituals can be used as weapons in the struggle for domination in a particular kind of stratified order. And indeed, an examination of political and religious history shows much of this sort of pattern.

But doesn't this interpretation land us back in the world of individual calculation that Durkheim earlier showed was merely a surface phenomenon, itself dependent upon the existence of deeper solidarities and propensities for order? I don't believe so. Durkheim makes a convincing case that our conscious sense of reality is a surface comprised of shared cognitive symbols; hence it makes sense that people do not generally think in terms of blatant calculation of personal advantage. On the contrary, we think, and talk, in terms of moral ideas, convincing ourselves and others that we act because of generally valid principles and that everyone should act as we do, since we act for the good of all as much as for ourselves. But these mental furnishings are not themselves to be taken as ultimate realities; they are themselves products of ritual situations which foster such world views. Hence, it is perfectly consistent to see human beings as animals struggling naturally and without conscious self-reflection for advantages, while at the same time subject to processes of emotional contagion and social cognition. People struggle, but they do not struggle alone, just as they do not do much else of social importance alone either. The rituals of solidarity are major determinants of how alliances in social struggles will line up and who will win what in these struggles.

The key to a more realistic and empirically satisfying analysis, then, is to focus Durkheimian's leads on the micro level, and to see the ritual creation of solidarity as a series of events that add up to a larger set of struggles over domination. The British tradition of social anthropology developed the Durkheimian model at least partially in this direction. With Radcliffe-Brown, Gluckman, and others, the focus was on rituals within tribal societies; funerals, marriages, initiations and the like were shown to contribute to re-creating group solidarity, especially in inevitable periods of transition due to individual life-careers. That the sum total of such interactions might be a structure of domination and conflict, though, was by and large glossed over (although one may find traces of this view in Lévi-Strauss' continuation of the French line of this tradition).[3]

Durkheim's work offers a good deal for filling out a bare stratification perspective, and later empirical developments have tended in this direction. Durkheim's model of variations in the division of labour, although originally couched in evolutionary terms and applied to entire societies, is capable of being applied analytically as a set of variables within any one society. Basil Bernstein,[4] Mary Douglas,[5] myself,[6] and others have proposed that a major difference among the cultures of social classes is that some of them approximate the conditions for mechanical solidarity, others for organic solidarity, and hence manifest corresponding differences in class outlooks. Bernstein, and Bourdieu,[7] argue that such cultural differences may be a key basis for maintaining domination, especially when the culture of the higher classes is used as a career selection device through the school system.

The contributions of Durkheimian analysis to our understanding of stratification can be made even tighter if we see that its detailed micro-basis is in the sphere of interaction ritual. Here Goffman's contributions are central. For Goffman's early work, in particular, draws heavily on empirical materials of occupations, social classes at work, and of leisure status groups and their idealised self-presentations. Although Goffman does not raise this dimension to explicit consideration, it is not difficult to do so.

That Goffman should be the one to make this connection is not surprising when we consider his biography. Goffman, a Canadian, was trained at the University of Toronto in the 1940s, notably by C. W. M. Hart, in Radcliffe-Brown style social anthropology. Goffman then went on to graduate work at the University of Chicago, where his anthropology background and perhaps also his British Commonwealth connection led him to work with W. Lloyd Warner, the Australian anthropologist-sociologist. Warner was a key figure in the development of empirical sociology in America. He began, very much in the Radcliffe-Brown tradition, with a field study of the Murngin bushmen in Australia, but then decided to transfer his anthropological field techniques to virgin territory – a modern civilized community. Thus the 1940s saw a long series of volumes by Warner and his associates on Yankee City (Newburyport, Massachussetts), then on Jonesville (a Midwestern town), Bronzeville (black Chicago), Deep South (a segregated southern city), eventually leading to efforts to capture the entire society beyond the community level, by studies of business executives' careers and of the structure of the corporate economy. Warner, in short, set out to map the entire structure of American society in anthropological detail.

In the process, Warner tended to lose much of his earlier Durkheimian analytical refinement, and to concentrate on sheer description. Perhaps it is for this reason that Goffman moved away from explicitly following Warner's concerns with stratification. Goffman's first paper (1951), published while still a graduate student, was on stratification, dealing with material displays of status ranking. But it was a pedestrian effort, staying close to the utilitarian surface, and Goffman must have felt the need to move farther afield for greater analytical punch. The line he chose was a combination of Durkheimian ritual analysis with the empirical materials of banal face-to-face interaction. Yet even here, in a sense, he was following Warner's lead. He took up the challenge to look at his own society with the detachment of an anthropologist in the most unfamiliar place, although on a more micro level than Warner. Nevertheless, a comparison with Warner's last book in the *Yankee City* series, *The Living and the Dead*,[8] shows what Warner could do, amidst all his other projects, with a straightforward ritual analysis of such American institutions as parades and cemeteries.

The Chicago tradition helped Goffman find his own empirical focus for his Durkheimian analysis; the symbolic interactionist emphasis on situations and on the social self gave him his early subject matter, although Goffman transformed the explanation of these phenomena in a strongly Durkheimian direction. But situations and selves are highly abstract notions; and with Goffman's drive for empirical grounding, it is not surprising that he emerged with a body of materials that revealed the differences in social situations and social selves of people in different positions in society, which is to say, differences in the class structure. For one of the great empirical strengths of the Chicago School was not only the Park-Thomas-Wirth tradition of studying urban ecology and ethnic relations; there was also a strong emphasis upon the ethnography of professions and occupations. *The Presentation of Self in Everyday Life*, in one respect, may be regarded as a synthesis of this literature.

In it, Goffman cites some twenty Chicago M.A. and Ph.D. theses, along with a number of other dissertations on occupations. We find studies of garbage collectors, shoe salesmen, pharmacists, labor union officials, bureaucrats, and many more; we find the names of Dalton, Wilensky, Blau, Becker, and virtually all the important researchers of the world of work. Everett Hughes, who organized and guided this line of research at Chicago, had already produced some synthesising ideas,[9] and we find echoes of them in Goffman: how occupations attempt to deal with their dirty work by shunting it off to subordinate occupations; relatedly, how the 'professions' build up an idealised public image, and how all occupations attempt to follow this self-idealising path.

The result is that when Goffman came to write on the ritual creation of selves, and hence of shared definitions of social reality, he had at his disposal an array of empirical studies showing how people at work manœuvre to present an idealised front, and showing as well what stage-setting resources they have to use in this dramaturgy of everyday life. Goffman's reflections remain on a high level of abstraction, covering the commonalities of all occupational experiences (and of analogous processes in the leisure realms of polite sociability); but it is not a large shift to see that he has illuminated as well the major differences among the immediate day-by-day experiences of social classes. Classes differ because of different kinds and amounts of self-presentational experiences. Moreover, solidarity within classes (i.e., their transformation into status *communities*) is to a large degree the solidarity of teams in putting on performances and guarding common backstages. And the overall structure of stratification, in the final analysis (the distribution of wealth, power, and prestige) is the result of the on-going activities by which some people idealise themselves better than others in the everyday encounters that make up the world of work and hence the organisational structure of society.

Why should rituals be important as a basis of power and material wealth? Because the solid economic and political organisations of society must nevertheless be enacted. Ordinary macro-level social theory tends to take such organisations for granted, as does everyday discussion, as if they were 'things', with a permanence that exists apart from the people who perform them; in the same way, we take 'positions' to be entities with an independence and solidity of their own. But these are metaphors, and hyperboles at that. Empirical reality, in the most detailed sense, is made up by a succession of minute-by-minute encounters. 'Organisations' and 'positions' are thing-like in their solidity only because they are continuously and repeatedly enacted in a series of micro-situations. They are solid to the extent that they are taken for granted and thus smoothly re-enacted, minute by minute and day after day; but without this process of *continual* social definition, they cease to exist. Now we can see the ultimate importance of interaction ritual: ritual creates sacred, solid-seeming realities, social symbols which are not to be questioned and which have a strong and compelling sense of exteriority. Organisations and stratified positions within them are prime instances of such things which take on coercive reality because we collectively believe them to be so. Thus well-performed rituals create and re-create the stratified order, and hence underlie the distribution of material, power, and status privileges.

We can go further into this line of analysis. It is possible to consider variations in the resources for producing and controlling rituals of various sorts: Goffman connects the Durkheimian to the Weberian and Marxian universes by showing us some of the crucial means of mental production, and the means of emotional production too. Such analysis would repay consideration of both its

191 of Modern Social Theory

vertical and horizontal dimensions, i.e., relations of domination and conflict *among* classes, and relations *within* classes by which solidarity is maintained and a common definitional line upheld. And Goffman's concern for the fragilities and contingencies of reality-construction tells us much about the difficulties under which people labour, both to dominate others consistently and to rebel success-fully. Goffman does not perform this analysis, and given his propensities for looking at the world from a particular angle, we should not expect him to do so. But his work nevertheless does situate itself in an extremely useful position. In this sense, Goffman fits naturally into the history of Durkheimian analysis in the twentieth century: from Durkheim's own original functionalist themes to its recent twist toward an analysis of stratification ritual and the ritual weapons of conflict.

NEO-RATIONALISM AND GAME THEORY

Goffman's early works culminate in a burst of publications at the turn of the 1960s. *The Presentation of Self in Everyday Life*, *Encounters*, and *Asylums* appear virtually simultaneously, *Stigma* and *Behaviour in Public Places* simultaneously a few years later. All push a Durkheim-ian line, emphasising the primacy of the social over the individ-ual, and the moral and functional nature of social arrangements. Then another note begins to emerge, as Goffman begins to pay more attention to the egoistic and calculative side of interaction.

This note is already present in *The Presentation of Self in Everyday Life*, but Goffman plays it down, considering the manipulation of impressions to be a secondary phenomenon produced by the demands of society itself for a clear definition of the situation. *Asylums*, again, takes mainly a functional stance, claiming that the self-destroying pressures upon inmates are due to the technical needs of the organisation processing masses of people. Ironically, this is the book that gave the sharpest impetus to the labeling theory of deviance: that what happens to one *after* one is apprehended by the authorities is fateful for the self, not what happens before. Yet Goffman himself does not enter this theme as a note of protest, but as an inevitable irony of social order.

But *Asylums* includes another note that pushes explicitly away from Goffman's socio-centric view. His explanation of the be-haviour of inmates working the 'underlife' of a total institution posits a non-social self as well, a kind of pure existential will that struggles for a sense of autonomy, most obviously under adverse conditions (see, 1961c, pp. 319-20). Goffman's essay on 'role distance' could take a similar line but doesn't. Here the argument is turned the other way, claiming that when one deliberately distances oneself from a social role, it is because that role is too demeaning in the light of some *other* role the individual also holds. Hence role-distance (of which the underlife of a total institution is an instance) does not mean the victory of the self over society, but simply the claim of part of society over another part. 'Fun in Games', the companion essay in *Encounters* to 'Role Distance', stresses the positive side of this interpretation: Euphoria, Goffman claims, is when one is fully absorbed into a social role, unself-conscious of any transformative staging rules involved.

Still, the more egotistical image of the self does not go away. 'Where the Action Is' recognises a widespread desire for individuals to show their ability to deal with competitive stress, even to the extent of manufacturing artificial situations in which to show this character. Nevertheless, Goffman proposes that such behaviour is at least half socialised, since society can make use of such personal strength, even if it is often used against social routine. And finally, in *Strategic Interaction*, Goffman explicitly takes on conflictual and calculative situations. Although he is critical of game theory, he nevertheless follows out its neo-rationalist modifications, making little effort to bring conflict back into the fold of funtionality and social morality.

This, then, is a legitimate second theme in Goffman, rising from its subsidiary place in the earlier works, while the Durkheimian emphasis recedes in his middle period. There is no sharp break; Goffman's early descriptive works on public interaction all include moves with relatively low levels of trust, just as the Durkheimian themes continue into *Relations in Public* and even later. But Goffman has clearly made an incursion into a different theoretical territory.

This territory, broadly speaking, might be called the utilitarian tradition. Game theory emerged from economics, and gives in explicit form the economic actor as a rational, calculating, egoistic individual, matched against other individuals in competitive and bargaining situations. In a sense, it is surprising that Goffman should have anything to do with this line of thought, for Durkheimian anthropology is explicitly and thoroughly critical of utilitarianism. Durkheim's starting point was his proof that rational economic exchanges could not take place without building upon a more basic pre-contractual solidarity. And Goffman does follow a version of this line in criticising game theory.

But intellectual alliance is still possible, for game theory itself had been taken in quite a different direction from its earliest stance by its second generation of theorists. Thomas Schelling, in particular, whom Goffman credits (in a discrete footnote) with creating the field of strategic interaction, re-oriented game theory away from the model of independent rational actors with clear knowledge of payoff matrices and toward the question of communications and meta-communications that go on in strategic bargaining, especially in the absence of clear information. This development was part of a larger intellectual shift occurring in the late 1950s. What may be called neo-rationalism emerged, especially within organisational theory and operations research. Such theorists as Herbert Simon developed a revised and more realistic model of the human actor as information-processor, stressing strategies used within cognitive limitations, and in the absence of direct sanctions to control others' behaviour. And as we shall see in the next section, there is an even wider trend in twentieth-century thought, arising above all in philosophy (although ultimately from mathematics), which points to the different *levels* of activity in which cognition is embedded. All across the board, the narrower model of individual rationality has given way to a more sophisticated version. It is this more sophisticated version to which Goffman brings his sociology.

In *Strategic Interaction*, Goffman takes up game theory and especially its application to conflict situations: spies and counter-spies, armed confrontations, and the like. And he argues that this sensational material nevertheless does apply widely to everyday life. 'In every social situation', he says, 'we can find a sense in which one participant will be an observer with something to gain from assessing expressions, and another will be a subject with something to gain from manipulating this process' (1969, p. 81). Thus every encounter between buyer and seller, employer and job applicant, supervisor and worker, will have some quality of strategic conflict; so will relations among friends and acquaintances, since one is often in the position of having feelings about another which cannot be admitted. Goffman does not develop any full-fledged conflict viewpoint, of course, but one can easily ground these points in a larger view of the processes that produce such conflicting interests. After all, it is competitive economic markets based on private property that undergird the manœuvring of buyer and seller of both commodities and labour; and the varieties of sexual property relations, and the market-like aspects of conversational networks in general, that underlie much of the pressures for duplicity in personal relations.

Goffman's major interest, though, is on another level. He is concerned to distinguish between communication, the messages that people explicitly send to each other; and expression, the impressions that people give off, whether they are aware of them or not. In general, expression is much more basic than communication. For, as Goffman points out, 'as a source of information the individual exudes expression and transmits communications, but . . . in the latter case the party seeking information will still have to attend to expression lest he will not know how to take what he is told' (1969, p. 9). A spy may be told certain information by a contact, but s/he still must assess not only (1) if the contact's statement is correct, but (2) whether it is believed by its maker; if the statement is about some future action, there are not only these questions of correctness and self-belief, but (3) whether the actor has the resolve to carry out the action; and (4) whether s/he has the capabilities to do so. In assessing most of these matters, one must pay more attention to how and in what context something is said, than to what is said itself.

Goffman goes on to consider the ramifications of strategic games, as players attempt to manipulate the other's responses to moves and communications. Since one makes an impression as well as transmits a message, a skilled interactional strategist attempts to control or fabricate impressions. The skilled observer tries to penetrate the 'cover' by discovering the opponent's strategy. Here, Goffman points out, game theory and the symbolic interactionism of George Herbert Mead converge. The game player takes the role of the other and interprets messages by reading the intent behind them. In classical game theory, these intentions are transparent; there is no difficulty in placing oneself mentally in the other's place.

But here, Goffman finds both game theory and Meadian social psychology to be naïve. In real life, it is often unclear who the opposing players are, or what their moves can consist in, until after the moves are made; imputation of social motives to others (and often to oneself as well) is more usually retrospective than prospective. In Garfinkel's term, it is an 'account' rather than a cognitive programme of action. And even where the Meadian role-taking model does fit better (in open, conflictual, game-like interaction) it is inadequate as a model for the actual performance of social action because it ignores the way in which people manipulate impressions to prevent successful role-taking.

Game theory and symbolic interactionism are both flawed, then, because they apply a single-level model to a two-leveled situation. Neo-rationalist game theory, though, is closer to an appropriate model, especially in Schelling's version of tacit coordination games.[10] Schelling's argument is that coordination can occur, in the absence of communication, if there is an *obvious* solution, a move that both players will see as much more likely than any other. Goffman tends rather to emphasise the ambiguities that exist, and hence the difficulty of arriving at clearly coordinated activity. Thus he explains that espionage and efforts to maintain secrecy are often failures, partly because information, being non-physical, is relatively easy to steal, but more importantly because of humans' inability to fundamentally control their *expressive* behaviour. People who wish to conceal something, he says, usually appear self-conscious, and 'it is this incapacity to inhibit warning signs of self-consciousness that makes an individual relatively safe to be near' (1969, p. 33). In effect, Goffman tells us that the human animal automatically gives off expressions in its postures, emotions, gestures, and that these telegraph one's intentions to act. Communication may be added into this process, even in the form of reflexive communications to oneself via internalised others (as in Mead's theory of verbal thought), and one's conscious thinking may be directed towards controlling and manipulating one's nonverbal expressions. Nevertheless, the expressive side remains fundamental and will control interaction whether or not communication takes place. In effect, Goffman is saying that Schelling's tacit coordination is brought about, when it occurs, because the most obvious signals are the unconscious, expressive ones, not the manifestly communicated symbols.

The argument can be made more generally. For problems of mutual assessment of motives are not confined to strategic conflicts. The 'game' may be one of coordinating the members of a social team, yet the issue still remains of how this is done, especially since overt communications, even when possible, always presuppose some tacit understandings of how these messages are to be taken. Goffman gives the example of ordinary sociable conversation. Friends often engage in the exchange of joking insults, with an attempt at witty repartée. Here, the manifest content of communication is *not* to be believed; nevertheless, the activity tends to be highly controlled, not by communication rules but by expressive standards. One does not judge such talk first of all in terms of objective truthfulness, sincerity, and candour, but of suitability to the situation and the personal relationships; in many situations, sincerity and candour would be highly unsuitable. And it is possible to go beyond Goffman's example to cite many other types of conversation that fit this scheme: not merely joking statements not to be believed, but the egotistical self-dramatisations or mutually self-indulgent complaints that make up so much of sociable talk, not to mention their counterparts in serious 'political' talk within organisations and governmental arenas of all kinds; all of the latter tend to be situationally *believed*, even though fairly inaccurate. 'What is enforced', says Goffman, 'is not words but standards of conduct' (1969, p. 134).

Goffman does give communication a place, but it is not on the level of face-to-face interaction. Where games are 'loose', i.e., where enforcement of payoffs is in the hands of someone other than the immediately confronting players, communications through organisational channels become important. Here *communication* itself may be manipulated; here efforts at cheating take the place of efforts at impressions management. Goffman's perspective on this point remains very conflict-oriented. It is apparent that the moral ties that bind people are fundamentally based only on the face-to-face level where the contingencies of expression are located.

But even here Goffman has become doubtful about how central a role moral obligations play. For although mutual trust has an obvious functionality in making social relations possible, trust in people's truthfulness as communicators touches only a relatively small part of what is involved in successful coordination of actions. As noted, actors must also assess each other's correctness of judgment, and their resolution and capacity to carry out promises and threats, as well as other situational factors that may make outcomes quite different from what any individual consciously intends.

Goffman in fact proposes several different reasons for the relative stability of social order, which go rather far afield from moral obligations and trust. There is people's relative inability to control their nonverbal expressions, which makes them more trustworthy than they themselves might wish. Moreover, the fact that people do not come completely clean with each other, and that yet other persons are aware of these duplicities among their acquaintances, often makes for a 'multiplicity of checks; everyone, in effect, is in a position to blackmail everyone else' (1969, p. 76). Hence overt conflict is not the usual state, but not because there is an overriding solidarity to offset the Hobbesian war of egotistical actors, all against all. Overt conflict occurs so seldom, rather, because conflict is a form of interaction as much as cooperation, and a winning strategy involves as many cognitive and coordinative difficulties as other forms of social order. Thus the game model is further circumscribed, primarily by human weakness. Whether because individuals are cowardly or because they are constrained by the difficulties of successful conflict, we find that the actor:

> does not use his turn to make a move; he gets by with half-actions. Instead of commitments and enforcements, he provides assurances and resentments. Instead of moves, mere expressions. To frame this gestural realm entirely into strategic equivalents is to violate its regrettable nature; we end by making sustainable imputations of complex play to persons who aren't quite players and aren't quite playing. (1969, p. 135)

Goffman's conclusion can be read as an expression of existential cynicism. Not only can we not maintain social order on a firm functional or moral foundation, but we cannot even maintain a decent and dignified level of conflict. But in a less evaluative vein, the argument may also be read as a striking extension of the arguments of neo-rationalism. One of the most important formulations is that of March and Simon.[11] In the classical model, the rational actor optimises the gains from each move. Realistically, however, in any complex situation this is usually impossible. Even a computer programmed to play chess cannot consider all possible moves and countermoves, as the set quickly becomes unmanageably large. Similarly, the manager of an organisation cannot plan for all possible contingencies. Instead, the rational strategy is to replace *optimising* with *satisficing*: to set minimally satisfactory levels for each area of operation and attempt to optimise only the most salient. The others are left to routine unless they fall below satisfactory levels, in which case one can attend to them for trouble-shooting.

This model of limited human cognition in a complex world has several implications. It fits with Simon's theory of organisational power,[12] (which builds in turn upon Chester Barnard's classical work, itself frequently cited by Goffman)[13] in which an organisation cannot be simply controlled from the top, programming all members' behaviour in advance. Rather, delegation of authority is inevitable, whether it is officially recognised or not. Hence real sources of power may be unofficial ones, and these exist wherever the outcomes of activities are most uncertain. In particular, technical advice-givers or trouble-shooters, even if they lack the official power to give orders, have effective power because they deal with the non-routine areas where choices must be made. What they express focusses non-experts' sense of the reality of the issue at hand, and this circumscribes what official decisions they can take.

The neo-rationalist model, then, envisages a world in which open-ended strategies for action are followed rather than iron-clad rules. In aligning himself with this position, Goffman has moved away from an earlier stance (in *Behaviour in Public Places*) in which rules govern public behaviour. Rather, the position taken in *Strategic Interaction* implies that the simple communication of rules, whether to others or to oneself, rests upon a deeper strategy of following certain lines of conduct. In an interactional situation, it is the expressive side (the ways in which people make moves and telegraph them in advance by their physical set) to which one must pay most attention. In effect, both Goffman and Simon converge on a model of human consciousness as figure and ground. It is impossible to attend to everything at once; so one satisfices in most areas and optimises only a few (Simon); one operates most basically upon expressions of real moves and judges the significance of explicit communications in this light (Goffman).

Schelling's contribution to neo-rationalism (which has explicitly influenced Goffman) was to point out what solution can be reached in an interaction in which each side has cognitive limitations and is aware that the other side has the same.[14] Two individuals, trying to meet in a large city on a given day but lacking more specific plans and unable to communicate with each other, will be able to meet if there is a sufficiently obvious landmark to orient to. Upper-middle class residents of the northeastern US generally can reach a solution for meeting in New York City: Grand Central Station under the clock at noon. Similarly, in an arms race or a military operation where communication is limited by mutual distrust, stability or escalation depends upon whether or not an obvious stopping place exists under the circumstances.

The sociological importance of this analysis is that it explains how political power can be simultaneously based upon threat and consensus. The political leader, whether military dictator or party influence broker, is powerful only because others obey his/her orders; but this in turn depends upon whether they believe the leader is powerful and thus able to reward acquiescence and punish defiance. The problem of every political actor, then, is to find where the winning coalition is, and to make sure they are with it rather than against it before a showdown occurs. The cumulative social definition of someone as powerful makes him/her powerful, and the same holds for powerlessness. Hence the neo-rationalist explanation of political authority points to the expressive symbols by which this tacit coordination game is resolved. As in Goffman's earlier dramaturgical model, the publicly accepted definition of the situation is all-important, above all in cases of potential conflict; a clear definition of the situation creates an 'obvious' solution to the coordination game, while the disturbance of this clarity can cause power to crumble. The stakes, then, in effective social dramaturgy are not only the general need for cognitive order of which Goffman speaks; they include the entire structure of domination.

The ramifications of this model are considerable, and mostly remain to be worked out. For in moving to a model of stratification, conflictual interaction, and tacit coordination, it is not necessary to abandon the earlier ritual model of the construction of social realities and moral ideals. These are two different perspectives on the same empirical phenomena. The ritual model is especially useful because it can be cast in terms of variables, notably variations in 'social density', which affect the strength and abstractness of shared moral symbols,[15] while the models of strategic interaction and cognitive limits upon overt communication point to the distribution of power and the contingencies for its change. Goffman, as usual, has left these lines for others, while his focus has moved on to a consideration of the levels of social reality itself. This is the subject of our final section.

SOCIAL EPISTEMOLOGY AND MULTI-LEVELED REALITIES

From Goffman's various works, we can compile a set of reasons why reality is not hard and simple, but multi-leveled and fragile. The list grows as he moves along, and by his latest book, *Frame Analysis*, it is easy to assimilate Goffman to the hyper-relativism of sociology's

epistemological radicals, the ethnomethodologists. Yet Goffman
began by stressing the hard external constraints of society upon
what individuals can afford to do and believe; and in *Frame Analysis*,
along with an explicit social relativism, there is an equally strong
stress upon why the world, although capable of shifting, nevertheless tends to find a solid resting place. In effect, Goffman wants to
have it both ways, and through the notion of frames, he finds an
elegant device which comes very near to allowing this. The world is
complex and shifting, but it is not infinitely so; Goffman sets out to
chart a finite number of levels among which shifts can take place.

Let us look first at the compendium of reasons why reality is
multi-sided. First, the early Durkheimian argument that reality is
socially constructed implies (although Goffman barely touches this
point) that different social conditions, such as different historical
eras, result in different realities. This is especially so since society is
so much organised around moral realities and their concrete
embodiments in sacred objects, such as the self, or as symbols of
society itself. The point Goffman does draw from this is that social
realities, as created, are in some sense artificial and arbitrary; yet
because they are (allegedly) so beneficial in their consequences,
people place great pressures on themselves and each other to
maintain these realities, to uphold a single strong definition of the
situation. The pressure to do is so great, and the difficulties which
crop up are so common, that people are forced into a second level of
reality right there: they are not only participants in a social reality,
but technicians manipulating the stage setting in order to uphold it.
Hence the first complexity: that of frontstage and backstage
realities.

Second, Goffman recognises that many sorts of social situations
are doubly artificial, as in the case of games, refined social etiquette,
and the like. Some of society, then, is a play within a play; and often
people's goal is to forget the transformative rules by internalising
them and taking them for granted. This is the source of euphoria, of
'fun in games'. This is not a primitive social achievement, but a
relatively sophisticated one.

Third, persons in complex societies tend to have multiple roles;
hence they may manifest displays of ironic or deprecating distance
from some of these roles, the better to uphold other ones. Here social
complexity (and especially the status differences among various
parts of one's role-set) produces yet another lamination of realities.

Fourth, social conflict and efforts at domination create further cognitive multiplicities. This is already implicit in the frontstage/ backstage distinction, where it can be seen that different occupations and social classes maintain misleading frontstages and deprecating backstages toward each other. The analysis of strategic interaction shows that one may manœuvre to throw off one's opponents or competitors by managing one's expressive behaviour. This gives us not only the complexity of what an actor really intends and what impressions s/he gives off, but also the distinction of communication versus expression. And to all this Goffman adds another subtlety, in the form of human cowardice or incompetence at playing strategic games to the hilt, leaving us in a slushy realm of gestures half-intended and half-retracted.

Finally, conversation itself is analysed as a realm in which people concern themselves with certain types of conduct and not primarily with the objective truth of what is said. Conversations create little realms of temporary belief all their own, for part of the approximate standard of conduct is to engross oneself in the world that is narrated. This produces pressures not only to insulate one's conversation from actual states of affairs in the world to which it allegedly refers, but to perfect and idealise the subject matter, to make it 'a good story'. In a final irony, Goffman can point out that professionally made 'conversation', such as the stories of commercial dramatists, appear truer than real life precisely because they have a clearness and elegance that ordinary life and our amateur efforts at recounting it seldom reach. Realities are not only multiple but are socially biased so that it is that which has been most transformed that often appears most real.

In *Frame Analysis*, Goffman assembles and formalises many of these themes. The 'frame' metaphor gives us the image of a picture (the content) and the perspective from which it is viewed (the frame). The metaphor can encompass various such distinctions: Goffman's communication versus expression, Austin's locutionary and illocutionary forces, or the distinction in formal logic between rules within the system and the formalities constituting the system. For Goffman's purposes, it is useful because it can encompass a series of shifts among levels. For if one can look at a picture with its frame around it, one might also draw another picture, which puts the picture and frame in the centre and adds the viewer inside another frame. But this in turn raises the possibility of drawing still another picture, including the viewer's perspective, and so on, ad infinitum.

Goffman is not concerned with infinite ramifications, but rather with spelling out the socially relevant number of levels. He suggests two primary frames people recognise: events occurring in the natural world and those within the social world. Upon these can be done a number of key shifts, to switch to a musical metaphor, transformations of primary settings into make-believe, contests, ceremonials, technical re-doings (practice sessions, exhibitions, replayings and the like), and other regroupings. Among these ought to be included the explanations and accounts, fantasies, intellectual commentaries, and other restructurings of life experience in ordinary conversations. Various laminations may be added by keyings of keyings (if one stuck to the earlier metaphor, one could say frames around frames), and possibly even further.

The theme of the potentially infinite regress of self-reflexivity is one which Goffman might seem to have taken from the ethno-methodologists. In a larger perspective, Goffman is only expanding a sociological version of a theme which has spread more and more widely in twentieth-century thought. Its origins might be traced to the paradoxes generated by late nineteenth-century mathematicians dealing with the concept of infinity, and which produced the turn-of-the-century battle between mathematical formalists and intuitionists, each with their own programme for avoiding such paradoxes. Bertrand Russell's efforts to produce a formal system of mathematical fundamentals, however, produced further paradoxes, and in the 1930s Gödel showed that any axiomatic system like Russell's always involves at least one principle which cannot be proven or refuted within the system; while a larger system containing a proof of this principle could be constructed, it in turn would involve another principle standing outside it, and so on, ad infinitum.[16] Moreover, Wittgenstein's revelations of the multi-leveled nature of language is not only an analogy, but also a cousin to Gödel's incompleteness theorem. For Wittgenstein was a pupil of Russell, and he first attempted to follow his teacher's footsteps, but in another field, by formalising a theory of language; later Wittgenstein played his own Gödel by turning about to show that language not only involves the level of explicit syntax and reference, but a metalinguistic level, later christened by Wittgenstein's imitator and rival, John Austin, as 'speech acts'. Thus Goffman's expression versus communication is rooted in an understanding that had built up through the first half of the twentieth century, and his concept of frames extends to social cognition via Gödel's recognition of the potentially infinite regress of self-reflexive thought.

Goffman's model, though, is especially satisfying because it combines the Gödel-type recognition of potentially infinite boxes within boxes with the Wittgenstein-Austin recognition of a finite number of incommensurable levels of human language, and it does this in a fuller context than either. For Goffman deals with types of *social* action, among which the purely logical or linguistic patterns of the mathematicians and philosophers might be placed. The activities of intellectuals, or even of ordinary language speakers, were previously given without any context, even though both the mathematicians and the linguistic philosophers point beyond themselves – Gödel in a purely formal sense, Wittgenstein and, especially, Austin coming near enough to see that symbolic communications are embedded in various social actions and indeed *are* a type of social action. The next step would be to a fully sociological perspective, and Goffman takes this step, if only rudimentarily. He takes it via the stepping stones of his previous works; hence we get a typology of frames and keys based on his familiar concerns with the theatre and with social dramaturgy, with spies and con men, conversationalists and managers of self-expressions. But surely Goffman's frame is the larger one and his social typology implies, somewhere within it, particular keyings of other realities that make up the productions of intellectuals and the expressiveness as well as the content of ordinary speech actions. In effect, Wittgenstein told us that speech acts exist; Austin gave the category a name, while Goffman provides the beginning of a systematic mapping of the territory.

In following this train of intellectual development, Goffman moves somewhat parallel to the ethnomethodologists. But whereas Garfinkel and his followers have tended to emphasise the paradoxical side of multi-leveled realities and their potential for infinite regress in the search for the ultimate ground, Goffman asserts that solid ground does exist in the contours of the levels themselves. Natural and social worlds may be transformed by various keyings, and social actors may explicitly play on these transformations in order to capture someone else in a constructed reality. Nevertheless, Goffman emphasises, there *are* real cops and real robbers (or real innocent suspects), and real military enemies with their espionage agents. And although they may play mutual containment games upon each other, with the infinite ramifications of drawing the trickster into a trick, discovering the trick and containing it with a further trick, nevertheless these matters are reduced back to ground zero when someone is shot, caught, or escapes with the goods. Goffman himself (1974, p. 316) notes that resolution of cognitive ambiguities often comes out of the barrel of a gun.

Thus, Goffman points to real sanctions in the material world as the ultimate grounding, and all transformations of it as secondary. More generally, he stresses that although the social world contains complex levels, people nevertheless usually know, or could know, what level they are on. One is practicing for a game (a keying of a keying); one is reminiscing conversationally about work experiences (another transformative keying of the natural and social world), and so forth. Goffman probably overstates the point, reiterating his earlier, functionalist-period position that the *rules* of any level of activity are sufficiently clear to most people most of the time. The point is undermined by Goffman's own arguments that expressions of conduct are more fundamental than explicit communications (among which rules are surely included), as well as Garfinkel's demonstration of a similar point which he refers to as the 'indexicality' of all social communications and rules.[17] But Goffman at least manages to capture both sides: not only the complexities and dynamics of the world, but also the ability of people (and of a sufficiently sophisticated sociologist) to settle on a clear reality much of the time.

Regrettably, Goffman once again misses the implications of his analysis for a theory of stratification and hence a link to the mainstream of macro-sociology. For the police and the con artist, with their defense of or attack upon property, the military and their spies, with their search for territorial power: these are ultimate realities indeed in the sense of controlling the sanctions before which all else will bow. In one sense, all the social game-playing is only superstructure to political and economic fundamentals. But Goffman himself, were he to follow his own assertions in this vein, might be ready to point out that the superstructure acts back upon the material base. For the police and the military, like economic and any other human organisations, are made up of physical bodies of persons *coordinated* for mutually supporting actions. And such coordination requires coordination games, dependent upon human communicative and above all expressive manœuvrings. Out of the shifting cognitions of the 'superstructure' are determined the alliances that make up basic social structure, and the shifts and breaks that make up the dynamics of human history. In this sense, Goffman's middle and early periods of theorising complement his later themes nicely. A synthesis of all three, reaching out to their surrounding intellectual traditions, would come very close to providing the skeleton of a very powerful general sociology.

SO, FINALLY: POPULARIST OR INTELLECTUAL?

Such a synthesis would not be very much in keeping with Goffman's own intellectual habits. We have seen that he has continually drawn upon powerful intellectual traditions and upon wide-ranging empirical research both of his own rather innovative procurement, and of the best of his contemporaries. But Goffman hides his intellectual elitism behind a theory-deprecating manner, producing a kind of undergound, hermetic theorising beneath a popularistic-seeming surface. Yet even the surface is paradoxical and mislead-ing; for although, as noted, Goffman's actual wording is restrained and judicious and his actual contents scholarly in a very elevated sense, his works have almost always been received as an iconoclasm that is virtually the opposite of his manifest messages. Yet the impression of iconoclasm is not exactly accidental. Goffman himself has warned us that manifest communicative content is less impor-tant than the expressive style in which it is presented. It is the frames through which Goffman's work has been presented that have attracted the attention, as, following his theories closely, we might have expected. The Durkheimian content of *The Presentation of Self in Everyday Life* has taken a back seat to the dramatic, if allegedly superficial, imagery of frontstage and backstage manœuvres, and the functionalism of *Asylums* to the implicit irony of a labeling theory in which mental illness is produced by the very processes that are supposed to cure it. And the relativism of the frame metaphor popularly overrides the conservative assertions studded through the contents of *Frame Analysis*.

One must suspect that Goffman, whether motivated consciously or unconsciously, has pursued a multi-leveled strategy of in-tellectual self-presentation. For he has not only kept up with the major intellectual action of the esoteric world of fundamental theory, he has also had a keen sense for where popular movements were going. His covert sponsorship of labeling theory predated the popularity of Thomas Szasz and R. D. Laing and the whole outburst of encounter grouping and other efforts to break through the conventional institutional frameworks of psychotherapy. *The*

Presentation of Self in Everyday Life, in its popularistic interpretation, foreshadowed the 1960s critique of the mindless conformity and social phoniness of the 1950s, just as *Frame Analysis* seems to reflect the living theatre of the hippie era.

Goffman even hit on a formulation of a phenomenon, that, if read correctly, could well have predicted the whole trend of onslaught upon traditional deference and demeanour patterns that made its sharpest cut in the casualness revolution of the hippie period. For Goffman's essay 'Role Distance', published in 1961, pointed directly to the trend, prominent even then among American youth, of ironic coolness of flippancy toward conventional social roles. Goffman was almost alone in bringing this to theoretical attention, while most sociologists described in boring detail the 'straight' roles of the conventional world, missing with textbook blandness the most salient feature for most young Americans: the distinction between the 'cool' and the 'finky', between the 'hip' and the 'square', between those confining themselves within the bland and blind world of traditionally proper conventionality, and those with enough energy and self-possession to distance themselves and eventually to catch a glimpse of the arbitrary and enacted nature of the whole social order.

Goffman, it must be said, seems to have captured the point more unconsciously than consciously. His explicit analysis of role-distance sees no historical significance in the phenomenon, and he explains it in an all-too-conventional fashion. The cause of this failure is not unlike the cause of his failure to push on through to full possession of the theoretical territories he has reconnoitered. Goffman seems hyper-reflexive; he himself manifests an extreme form of role-distance, separating himself from any clear, straightforward position, be it theoretical or popular. In this sense, he appears as the epitome of the 1950s intellectual; hip to the point of unwillingness to take any strong stance, even the stance of his own hipness.

In a larger perspective, Goffman represents a kind of extreme point in the moral career of the twentieth-century intellectual. The modernism and self-glorification of the creative intellectual early in the century had long since given way to unbridled experimentalism and to an esotericity that left the intellectual entirely free of popular pressures, and at the same time progressively more and more nihilistic about having a meaningful social role. Goffman's intellectual youth coincides with existentialism and the theatre of the absurd, with idolisation of the ultra-cool, heroin-fed jazz musician and the nihilistic cynicism of the beatnik painter. Goffman, I think, is their sociologist counterpart, like a good many of his sociological generation who expressed their own hipness by confining their research to the backstages of society, to pool halls, jazz musicians, con men, and 'deviants' generally. Where Goffman stands out is in his intellectual superiority, his ability to use links with the elite intellectual mainstreams (with the Durkheimians and the game theorists, philosophers and organisational researchers) to provide an extra measure of role-distance from his hip exposé role itself. And one might add, unfortunately, vice versa, as far as the systematic advancement of theory goes.

But that would be to judge Goffman by a type of *engagé* standard that is more characteristic of another intellectual generation. In his own terms, Goffman has been eminently successful. That he might prove to be even more successful on terms alien to his own would be an appropriately Goffmanian irony.

EDITIONS OF GOFFMAN'S WORK USED IN THIS CHAPTER

(The dates are taken from the bibliography provided in the *Editor's Introduction*; the pagination for quotations cited in this chapter from the editions shown below).

(1955)   'On Face-Work: An Analysis of Ritual Elements in Social Interaction', in Goffman, (1967).

(1956a)   'The Nature of Deference and Demeanour', in Goffman, (1967).

(1957)   'Alienation from Interaction', in Goffman, (1967).

(1959)   *The Presentation of Self in Everyday Life*, (Garden City, New York; Doubleday Anchor).

(1961c)   *Asylums: Essays on the Social Situation of Mental Patients and Other Inmates*, (Garden City, New York; Doubleday Anchor).

(1967)   *Interaction Ritual: Essays on Face-to-Face Behaviour*, (Garden City, New York; Doubleday Anchor).

(1967a)   'Where the Action Is', in Goffman, (1967).

(1969)   *Strategic Interaction*, (Philadelphia; University of Pennsylvania Press).

(1974)   *Frame Analysis: An Essay on the Organisation of Experience*, (New York; Harper and Row).

CHAPTER ENDNOTES

1. There is a footnote at the end of the penultimate sentence of this passage in Goffman's original. It reads (1956a, p. 47, fn. 1): 'Emile Durkheim, *The Elementary Forms of the Religious Life*, (Allen and Unwin, London, 1916)'. Goffman is here referring to Book 2, chapter 8 of Durkheim's work.

2. Kai T. Erikson, *Wayward Puritans*, (J. Wiley and Sons; New York, 1966).

3. Claude Lévi-Strauss, *Les Structures Elementaires de la Parenté*, (Paris; Presses Universitaires de France, 1949). [*Trans.: The Elementary Structures of Kinship*, (New York; Beacon Press, 1969)].

4. Basil Bernstein, *Class, Codes, and Control*, (London; Routledge and Kegan Paul, 1971).

5. Mary Douglas, *Natural Symbols*, (Harmondsworth; Pelican, 1973).

6. Randall Collins, *Conflict Sociology*, (New York; Academic Press, 1975), pp. 67–79.

7. Bernstein ibid., and Pierre Bourdieu, *Esquisse d'une Théorie de la Pratique*, (Paris; Librairie Droz, 1972). [*Trans.: Outline of a Theory of Practice*, (Cambridge; Cambridge University Press, 1977)].

8. W. Lloyd Warner, *The Living and the Dead*, (Princetown; Yale University Press, 1959).

9. Collected in Everett C. Hughes, *Men and Their Work*, (New York; Free Press, 1958).

10. Thomas C. Schelling, *The Strategy of Conflict*, (Harvard; Harvard University Press, 1963).

11. James G. March and Herbert A. Simon, *Organisations*, (New York; J. Wiley and Sons, 1958).

12. Herbert A. Simon, *Administrative Behaviour*, (New York; Macmillan, 1947).

13. Chester I. Barnard, *The Functions of the Executive*, (Harvard; Harvard University Press, 1938).

14. Schelling, op. cit., pp. 53–118.

15. Cf., Collins op. cit., pp. 75–6, 153–5.

16. Edna E. Kramer, *The Nature and Growth of Modern Mathematics*, Volume II, (New York; Fawcett Books, 1970) pp. 444–62.

17. Harold Garfinkel, *Studies in Ethnomethodology*, (Englewood Cliffs, New Jersey; Prentice-Hall, 1967).

7: Goffman's Sociology of Talk

By Robin Williams

All of Goffman's most detailed studies of conversational interaction have been published since 1970, (see, Goffman 1971, 1974 and 1976), and perhaps because this period has also seen the publication of large amounts of work by the late Harvey Sacks and his colleagues, Goffman's work in this area has been somewhat overlooked. Such an oversight seems all the more remarkable in view of the indebtedness often expressed by conversational analysts to Goffman's pioneering work in this field of study, and.so, in this chapter, I hope at least to indicate the extensiveness of Goffman's contribution.

Now, while it is only recently that Goffman has published studies which concentrate exclusively on conversational interaction, the origins of this work lie in his much earlier studies, and in fact one major resource for his current analyses has been his doctoral thesis, *Communication Conduct in an Island Community*. It would be inaccurate to suggest that the basic framework adopted in that study has remained unchanged during twenty-five years of work, but it is fair to claim that some of the continuities between that and current work are quite astounding. For this reason, I shall begin this account of Goffman's treatment of talk with a brief glance at his initial study of the Shetland Island Community he called 'Dixon'.

The model of conversational interaction presented in that study stressed a number of aspects that were later taken up in detail. This initial formulation presented conversational interaction as a form of social order organised by reference to rules which specified the structure of message exchange and integration, the enforcability of legitimate expectations concerning participation, and the relationship between any situated conversation and its context. While negative sanctions were seen as applicable to those who persistently failed to conform to this order, rule circumvention and rule breaking were seen as essential to the model, rather than as deviations from it.

All of Goffman's work has been concerned with the study of naturally occuring interaction, and in the absence of any satisfactory prior excursions into this field, he has always needed to expend a great deal of effort in the generation of concepts that are adequate to such a study. One of the main requirements that has guided his choice of such concepts, and their development, is that each of them facilitate the capture and analysis of aspects of social interaction that comprise, for participants, unremarkably organised and separately identifiable 'units' of interaction which permit both horizontal and vertical differentiation of events. Accordingly, in his various presentations of the concepts that I shall explicate below, he has referred to them as: 'naturally bounded units', 'basic interaction units', 'concrete units of interaction', 'natural units of social organisation' and 'members of a single natural class'. His system of concepts, then (if system it is) is not one which has been built in accord with the rules of deductive logic, but rather, one which has been built from the dictates of observational and descriptive necessity. In this way, subtleties and distinctions have emerged and been allowed to develop over the course of their application and reapplication to real world events, but developments in the use of one concept have not always had any implications for the use of another. Some of that subtlety will undoubtedly be lost in the course of this account, but the alternative would be to increase its length too grossly.

The most inclusive concept in the whole apparatus is that of 'social occasion', and in some ways, it is the least satisfactory. The concept is defined by Goffman in the following way:

> When persons come into each others immediate presence they tend to do so as participants in what I shall call a social occasion. This is a wider social affair, undertaking or event, bounded in regard to place and time and typically facilitated by fixed equipment; a social occasion provides the structuring social context in which many situations and their gatherings are likely to form, dissolve and reform while a pattern of conduct tends to be recognised as the appropriate and often official and intended one. (1963a, p. 18).

Earlier, he had identified a series of constant and variable characteristics of social occasions, and there, (i.e., 1953), he concentrated largely on the nature of different rules and expectations which could govern the conduct of occasions as a way of providing criteria both for the limit of application of the concept as well as for effecting discriminations within different types of occasions. According to Goffman then, social occasions may be expected to have the following characteristics in common: a stable way of distinguishing between and separating off those eligible for participation in the occasion from those ineligible to participate; a specification of the major activity expected of participants as well as the permissibility and extent of subsidiary activities open to them during the occasion; a designation of those responsible for its organisation, and finally, the identifiable 'shape' which provides, for participants, an indication of the occasion's beginning, course, and end, as well as the shifting requirement of their own involvement (see, 1953, pp. 127–28; and, 1963a, pp. 188ff).

At the same time, the class of occasions does exhibit some internal differences according to Goffman's conceptualisation. An occasion may be treated by participants as either a means-to-an-end, or as an end-in-itself; although this orientation may differ between different groups of participants who are party to the same occasion. In addition, he has pointed to the presence of an informal/formal dichotomy so that occasions may be seen to be informal to the extent that participant involvement is loosely specified, subject to their own internal and ongoing programming of events within the occasion, and subject only to the authority of those nominated during its course. Indeed, no formally constituted authority need necessarily be present, and no explicit social control system need be in operation. On the other hand, occasions are seen as formal to the extent that participants are required to engage in actions that are specified in advance, directed by nominated individuals, and are under the supervision of a control system which is available in detail. The final aspect of social occasions that is subject to some variation, is that which deals with their relation to other events, so that some occasions may be clearly demarcated from 'ordinary' everyday events, even though the occasion itself may form part of a series of such 'extraordinary' occasions. On the other hand, an occasion might be wholly integrated into the normal flow of events from day to day (1953, pp. 131–5).

Although in the quotation from Goffman defining 'social occasion' used above, he suggests that we might look to the nature of the occasion to understand the nature of more local events within it; the notion of context that is being applied here is rather diffuse. One serious problem is posed by the attempt to demarcate the limits of the applicability of the concept, and since there is a problem in this regard, the concept occasion clearly cannot be taken as coter-minious with that of context. He has commented himself, that the closer we approach the informal and diffuse end of the continuum of occasions, the more likely are we to drift into another concept which might be better suited to the analysis of less demarcated social arrangements – that of 'behaviour setting' (1964, p. 145). Even in that early work in which he devoted most time to the articulation of this concept, he tended to declare a limited and largely definitional interest in this particular level of social organisation:

> In the research reported in this study, social occasions and series of occasions were not, as such, the focus of attention. The concept of social occasion has been considered because it is helpful to give some attention to what one is not, specifically, studying in order to speak more clearly about what one is studying. (1953, p. 135)

Although he did, in a later work (1963a, p. 21), provide more detailed analyses of one element of social occasions – that of the nature of participant involvement – here he maintained a cautious distance from the concept in general, preferring, it seems, to make it the background rather than the foreground of his study.

His later definition of social occasion includes references to two other concepts which locate elements within it. The first of these two deals with the character of participants, the second with the setting of their participation. Participants in social occasions constitute a 'gathering', where gathering is defined as: 'any set of two or more individuals whose members include all or only those who are at the moment in one anothers presence.' (1963a, p. 18) In a separate article published in the same year, (1964a, p. 63), he argues that the term can be applied whatever the temporal span of such mutual presence, and whether or not actual communication happens to take place between any of those who are co-present. A gathering then refers to a collection of people who have an increased potential for interaction by virtue of their common occupation of some social and physical scene. Such mutual availability is an element in the second concept to be introduced at this stage – that of 'social situation':

> I would define a social situation as an environment of mutually monitoring possibilities anywhere within which an individual will find himself accessible to the naked senses of others who are 'present' and similarly find themselves accessible to him. (1964a, p. 63)

The concept of social situation, then, is formulated by Goffman as an 'ecologically or environmentally based unit', which refers to the settings within which gatherings form under the auspices of some social occasion. The concept is not wholly environmental, however, since it involves both the presence of participants, and at least a minimal kind of relationship between them. In yet another article, he says: 'Situations begin when mutual monitoring occurs and lapse when the next to last person has left.' (1964, p. 144)

So far, however, the concepts that I have been presenting are indicative of background considerations which do figure in the production of communicative interaction, but do not report on that production directly, Each has been couched in the language of 'possibility' and 'accessibility', referring to a structure in which certain kinds of event *can* happen rather than necessarily *do* happen. A progressive 'descent' of Goffman's heirarchy of concepts, however, will soon bring us to those which deal with direct interpersonal contact as an actual, rather than as an imaginable event.

It will be recalled that social occasion comprised both a reference to the character of participants and also to the setting of their participation. In the same way, 'encounter', the next unit of interaction to be considered, is also bifurcated. Encounter (or 'engagement', or, 'face engagement', or, 'focused gathering', or, 'situated activity system') is defined in the following passage:

> it is possible for two or more persons in a social situation to jointly ratify one another as authorised co-sustainers of a single albeit moving focus of visual and cognitive attention. These ventures in joint orientation might be called *encounters* or face engagments. A preferential mutual openness to all manner of communication is involved. (1964a, p. 64, emphasis in original)

The first criterial feature of the concept of encounter, then, is that of the joint ratification of authorised participation, earlier referred to by Goffman as 'accredited participation' (in 1953), and this feature of encounters has been considered in detail in a number of his essays (especially in his collections dated 1961 and 1969, and in 1971). Authorised participation is described as a 'type of social status' under the auspices of which participants accord to themselves and others a dual set of rights and obligations – the first to generate their own situationally meaningful and normatively appropriate conduct; the second to pay proper attention to the conduct of those others present. What will count as proper attention, and to what elements of participants' conduct, such an orientation is expected will be the result of collective descisions amongst those present, although much will already be prefigured for them by their presence as a gathering within a specific type of occasion (for a detailed account of the structure of attention and disattention in encounters, see: 1961, pp. 19–24).

In addition to the issue of participant ratification, however, there is that which Goffman has identified as 'unfocussed' and 'focussed' interaction. The former term is reserved for use in those situations in which participants have largely to deal with one another in terms of their management of copresence, and therefore refers to forms of interaction which are conventionally regarded as distant, fleeting or inconsequential – scanning, glancing, and other cursory and temporally limited forms of interpersonal involvement. It is, however, with the use of the latter term that we first come near to approaching Goffman's sense of the place of talk in his whole framework. Focussed interaction refers to those situations in which participants choose to sustain a 'single focus of attention'. Such a single focus of attention produces for participants and observers alike the appearance of a mutual activity amongst those so engaged, and what Goffman calls a 'we-rationale' (1963a, p. 98) tends to develop amongst such participants. Indeed, it is only in the situation of focused interaction that mere co-presence can turn into full-participation. it is the encounter then for Goffman that is the 'natural home of talk', for it is within an encounter that provision will be made for communication between individuals as well as for the reception of new participants, the continuation and termination of the mutual activity, and the departure of those who are no longer able to participate. The unit of the encounter is centrally organised around a concern with communication between those engaged

within it: 'encounters are organised by means of a special set of acts
and gestures comprising communication about communication'.
(1963a, p. 99) The very terminology used in this formulation of the
organisation of encounters however suggests something distinctive
about the approach taken by Goffman to the place of talk in such a
unit. Talk is to be treated as a type of *activity* and not merely a
medium of communication, and because of this, the features of
participation within encounters are taken to be features of talk too.
In Goffman's own words:

> the study of behaviour while speaking and the study of the
> behaviour of those who are present to each other but not engaged
> in talk cannot be analytically separated. (1964a, p. 62)

The analysis of talk has to be carried out in terms of the rules
which regulate the actions of individuals within face to face
encounters, and in making this claim, it is not that Goffman is
reiterating a more frequent demand that verbal and non-verbal
communication have necessarily to be treated at the same time and
in the same way, but rather that the anlysis of both of these has to be
subsumed by one which can take into account the various ways in
which participants in face engagements are able to demonstate and
control their joint alignment to the situation and to each other
during the course of an encounter. Often, this will of course be done
in and through talk, but not exclusively so; and talks' rules lie not in
talk itself, but in the *state* of talk. What then are the directions in
which an analysis of talk as a form of action, or conduct take in
Goffman's work, and what units of interaction are available for us to
describe the working of such a form of interaction below the level of
the encounter?

In his earlier work he had introduced the term 'interplay' to refer
to: 'the total communication which occurs on the part of accredited
participants during the time that they are aligned together in one
definition of the situation and one focus of visual attention.' (1953,
p. 141) Interplay then refers to events that happen within
encounters, in fact, to the total content of communicative events,
although defined in this way, the term seems to suggest a move away
from Goffman's interactional approach to talk. Nevertheless, later
work makes it more clear that interplay is to be taken as referring to
acts in general rather than specifically communication (see
Goffman, 1964a), and perhaps the elision arises because of the

possibility that any act within an encounter is treatable as a form of communication by those present. Within encounters, the total interplay is itself built up from a number of smaller units of exchanges tending to occur in groups which are unevenly distributed throughout the course of the encounter. Such exchanges need not involve all the participants to an encounter at one time, so that for any exchange, there can be direct and indirect participants. Goffman calls these exchanges 'interchanges', and his first formulation of this concept startlingly prefigures his most recent and detailed discussion of this topic:

> Frequently the first message in one of these groupings presents a 'statement' of some kind and the following messages in the grouping provide a reply, then a reply to the reply and so on. A communication spurt of this kind may be called an interchange. (1953, p. 170).

In examining what makes up these 'communication spurts', it is possible to arrive at the most basic unit of Goffman's whole heirarchy of concepts. The interchange consists of at least two 'moves' where move is defined as 'everything conveyed by an actor during a turn at taking action' (1955, p. 20). The term move is to be contrasted with two main alternatives: those of 'message' originating from communication theory, and of 'turn' taken from conversational analysis. Goffman's argument against the first alternative is as follows: a commonsense view of conversation would suggest that a serial exchange of messages takes place between those co-participants who make themselves available for such an exchange. These co-participants may be conceived as sender and receiver, and the messages are exchanged between them. Each message has two elements; a linguistic element which comprises what the speaker says, and an expressive element which comprises the way in which what is said is done. Such a conceptualisation, however, is not able to do justice to the interactional basis of talk, for how could such an approach deal with (for example) the requirement of participant attentiveness to each speaker during the course of his talk, or more generally, the way that the actions of those speaking are aligned to the actions of those not so engaged, and to their own actions once their own speaking has finished? In a state of talk, recipients are required to demonstrate the successful receipt of a message during the course of its transmission, and the work done by the receiver in this regard is referred to by Goffman as the 'take', a visual and postural display on the part of the recipient which informs the sender as to the reception of his message. A response to a message (say in the form of a question), has at least two very closely integrated parts then, for even before the recipient has begun to produce a verbal second to the senders first, at least part of his response has already been accomplished by the 'take'. And this is a simple example, for in other situations:

> where messages are very brief and where participants feel they need not exercise much control over the expression of their responses, the take and reply in a message may become merged and may overlap considerably. (1953, p. 168)

'Move' is also to be distinguished from the unit of analysis used by those engaged in conversational analysis. 'Talk during a turn', refers to what is said (the utterance); while 'turn', or 'turn at talk' refers to the opportunity to say it. While the latter two of these three terms does seem substantially similar to that of Goffman's, at least insofar as it appears to retain an essentially interactional view of talk, Goffman is clearly dissatisfied with its use as a primary unit of analysis in his own investigations. He does, of course use all three of these terms, but he also clarifies the difference between move, and turn, in one of his more recent studies. There are circumstances, he argues, where a move is equivalent to a turn, but equally, a turn can be both less than and more than a move. Two moves can be contained within one turn as in the case of an individual who gives an answer to one question and asks another within the same conversational slot. Two turns can be contained in the one move as when two individuals each contribute to a single answer to a third person's question. While turn then seems to align individuals and their talk, move aligns situations to talk. His most recent definition of move is that it comprises:

> any full stretch of talk or its substitute which has a distinctive unitary bearing on some set of circumstances in which participants find themselves (some 'game' or other in the peculiar sense employed by Wittgenstein). (1976, p. 272)

The definition, it will be noticed, provides not only for more attention to be given to the substitutability of not only non-verbal counterparts for verbal utterances, but also for the possibility of the execution of moves by taking physical action in a more direct way (1976, pp. 283–290). For Goffman then, the analysis of talk as a form of conduct is to be focused on moves and their organisation within social encounters. We may legitimately go on to ask: what are the organising or structuring principles which lie behind patterns of moves such that they occur in the way that they do within such settings? An answer to this question requires us to take into account two direct principles of their structuring as well as a mediating condition. The two direct principles are those of communicative and ritual requirements, and the mediating condition is that of 'context' or 'frame'.

Communicative requirements or constraints on the organisation of conversational interchanges are dealt with by Goffman in a fairly summary way. In his earlier, (1955), treatment of this topic he merely detailed the most basic requirements for the exchange of messages as those which provide for the sender's need to know whether or not his message has been received adequately by the recipient, so that each sender in turn may assure himself as to the usefulness of sending further messages or not. Later, however, communicative requirements were specified in more detail. He suggests that they fall into three categories: basic capacities of operators, a repertoire of available signals for use by operators, and some apparatus for ensuring the maintenance of a communication system. The basic capacities required are those of adequate transmission, reception and feedback, and in addition, the capacity to distinguish between different frameworks which provide for a variety of ways in which some specific communication is to be generated or understood. Signals required to ensure the organisation of these capacities and their use during the course of communicative interaction include: 'contract signals', which provide for the display of individual and mutual openness of a given channel, as well as for its closure at appropriate points; 'turn-over signals', which signal changes from transmitter to receiver and vice versa; and 'pre-emption' signals which provide for the reorganisation of transmissions during their course. Finally, operation requirements specify a series of necessary internal and boundary features of effective communication, including those of participant honesty and relevance and a series of ways in which any encounter may be protected from outside interference so that a single focus of attention may be sustained amongst those present. (For details of all these requirements, see 1976, pp. 262–265).

Goffman's treatment of the ritual dimension which governs the organisation of conversational interaction is rather more extensive than that accorded the purely communicational. Encounters provide settings within which participants unavoidably align themselves, and can be seen by other to align themselves to a view of, among other things, the situation, others present within the situation, and themselves. The availability of such alignments being present for others, means that participants are expected to exercise a degree of tact and care during the course of an encounter:

> just as there is no occasion of talk in which improper impressions could not intentionally or unintentionally arise, so there is no occasion of talk so trivial as not to require each participant to show serious concern with the way in which he handles himself and the others present. (1955, p. 33)

Such concern has to be shown towards a number of different social entitites, including of course, some of the units of interaction already identified in this account (1967, p. 169) and this concern is itself subject to organisational production and recognition. It is referred to by Goffman as 'ritual care', and he has defined ritual as: 'a perfunctory, conventionalised act through which an individual portrays his respect and regard for some object of ultimate value to that object of ultimate value or its stand-in.' (1971, p. 88). While it is the case, as I have suggested above, that ritual care needs to be exercised in relation to a number of 'sacred' entities, Goffman argues that chief among these is that of the self. At each stage of any conversational engagement, participants are required to be sensitive to the consequences of the details of their interaction and participation on both their own and others selves. Such sensitivity is difficult to maintain with exactitude, for while it is necessary for individuals to convey sufficient self possession and respect for others (by, for example, providing and demanding attention proportional to the speaker's importance, by their handling of interruptions, delays and conversational lulls), at the same time, these accomplishments are expected to be achieved without apparent effort and without themselves becoming conversational topics. For this reason, the performance of the over-sensitive or over-concerned conversational participant is as problematic to his co-participants as that of the unskilled and incompetent. Nevertheless, it is through the management of self that ritual elements can be seen to impinge upon, and structure the organisation of talk.

Goffman provides two technical terms to specify how these ritual constraints work in more detail: 'line' and 'face'. Within encounters, individuals are said to act out a line, where line is defined as: 'a pattern of verbal and non-verbal acts by which [a participant] expresses his view of the situation, and through this his evaluation of the participants, especially himself.' (1955, p. 5) At the same time, 'face' is defined as, 'an image of self delineated in terms of approved social attributes' (ibid.). This image is located, according to Goffman, not in the person, but in the events of the encounter. Lines are chosen from a set of institutionally available and approved possibilities, and it is by the judicious choice of such lines that individuals are able to display situationally and morally appropriate action. The orientation to face expressed in the production and reaction to lines is for Goffman, the 'point of leverage' that the ritual order exerts on the person, and it is the immediate co-participation of persons that are involved in a ritual relationship which comes to determine that peculiar form taken by conversational interaction. This happens in the following way. In general terms, our contacts with objects of ritual value or significance are mediated. In the case of deities, our contacts are mainly limited to their images or representations, and in the case of interaction units, the nature of the 'contact' is even more difficult to formulate. In the case of interpersonal ritual which has as its sacred object, that of anothers' self, however, the object can be physically present, and at the same time that this tends to produce a reduction in the object's sacred power (1953, p. 104), it also generates the possibility of exchange between parties in a way that was previously not possible:

> In human interaction, however, the idol which we are ritually careful of is also ritually careful of us. If we offer him up a prayer or perform a gesture of obeisance, he, unlike other kinds of idols, can answer us back, blessing us, or returning the complement of worship. Thus, instead of a single act by which a devotee expresses his attitude towards a graven image, we get a double act, a statement and reply for the graven image is in a position to respond to the offering that has been made to him. (1953, pp. 173–4)

An offering, once made then, obliges its recipient to acknowledge:

its receipt, its proper appreciation, its appropriateness as a reflection of the relationship between the persons involved, and finally, the gratefulness of the recipient. Goffman has referred to the moves that correspond to these requirements as constituting 'a little ceremony', and he has argued that this requirement of ritual structure provides for the organisation of conversational interaction equally well as does the previously outlined set of communication requirements. In a sense, then, conversation may appear to be overdetermined by these two sets of requirements. Both lead to the necessity for the organisation of conversation as a series of more or less bounded interchanges, which, while they may be said to form an interplay by virtue of its definition as comprising all the acts passing between co-participants to an encounter, that interplay itself: 'is not a continuous flow of communication; it proceeds by discontinuous jerks or steps, an interchange at a time.' (1953, p. 174)

The third important feature of conversation – that of con-versational context has already been mentioned in passing, for built into the concept of the encounter was the claim that this unit of interaction involves a single focus of attention to be sustained amongst its participants. Part of this focus of attention, was, according to Goffman, a definition of the situation which both makes possible a shared understanding of the talk between participants and at the same time is sustained throughout their participation within the encounter, (1953, pp. 136–40). A feature of encounters is, then, that they 'generate a world of meanings' (1961, p. 26), and one way in which Goffman has formulated his concern with this world of meanings is by his use of the term 'frame':

> I assume that definitions of a situation are built up in accordance with principles of organisation which govern events – at least social ones – and our subjective involvement in them; frame is the word I use to refer to such of these basic elements as I am able to identify. (1974, pp. 10–11)

While frames then are built in accordance with 'principles of organisation', and thus there are limits both on their number and the methods for their construction in the assignment of sense within encounters; it is the work of individuals within encounters to construct and maintain such frames as they are able to bring into play for the context of their activities. Talk then both requires a frame, and at the same time is a medium for the creation, maintenance, alteration and destruction of frames. In the remainder of this chapter I will demonstrate the ways in which Goffman has used the concepts that I have outlined above in the course of his empirical investigations of talk.

In one of these investigations (1971), he has provided an analysis of two types of interchange – 'supportive' and 'remedial' – which he describes as 'among the most conventionalised and perfunctory doings we engage in' (1971, p. 90). His analysis of the first class of these naturally bounded interchanges concentrates largely on one group within it – that of 'access rituals', which highlight for participants changes in the degree of access between one another; the most common of these are greetings and farewells. Such access rituals consist of a minimum of two moves (e.g. greeting, greeting), but may also include more. The expectation of the performance of an access ritual creates, according to Goffman, a 'time-person slot' such that whatever is done by the participant within that time-person slot is to be inspected by others present to determine whether or not it is understandable as part of that ritual. What may be found in the slot then can include talk which is lexically identifiable as a greeting, talk with other lexical components which can be made to substitute for a conventional greeting, non-verbal substitutes, and physical gestures and posture in general. While, however, there is a basic similarity between greetings and farewells in this respect, that is that they share a structure known as that of the 'adjacency pair', there are also a series of ritually relevant distinctions between the organisation of these two types of access rituals.

Farewells can be expected to be more expansive and less restrained than greetings, since the issue of what is to follow the former ritual, and whether or not it will meet the standards of communication promised by its delivery will not really arise since participants will no longer be in one another presence. This latter fact, however, also contributes to another difference between the two rituals: both greetings and farewells are determined in their content by the nature of the relationship between the persons involved. Greetings are also determined by the time which has passed since the participants were last together, while farewells are determined by the time which will pass during which they will be apart. While the attenuation rule can be used to select the level of greeting so required, once a greeting has been made it 'holds' for the course of an encounter; farewells cannot be said to 'hold' in the same way, for the fact that an encounter is actually necessary for a farewell to take place means that there is always the possibility that such a face engagement may continue after the farewell has been done. Such cases of 'failed' farewells are a cause of considerable unease to participants, and although it could be argued that a greeting can 'fail' insofar as participants do not stay in touch for a period sufficiently long for interaction promised by the greeting to take place, at least the two parties do not remain in close personal contact. Goffman also mentions another source of ritual difference between the two access rituals, which resides in the fact that relationships are conventionally understood to develop (positively or negatively) over time. Thus greetings may be selected which reflect the status of a relationship at any single point. On some occasions, however, farewells have to do a double job which greetings do not: they not only have to end encounters, but they also have simultaneously to end relationships. While greetings placed at the beginning of a relationship can be properly tentative, chosen to reflect that status, farewells done to end both encounters and relationships have no such option. Such 'poignancy', argues Goffman has neither an equivalent nor an opposite in the case of greetings. Finally, he demonstrates that the scheduling of farewells is more complex than that of greetings; in the former the necessity for joint alignment is more consequential since to begin a farewell before the other party is ready to depart is to create serious interactional problems for the departer and the one to be departed from.

In these ways (and in some others), Goffman makes it clear in his analysis of supportive interchanges, that while both greetings and farewells have a common structure in that they both take the basic form of 'adjacency pairs', the requirements of their operation as 'ritual brackets' which surround an encounter create different limitations on, and problems for, their employment by participants during the course of their actual use.

While supportive interchanges are reasonably simple, comprising a pair of moves each of which tend to be broadly similar to the other, remedial interchanges are more complex, being comprised of rather more moves which are structurally dissimilar from one another, and being organised as a system of 'immediate remedial interaction', (1971, p. 171). The remedial work involved arises in response to an anticipated or occurred interactional offence, which for Goffman, is normally equivalent to an offence against the self of some participant. His first, and rather preliminary, approach to this phenomenon largely concentrated on face-saving practices. (1955, p. 20). The complete face-saving sequence was said, by Goffman to involve four moves, excluding from consideration the offence which comprised the threat to face: calling attention to the misconduct (the 'challenge'); an opportunity for the offender to correct the offence either by redefining the act, redefining himself, compensating the threatened or by self punishment (the 'offering'); the ratification of the offender's offering by the offended person (the 'acceptance'); a display on the part of the offender of his proper alignment to those who have now forgiven him (the 'thanks').

In subsequent work, however, Goffman attempted to extend the temporal dimension of remedial interchanges so that he could account for the performance of such ritual obligations that actually occurred before an offence could take place. This necessitated the development and modification of his original framework. In this later study, he claims that:

> The function of remedial work is to change the meaning that otherwise might be given to an act, transforming what could be seen as offensive into what can be seen as acceptable. (1971, p. 139)

In order to deal with the analysis of such remedial work, Goffman proposes the general assumption of 'worst possible readings' of any potentially offensive act; from that assumption, he generates a concept to deal with the act itself and two concepts to deal with those involved in the act: 'virtual offence', 'virtual offender' and 'virtual complainant'. Three main devices are conventionally available as the basis of remedial work: accounts, apologies and requests. Included in the first of these categories are: 'rejoinders', in which the offender can argue that the act never occurred or that he wasn't involved in any act which did occur; 'counters', in which the individual claims that the act has been incorrectly categorised; and 'mitigations', of ignorance, reduced responsibility, lack of competence or the absence of sufficient self control. Apologies work, according to Goffman by means of a bisection of the offender into two parts, the first of which admits responsibility for the offence, while the second recognises the offensive nature of what has happened and appropriately sanctions the first. Unlike either of the first two type of remedial devices, the third type, that of requests, occur prior to the event rather than after it, and thus is defined by

Goffman as: 'asking licence of a potentially offended person to engage in what could be considered a violation of his rights.' (1971, pp. 144–5). Despite such differences in the details of different types of remedial work, however, Goffman provides a term which covers all three in terms of the part they play in any remedial cycle – 'remedy'. In addition to the delivery of such remedies, there are several other parts to the basic remedial interchange: 'relief', which may be expected to follow the provision of a remedy; this second move being normally made by the victim of the offence in response to the remedy, and displaying to the offender that the remedy offered has been both acceptable and accepted. This move can be followed by a next move which consitutes 'appreciation' wherein the offender shows his gratitude for the acceptance of his remedy contained in the relief, and this move too may be followed by a final 'minimisation' move in which the offended provides an attenuated version of the relief which serves to demonstrate his 'appreciation of the appreciation shown to him and rather fully terminates the interchange' (1971, p. 177).

Two of the most important features of his treatment of this type of remedial interchange, however, both suggest some difficulties in the further formalisation of the analysis. The first feature is that the moves as detailed above do not correspond to turns at talk, and the second is that the basic cycle undergoes a series of modifications in practice. The first feature is best demonstrated with one of Goffman's own examples:

A: 'I'm taking the rake. Okay? Thanks'
B: 'Sure. Nothing at all' (1971, p. 178)

In the above interchange, we have all four elements of the remedial cycle: a remedy which takes the form of a request, 'I'm taking the rake. Okay'; a relief, 'Sure'; an appreciation, 'Thanks'; and finally the minimisation move, 'Nothing at all'. The sequential order of these moves, however is rather different from that which has already been detailed, and what is more, each turn at talk has contained two moves:

A: request/appreciation
B: relief/minimisation (1971, p. 178).

In addition to the disjunction between turn and move and the laxity of sequential organisation Goffman provides accounts of a number of 'transformations' of the remedial cycle too. The first issue is that it is unnecessary for all, or indeed, any of the moves to be accomplished by speaking at all, for it is talk as a form of conduct that does the work of occupying specific slots. Such slots can be occupied by a number of other actions that an individual is capable of performing in addition to or instead of speaking actions. Secondly, it is not only in the case of requests that the remedial cycle can be started up before the virtual offence has taken place; in many encounters, it will be clear to those present that an intended act may well constitute a virtual offence, and in such cases, remedial work may well be carried out in advance of its commission. There are also situations in which the full remedial interchange may be unnecessary, this possibility being particularly likely where, following the provision of a remedy, subsequent moves can be taken for granted by the way in which those present are then re-aligned. The same incomplete cycle can arise in situations where both parties present themselves as virtual offender to the other, a dispute which often lapses rather than being resolved, and in such a circumstance, for one participant to supply a relief would be to resolve a dispute which both might prefer unresolved. There are, finally, two additions proposed by Goffman to the set of moves thus far outlined: a 'priming' move whereby one participant can remind another of the next move required at any stage in the complete interchange; and 'recycling', whereby a move, shown to be insufficient to its task, has to be redone for the sake of whatever party happens to be its intended recipient.

In a more recent work, (1976a), many of the observations made in the two studies reported above have been deepened, and the implications of this type of analysis clarified. In the work reported so far, the analysis of moves has been carried out by examining their sequential placement within an interchange, and by examining the ways in which interchanges are built from a sequence of moves. The simplest examples of this occurred in the case of access rituals considered as adjacency pairs, and the more complex sequences involved in remedial interchanges broadly followed the same procedure. The principle of the sequential organisation of moves in general had not been much considered, however, apart from the observations to the effect that the moves that comprised a remedial interchange did not always occur in the standard order assembled for the purposes of analysis. It seems, however, that the very notion of the sequential organisation of talk requires a more critical approach than that accorded it up to this point. There are a number of factors that have to be taken into consideration in the attempt to formulate the sequential structure of talk, and to make that structure account for its orderly character. The first of these has already been suggested – some sequences of moves involve changes from talk to action from move to move and vice versa. A second has to do with what Goffman refers to as the 'reach' of responses (where a response is a generic term for a move which follows some prior move). The point is illustrated with the example of a proper response to a request for the time: such a proper response includes two parts, the first being the inspection of some time-piece, the second comprising a report of that inspection delivered to the questioner. Some individuals, however, on being asked the time will already know what it is in the sense of having only very recently having inspected a watch. In the case of their response, it is common for such individuals to provide the now strictly unnecessary action-element in the response or employ a verbal substitute for that action. The response may also reach further back that the last utterance of the speaker (as in the case of a response to a completed story which, during its telling had also elicited a series of 'buried responses', ignored or overridden by the response following the story completion) and may only reach as far as one part in the previous utterance, rather than incorporating it as a whole. (Speakers, it seems, have licence to address pieces of a prior turn, including a selection of its linguistic, intonational, or non-verbal aspects). That such licence exists is part of a larger facility permitted to speakers – that of choosing one of a number of meanings that might be provided for the move in question, and this choice might be exercised either by a rekeying of the whole content of the move, thus transforming an intended meaning completely, or, by selecting elements of it to respond to as in those cases mentioned above.

The question arises for Goffman therefore, of what the 'response' can be seen as 'responding to', if such licence is permitted those who are responsible for building and delivering it. What is required then is a characterisation of the move prior to a response. The term Goffman chooses to use here is that of 'reference', arguing that the alternative 'statement', while providing for one basic feature of this type of move – its forward looking character – is insufficiently sensitive to deal with the range of things that can have been done to such a move by the response which follows it. In place of statement he suggests that we need: 'a word encompasing all the things that could be responded to by a person presenting something in the guise of a response. Call that the reference of the response.' (1976, p. 292).

A peculiar feature of this formulation is immediately brought to our notice – that it, 'recommends a backward look to the study of talk' (ibid). It is not merely then that a response follows subsequent on what has been said or done in an immediately prior move, but rather that it simultaneously provides a sense of what has been done or said by virtue of its selection from a number of possibilities. The nature of any single reference then is not decidable until a response has been accomplished, although its potential can of course be broadly sketched in, and the individual who makes a reference available may attempt to limit the type of response that is demanded of it. In this version then, conversational interaction is formulated as being constituted by: 'a sustained strip or tract of referencings, each referencing tending to bear, but often deviously, some retrospectively perceivable connection to the immediately prior one' (1976a, p. 309). This formulation is put to work on a series of illustrative two part interchanges, each of which begins with, 'Do you have the time?' and includes responses which vary from 'Yes I do. Its five o'clock', through 'No, I left it with the basil', 'What dime', 'Dont you remember me', to 'Yes, do you have the inclination', and, 'Stop worrying, they'll be here' (1976, pp. 306–8). In demonstrating the variety of possible responses to such a simple move, Goffman is able to show the various ways in which speakers can use parts of what has been said, and other actions performed by the other party, (as well as features of the context of the interchange) as the reference for their own response, thus creating a new context for that which may expectably follow. It may well be, as Goffman points out, that regularities exist as to the ways in which references are established, contexts selected from, and responses constructed; but at the same time, the choice open to speakers is vast, this choice being bounded only by the limits of 'intelligibility and decorum'.

Thus while talk is said to be governed by the constraint of both communicative efficiency and ritual respect for others, these constraints specify merely what seem to be very broad limits of its performance. This suggests that an analysis of talk which concentrates on the close details of its sequential organisation may mislead us into the attribution of determinacies which simply are not present during the course of that talk's production. He says:

although any conversational move is apparently determined by
the preceding moves of other participants, and appreciably
determines the moves that follow, still much looseness is found;
for at each juncture, a whole range of actions seems available to
the individual, and his particular selection is a matter of free
choice – at least at a given level of analysis. (1974, p. 501)

In conclusion then, it is this accommodative feature of conversational interaction that is one of its distinguishing features, this
feature being brought about through the concatenation of ritual
and communicative elements. The rules of self respect and considerateness which govern the establishment, maintainance and
responsiveness of participants to the 'face' claimed by others assures
a working acceptance of the claims that others make on their own
behalf, and while such an acceptance may not extend beyond the
boundaries of any single encounter, it is, according to Goffman, a
structural feature of occasions of talk, and remains in force during
such an occasion. The nature of social control and the invocation of
sanctions against deviance at the level of conversation also rein-
forces the accommodative nature of this form of interaction, for if
conversational deviation is to be sanctioned in such a way that the
encounter itself can remain a going concern, such sanctions have to
be operated selectively and with much care.

The communicative element of conversation provides the ideal
material for just this rather special kind of social control, however,
for if the continuation of an encounter depends on the forebearance
of some participants of the actions of others, it is convenient that
communications, unlike facts: 'can be by-passed, withdrawn from,
disbelieved, conveniently misunderstood, and tactfully conveyed.'
(1955, p. 43). Indeed, at one point, Goffman argues that this
accommodative emphasis of conversational interaction is so pervasive that it can be used to account for a common feature of such
talk – that it often constitutes less of a direct action (or what
Goffman calls a 'doing'), and more of a report of some other action,
a form of 'display', for such displays are of course much more easily
accommodated by participants than the production of direct and
immediately consequential doings. A display then is a 'review of
action', and the responses required of those present to witness such
displays do not consist in a favour direct action, but merely in
appreciation of the display offered. As he puts it:

What the individual spends most of his spoken moments doing is providing evidence for the fairness or unfairness of his current situation and other grounds for sympathy, approval, exoneration, understanding, or amusement. And what his listeners are primarily obliged to do is to show some kind of audience appreciation. They are to be stirred not to take action but to exhibit signs that they have been stirred (1974, p. 503).

Only one comment needs to be added in conclusion to this account of Goffman's framework for the analysis of conversational interaction. While I have reported his emphasis on the accommodative nature of such interaction, culminating in the concept of display, it should be remembered that the accommodation that Goffman presents us with is not an especially benign one, for ritual respect and consideration is precisely ritual – it is a requirement for interaction and not necessarily a 'genuine' reflection of concern of the participants. Rules of interaction are constantly being taken, and offenders and offences are chronically present in all kinds of conversational encounters. A good deal of remedial work is constantly under way, and for this reason, it is appropriate to conclude on a relatively gloomy note; taken from Goffman himself:

It is often better to conceive of interaction not as a scene of harmony, but as an arrangement for pursuing a cold war. A working acceptance may thus be likened to a temporary truce, a modus vivendi for carrying out negotiations and vital business. (1963, p. 40)

EDITIONS OF GOFFMAN'S WORK USED IN THIS CHAPTER

(The dates are taken from the bibliography provided in the *Editor's Introduction*; the pagination for quotations cited in this chapter from the editions shown below).

(1953)   *Communication Conduct in an Island Community*, Unpublished Ph.D Dissertation, (Chicago; University of Chicago).

(1955)   'On Face-Work: An Analysis of Ritual Elements in

Social Interaction', in Goffman, (1967).

(1961)   *Encounters: Two Studies in the Sociology of Interaction*,
            (Harmondsworth; Penguin).

(1963)   *Stigma: Notes on the Management of Spoiled Identity*,
            (Harmondsworth; Penguin).

(1963a)   *Behaviour in Public Places: Notes on the Social Organisation
            of Gatherings*, (New York; Free Press of Glencoe).

(1964)   'Mental Symptoms and the Public Order', in
            Goffman, (1967).

(1964a)   'The Neglected Situation', in Pier Paolo Giglioli (ed)
            Language and Social Context, (Harmondsworth;
            Penguin, 1972) pp. 61–66.

(1967)   *Interaction Ritual: Essays on Face-to-Face Behaviour*,
            (Harmondsworth; Penguin).

(1974)   *Frame Analysis: An Essay on the Organisation of Experience*,
            (Harmondsworth; Peregrine).

(1976a)   'Replies and Responses', *Language in Society*, Volume 5,
            No. 3, (December, 1976) pp. 257–313.

8: Goffman's Version of Reality

By Steve Crook and Laurie Taylor

Goffman's books and articles have frequently been read as substantive contributions to a number of different, if related, areas of sociology. *The Presentation of Self in Everyday Life* regularly appears on the booklists for 'Self and Society' courses; *Asylums* is a constant reference for 'Penology' and 'Mental Illness' options; the essay 'Where the Action Is' is invoked by writers on gambling; *Strategic Interaction* is cited by students of spying; and *Encounters, Behaviour in Public Places, Interaction Ritual* and *Relations in Public* are combed for insights by those concerned with the intricacies of face-to-face interaction.

Such appropriations have done much to illuminate the subjects under consideration. We know more about the self, institutions, gambling, bluffing, and body language, as a result of Goffman's work. But this use of the texts as a variegated resource for a range of substantive enquiries has tended to obscure certain general, and less substantive emergent features. Ironically, perhaps, it has particularly allowed us to overlook the shift away from 'content' in Goffman's work, and increasing recourse to a formalistic, more 'content-free' analysis. The most dramatic development of this tendency is to be found in *Frame Analysis*, a book in which the background methodological devices (models, perspectives, frameworks) which were originally employed with varying degrees of explicitness in the earlier works to gain some purchase upon substantive features of the world, have themselves been transformed into the central topic of enquiry. The traditional claim that there was a certain heuristic value in treating particular social arrangements as a ritual, a drama or a game has been replaced by the considerably stronger claim that these models may not only constitute modes by which experience can be organised, but that this possibility forms the basis for a general theory of the organisation of all experience.

Frame Analysis addresses itself not to any specific subject matter (to prisons, public behaviour, mental illness or physical disability), but rather to the experiential modes to which we make reference when seeking to establish what is going on in the world. Goffman himself makes an early claim in that book:

> My aim is to try to isolate some of the basic frameworks of understanding available in our society for making sense out of events and to analyse the special vulnerabilities to which these frames of reference are subject. (1974, p. 10).

These experiential modes, types of subjective involvement (or 'frames') include play, drama, ritual, game and fabrication – the devices which Goffman has used at various times to illuminate particular frameworks of social interaction. But now, in *Frame Analysis*, the illustrative functions disappear and they emerge as general aspects of human cognition of the social. Their relationship to specific compelling features of the world becomes tenuous and at times arbitrary. Whether a particular 'strip' of activity is 'really' a game, a play, a rehearsal, a ritual, or a fabrication is not decided exclusively by reference to its intrinsic features. It can instead become any of these things provided the participants can utilise the 'keys' which enable appropriate transformations to be effected.

Goffman claims that the frameworks which organise our experience are something more than just a 'matter of mind', but his attempts to articulate the ways in which they are related to the organisation of the activity itself indicate that they are structures which are somehow prior to the events themselves. In fact, he says:

> Organisational premises are involved, and these are something cognition somehow arrives at, not something cognition creates or generates. Given their understanding of what it is that is going on, individuals fit their actions to this understanding and ordinarily find that the ongoing world supports this fitting. (1974, p. 247):

Now of course in earlier texts, it was precisely the ongoing world which prompted the perspective, not the perspective which organised the world and then 'ordinarily' found support for itself within that world. In *The Presentation of Self in Everyday Life*, for example, Goffman makes it quite clear that the dramaturgical perspective is to be used as an heuristic device which will not necessarily fit all features of the subject matter to which it is to be applied. He there tells us , 'In using this model I will not attempt to make light of it's obvious inadequacies', (1959, *preface*), and when the analysis is complete, Goffman is happy to agree that the model has now served its purpose, by saying:

> And so here the language and mask of the stage will be dropped. Scaffolds, after all, are to build other things with, and should be erected with an eye to taking them down. (1959, p. 224)

However this particular scaffold, the dramatic metaphor, was soon reassembled. It appears in much of Goffman's subsequent work with varying degrees of heuristic explicitness until, finally, in *Frame Analysis*, it loses its heuristic character altogether and becomes constitutive of reality itself: a subject for analysis in its own right. No longer is it a question of how far life, or the presentation of self, or social interaction could usefully be seen to be modelled upon drama but rather how far theatrical presentation itself was accounted for by our everyday tendency to dramatise ourselves and our lives. Goffman here makes this claim:[1]

> One could, in fact, argue that popularly recognised life-course themes do not merely make scripted presentation possible but are conceived of *in order* to make those entertainments possible. Human nature and life crisis are what we need to make life stageable. How else account for how well adapted life appears to be for theatrical presentation. (1974, p. 557)

The dramatic and the theatrical are now no longer a model but a frame – a particular transformation of concrete actual activity with its own claims upon our attention and its own felt sense (however transient) of somehow being the 'real world'.

It is not just the 'theatrical' and the 'dramatic' which change their status in *Frame Analysis*. Other previously adopted heuristic devices, 'ritual', 'play', 'game', and 'fabrication', make a re-appearance as experiential modes. They are now frameworks which taken together constitute a 'framework of frameworks'; a delimited set of organisational principles to which we refer when we seek an answer to the question, 'What is *it* that's going on here?' We have already seen that Goffman holds frameworks to be extra-cognitive and although he makes the usual apologies for the clumsiness of his conceptual armoury, he insists that they are grounded in reality, by claiming that, 'Some of the things in the world seem to urge the analysis I am here attempting' (1974, p. 13). In this way *Frame Analysis* extracts the organising features from the earlier Goffman texts, but leaves their substantive concerns behind. As Jason Ditton has observed, the book, 'generate(s) an analytic parenthood for all the orphaned Goffman minor works which littered the decade after the publication of *The Presentation of Self in Everyday Life*.'[2]

THE QUEST FOR REALITY

Our major concern in this chapter is with the relative success of this shift from 'perspective and substantial topic', to 'experiential form', with Goffman's ability to make the apparent 'contents' of the world analytically recede before the modes of their apprehension. We select this topic, not just because it represents Goffman's most recent (and most comprehensive) exercise in theory, but also because it necessarily involves a discussion about a range of epistemological problems which some of the earlier works have raised rather than resolved. In particular it introduces questions about the concept of 'reality' and its relation to social experience, and thereby about the relative compatibility of Goffman's analysis with those theoretical approaches which have been labelled 'interactionist', 'phenomenological', 'semiological' and 'structuralist'. In all this we are not aiming to correct Goffman's formulations – his own happy acknowledgement of the tentativeness of many of his ideas would make this a pedantic exercise – but rather to use them as a stimulus to discussion. We start with the problem of 'reality'.

Goffman's work has not always been notable for its extended discussions of other writers, but in the introduction to *Frame Analysis* he is at some pains to locate himself within a tradition of theorising about experience whose principal representatives are William James and Alfred Schutz. Both of these writers were centrally concerned with analysing the conditions under which experiences are said to be 'real' and it is this aspect of their work that Goffman wishes to develop. He says 'Within the terms, then, of the bad name that the analysis of social reality has, this book presents another analysis of social reality' (1974, p. 2). Concern about what should count as 'real' has consistently interested Goffman since *The Presentation of Self in Everyday Life*, where the actual choice of a dramatic model served to increase the salience of certain paradoxes: As he put it then:

> An action staged in a theatre is a relatively contrived illusion and an admitted one; unlike ordinary life nothing real or actual can happen to the performed characters – although at *another level* of course something real and actual can happen to the reputation of the performers whose everyday job it is to put on theatrical performances. (1959, p. 246, emphasis added).

Now, when Goffman is using drama as a partial heuristic tool to suggest what *might* be going on, the question of its relationship to 'other levels' is not apparently problematic. Indeed, there is a sense in which Goffmanesque models have become so much a standard resource of middle-class self-consciousness that their status vis-a-vis other resources seems unproblematic. But in *Frame Analysis* matters are different in that Goffman is no longer merely illuminating particular aspects of social interaction, but is attempting to account for the possibility of social experience in general. This means that questions about the reality-status of the various domains of experiential possibilities cannot be bracketed: 'the reality' or otherwise of an experience is obviously one of its most critical characteristics.

Goffman is too subtle an analyst to construe the question 'what is real?' as a demand for a metaphysical distinction between the real and the unreal. That sort of demand would draw him away from his central concern with the way in which social experience is produced, and this is why William James is so useful to him. As he says on page 2 of *Frame Analysis*, 'Instead of asking what reality is [James] gave matters a subversive phenomenological twist, italicising the following question: *under what circumstances do we think things are real?*' Although Goffman applauds the way James poses the question of the reality of experience, he is less sanguine about the answer, which he gives on page 3 (to which we have added emphasis): '*James copped out*; he allowed that the world of the senses has a special status, being the one we judge to be the realest reality.'

It is interesting to examine this alleged 'cop-out' more closely. Essentially, James works as a psychologist, basing his account of the sense of reality on the observation of 'mental facts'. Experiences are held to convey a sense of reality, in the first instance, in so far as they are not contradicted. Contradiction occurs when an individual's experience of an object is incompatible with the knowledge of that object which previous and cumulative experiences have given him. Faced with such a contradiction, the individual must choose whether to believe the evidence of his senses or his prior knowledge. James himself said:

> The whole distinction of real and unreal . . . . is . . . . grounded on two mental facts – first, that we are liable to think differently of the same; and second, that when we have done so, we can choose which way of thinking to adhere to and which to disregard.[3]

Although the individual will not consider a disregarded experience to be of a 'real' object; from the point of view of the analyst the experience itself is real enough, it has 'actually' occurred and must be accounted for. In order to facilitate such accounting James introduces the concept(s) of 'various orders of reality', 'sub-universes', or 'the many worlds'. Contradicted experiences; illusions, fantasies, errors, dreams and such:

> still have existence, though not the same existence as the real things . . . . they are in their way . . . . as undeniable features of the universe as the realities are in their way .[4]

The total world is composed of a number of smaller worlds, modes of containment for the diverse contents of variegated experiences. Meinong's jungle becomes a neatly classified botanical garden.

So far we have a formal model of the constraints within which the sense of reality is produced, and if James stopped here we would be left with experiential pluralism – and complete relativism. But he didn't, and he continues: 'Each world *whilst it is attended* to is real after it's own fashion; only the reality lapses with the attention'.[5] This notion of attention is however the way in which James eventually escapes from total relativism. For if the ascription of reality to experience only becomes a problem when a putative object of experience is 'contradicted', it is surely possible to identify those characteristics which can index: 'the success with which a contradicted object maintains itself in our belief.'[6] And he eventually produces a list of such characteristics:

1. Coerciveness over attention . . . .
2. Liveliness, or sensible pungency . . . .
3. Stimulating effect upon the will . . . .
4. Emotional interest . . . .
5. Congruity with favourite forms of contemplation . . . .
6. Causal independence and effectivity . . . .

The paragon of such experiential virtues is, of course, the world of sensible objects, and it is this, therefore, which comes to represent, for most people at least, the 'paramount reality'. Now, James's account would be circular if it were taken to be an explanation – if he were saying, for example, that we attend to certain experiences *because* features of those experiences coerce our attention. But, (as Goffman himself points out), the 'twist' which James gives to the question of reality is phenomenological, and it is phenomenological description rather than causal explanation that we are offered in James's *The Principles of Psychology*. James is giving an account of the features of individual experience which produce and maintain the 'sense of reality': it is difficult then in these terms to see how he could be 'copping-out'.

Goffman, however, is interested in experience in and of the *social* world and this difference of focus goes some way to explaining his dissatisfaction with James's account. For Goffman's purposes, James was certainly correct to identify the *sense* of reality as the central problem, but the authority which he imparts to the world of the senses is less helpful: sense experience doesn't in the first instance decide what sort of social event is going on. As far as the social world is concerned, James's vision carves out provinces of meaning which are too large, too rigid and too autonomous to account for our ability to cope with the constant and subtle shifts to which the sense of social reality is prone. An alternative stress in *Frame Analysis* is the suggestion that a good deal of our activity – or our experience of activity – is reflexive. A given 'strip' of activity is likely to depend for its sense – the sense of reality which it conveys – upon the understanding we have of other strips of activity (or perhaps the same strip in a different key) whose sense of reality is already established for practical purposes.

This reflexivity of experience is articulated in *Frame Analysis* through the concept of 'transformation', concretised through the image, or figure, of 'lamination': In Goffman's own words:

it becomes convenient to think of each transformation as adding a
layer, or lamination to the activity. And one can address two
features of the activity. One is the inner-most layering in which
dramatic activity can be at play to engross the participant. The
other is the outer-most lamination, the *rim* of the frame, as it were,
which tells us just what sort of status in the real world the activity
has. (1974, p. 82)

Here, then, is a spatial metaphor for the way in which the sense of
reality is maintained in a world of social experience subject to
continual transformation. In the centre is activity and
'engrossment' – a clear analogy to James's 'attention' – on the rim,
is structure and definition.

Goffman does not claim in so many words that some experiences
are more real than others, to do so would be to fall explicitly into the
Jamesian cop-out which he has attacked. But the text reveals that
not *all* activities are transformations of other activities and indeed
Goffman frequently suggests that some sorts of activity have a
special status by virtue of their lack of dependence on transformational processes. A notion of something which is more 'real', or is
'sensed as more real', is lurking in the background. So we find
references to 'untransformed activity', 'activity which is meaningful
in it's own right', and 'untransformed reality'.[7] 'Untransformed'
does not, of course, mean 'unframed'; what Goffman terms *primary
frameworks* are at work in untransformed experience. Goffman
claims that 'primary framework' is, 'The first concept that is
needed', for frame analysis (1974, p. 25), a primacy which is held to
derive from the fact that the:

> application of such a framework or perspective is seen by those
> who apply it as not depending on, or harking back to, some prior
> or 'original' interpretation; indeed a primary framework is one
> that is seen as rendering what would otherwise be a meaningless
> aspect of the scene into something that is meaningful. (ibid.,
> p. 21)

Now, this does little more than assert that primary frameworks are
not reflexive in the sense that transformations are and that they have
something to do with the way events are interpreted.[8] There are as it
were the cognitive building-blocks of experienced social reality;
they render experience (formally) possible and are self-explanatory

in the sense that they may be legitimately posited without reference
to any other experience-ordering devices. A given primary framework, 'allows its user to locate, perceive, identify and label a
seemingly infinite number of concrete occurences defined in its
terms'. (1974, p. 21).

But it is not only primary frameworks which have this enabling
power; any frame, be it a keying, re-keying or a fabrication serves to
'locate, perceive, identify and label' the material of social experience in varying degrees of specificity. The defining characteristic of primary frameworks is that the relation between such a
framework and the material which it orders is the most 'primitive'
relation possible in social experience; primary frameworks offer us
real, literal events:

> Actions framed entirely in terms of primary frameworks are said
> to be real or actual . . . . a keying of these actions performed, say,
> on stage provides us with something that is not literal or real or
> actually occurring. (1974, p. 47).

But to complicate matters, on the same page, Goffman's favourite
paradox rears it's head, 'none the less we would want to say that the
staging of these actions was really or actually occurring'. The
postulate of primary frameworks, then, serves to define a concept of
literality which in turn allows Goffman to assert the unity of a world
of experience which incorporates the possibility of transformation.
Goffman wishes to characterise large areas of experience as
essentially transformed; at the same time he wants to avoid the
dizzying, ultimately banal, image of experience as an ungrounded
flux of mutually determining transformations. In order to satisfy
both of these conditions Goffman must identify a relatively stable
stratum from which transformations take the basic experiential
material upon which they work and to which they remain
reassuringly, if often tenuously, linked. The nexus at which
cognitive operations produce social experience solely through the
mediation of primary frameworks constitutes this level in *Frame
Analysis*. So while Goffman's emphasis upon the formal relationships
between frameworks may prevent the Jamesian positing of distinctive and autonomous worlds defined in terms of their contents, he
seems unable to cope analytically without reference to a paramount
sense of reality in the operation of primary frameworks. Any framed
experience must in principle bear a relation to the proto-typical

generation of experience in primary frameworks. He later says:

> Whatever goes on in an interpreted and organised stream of activity draws on material that comes from the world and in some traceable continuation of substance must go back into the world. (1974, p. 287)

Although primary frameworks are defined in formal terms, it seems that Goffman wants them to do substantive work as well when he asserts that 'taken all together, the primary frameworks of a particular social group constitute a central element of its culture' (1974, p. 27). But instead of offering an account of what such a 'central element' might look like, Goffman selects illustrations from his usual stock of would-you-believe-it media reports. All one can say is that primary frameworks seem on the substantive level to be a rough analogy to the phenomenological 'Lebenswelt'. Goffman again:

> To speak here of 'everyday life' or, as Schutz does, of the 'world of wide-awake practical realities' is merely to take a shot in the dark . . . . To proceed, however, an operating fiction might be accepted . . . , namely, that acts of daily living are understandable because of some primary framework (or frameworks) that informs them. (1974, p. 26)

Primary frameworks are a necessary postulate within frame analysis, serving to make other concepts workable. Outside that context there seems little reason to prefer Goffman's 'operating fiction' to Schutz's 'shot in the dark'. Even in the context of Goffman's work, primary frameworks are odd beasts. They are defined negatively in contrast to transformations; they capture real events in some unexplicated way and present them to actors (how does an actor know that he is using a primary framework?, could he mistakenly think that he was?), they are defined formally and yet delineate a central area of social reality.

FRAMES AND FRAMING

The discussion of primary frameworks and the sense of reality has another aspect which throws some light upon the complex question of the actual status of 'frames' in Goffman's account. As we have seen, 'actions framed entirely in terms of primary frameworks are said to be real or actual'. Now this sense of reality appears here to be a product of the frame itself. Primary frameworks by their nature are more liable to induce a sense of reality than other frames. But our relative sense of reality is not simply the result of a passive reaction to the intrinsic features of various frames; it is also actively generated by our use of those frames. Particular frames may be more vulnerable to others (fabrications, for example, are definitionally more vulnerable than primary frameworks) but it also is the case that individuals suffering from frame-insecurity may actively effect re-keying or transformations of the original frame in order to secure their sense of reality – in order to satisfy themselves more thoroughly 'that this is what is really going on'.

This point can most usefully be elaborated by reference to an article cited by Goffman: 'A Theory of Play and Fantasy' by Gregory Bateson.[9] Bateson considered the following paradox. If two individuals are 'playing' at fighting, they must be able to assert at a meta-communicative level that, 'this is play'. But playing is playing at something (in this case a fight) and hence the paradox. Bateson says: 'These actions, in which we now engage, do not denote what would be denoted by those actions which these actions denote'.[10] The playful punch denotes a punch, but it does not denote what would be denoted by the punch. Bateson regards our ability to handle such paradoxes as a central component of human communicative competence: it is an example of the 'meta-communicative' skill which enables us to operate at a, 'multiplicity of levels of abstraction'. Bateson then proceeds to introduce the term 'frame':

> Every meta-communicative . . . . message defines, either explicitly or implicitly, the set of messages about which it communicates, i.e. every meta-communicative message is or defines a psychological frame.[11]

Such messages, for example, say that, 'this is fighting', or, 'this is play': they not only suggest the way in which the activity should be apprehended but comment upon its reality status. Bateson does refer to a number of possible 'frames' – 'play', 'movie', 'interview', 'job', or, 'language' which are consciously recognised but also acknowledges that, 'in other cases . . . . the subject may have no consciousness of it.'[12] As this casual eclecticism suggests, Bateson is not so much interested in actually listing a delimited set of frames, but is rather concerned by the communicative implications of such varied forms of experiential evaluation. The notion of frame captures the ambiguous relations between communication and meta-communication. And so, 'The frame is involved in the evaluation of the messages which it contains.'[13]

Goffman acknowledges that Bateson employs the concept of frame in 'roughly the sense in which I want to employ it', (1974, p. 7) and his chief debt is to precisely this ambiguity in Bateson's concept. Goffman's favourite paradox – events on stage are 'not real', but their 'stagings' are – is caught and tamed through frame. Goffmanesque frames both classify activities, making them available to actors and interpret them, telling actors 'just what sort of status in the real world the activity has'. This ambiguity does interesting work in primary frameworks. As we have seen, the classificatory or communicative functions of primary frameworks are not unique, all sorts of framework serve to, 'locate, perceive, identify and label'; what *is* unique is the unambiguous interpretive, or meta-communicative message: 'this is *real*'. The ambiguity between the communicative and meta-communicative messages of frame indicates that there may be more than one way of considering frame theoretically. From one perspective it can become a tool of interactionist analysis, drawing attention to the ways in which actors negotiate and structure the meaning of experience through the *use* of frame. Looked at from a different angle, frame can be used to present a more 'formalist' image of experience which focuses on what we have termed the 'framework of frameworks' – the formal relations between framing possibilities. This duality of focus is hinted at in Goffman's spatial model of transformation; we find engrossment and activity at the centre, form and structure at the rim.

Bateson's use of 'frame' inclines him to the former perspective. As he concludes:

> Our central thesis may be summed up as a statement of the necessity of the paradoxes of abstraction . . . . without these paradoxes the evolution of communication would be at an end. Life would then be an endless interchange of stylised messages, a game with rigid rules unrelieved by change or humor.[14]

This is a thoroughly interactionist perspective, one in which different versions of reality and different 'senses' of reality are continually up for grabs as communication proceeds. So, although Goffman asserts that Bateson employs the concept of frame in roughly the sense in which he wants to employ it, it is clear that he differs from Bateson by virtue of his additional emphasis upon what we might call *frame-as-structure*, as distinct from the more interactionist *frame-in-use*. I frame my experiences, but the structure of frame is prior to my experiences.

Whereas Bateson and Goffman regard frame and frame vulnerability as in index of interactional communicative competence (the schizophrenic, for example, fails to recognise the metaphoric nature of his fantasies) Goffman places much more emphasis than Bateson upon the distinctive characteristics of the actual frame (its sense of reality, its vulnerability). So much so in fact that some readers of Goffman's work have been able to disattend to the more interactional elements of the analysis and suggest that the frames which Goffman describes are part of a structural or semiological theory of experience. The most persuasive advocate of this reading is Jameson who reviewed *Frame Analysis* for *Theory and Society*. Jameson argues that the book is; 'further testimony to the growing rapprochement between ethnomethodology and semiotics';[15] that Goffman is trying to replace, 'the older skeletal structure of custom . . . [with] the firm cartilege of his socio-economic frames',[16] with the effect that his concepts, 'tend to displace our attention to the *process* of semiotic transformation and away from the materials transformed.'[17] These are insightful remarks and no doubt much is to be gained by tracing the extent of Goffman's debt to semiotics, but we would argue that it is a mistake to give a totally semiotic reading of *Frame Analysis*.

In a classic statement of the analytic thrust of semiotics Lacan argues that, 'No meaning is sustained by anything other than reference to other meaning'.[18] Now, this is not Goffman's position. The primacy of primary frameworks is indexed precisely by the fact that the meanings which they generate *are* independent of other meanings at the level of their production. To read *Frame Analysis* as an essay in semiotics is to read it from the outset as a fundamentally flawed text. As Barthes has remarked:

The danger . . . . [for semiotic analysis] . . . . is to consider forms as ambiguous objects, half form and half substance, to endow form with the substance of form.[19]

Goffman's formal figures (frames, keys, and fabrications), are ambiguous in just this sense, and this ambiguity is most reasonably regarded as an essential component in Goffman's theory of experience and not merely the product of a mis-begotten semiology.

Gonos has recently attempted to 'firm up' Goffman's 'frame-as-structure' approach by proposing a structuralist reading not just of *Frame Analysis* but of much of Goffman's earlier work.[20] He argues:

> The structure of frame . . . . is fixed and left essentially untouched by everyday events. Thus, when some commentators insist that Goffman depicts a social reality that is precarious and fragile we must specify that it is the individuals security and *sense* of reality that, in Goffman's world may be so described, not the social structure.[21]

'Frame' is the only frame-analytic concept which Gonos refers to and this limitation invites over-simplification. A more balanced view of frame and reality-troubles must take account of three of the features of Goffman's analysis which we have noted here. First, there are different types of frame and some of them seem more vulnerable to collapse than others (compare primary frameworks with fabrications). Second, individuals suffering from frame-insecurity do not simply select a more comfortable frame from a pre-given range, they effect re-keyings or transformations of the original frame. Third (and more generally), the vocabulary of frame; frame itself, keying, transformation, fabrication, is systematically ambiguous between the passive and structured on the one hand and the active and structuring on the other. (Experiences are framed, but I frame my experiences.)

Gonos identifies two definitional themes in contemporary structuralism – the de-construction of 'self', and a concern with language and textuality – and claims that these themes characterise Goffman's work. Taking 'self' first, the structuralist de-construction views the subject as a textual effect, a perspective that reaches a peak of sophistication in Lacan's interpretation of Freud. Now, Goffman has often found it useful to break down the unitary concept of self; in *The Presentation of Self in Everyday Life*, for example, he makes the distinction between 'performer', and 'character' (1959, p. 244). In *Frame Analysis* the breakdown is more complex and we are offered, 'figures, strategies, animators, principals' (1974, p. 567), but these are termed 'functions', and display the usual

Goffmanesque ambiguity. On one level they *are* images, or constructs, but on another level they are active categories, functions performed under the aegis of the 'central but very crude concept of participant (or player or individual)' (1974, p. 566). This is some way from the perspective of Barthes or Lacan. Gonos' emphasis upon a concern with language as indicative of a structuralist perspective is unhelpful: structuralism has no monopoly of analytic concern with language; virtually every contemporary school of social theory has its linguistic analogue. Goffman may be concerned with language, or more specifically with 'talk'; indeed, he considers that frame analysis is at its most obviously effective when dealing with talk. But this does not make him a structuralist. The point can be illustrated from his 'Replies and Responses', a paper which Goffman first presented in 1974, the year that *Frame Analysis* was published. The paper reviews 'ethnomethodological' perspectives on aspects of talk, and finds them wanting because: 'Natural conversation is not subject to . . . . recording bias – in a word not subject to systematic transformation into words.' (1976a, p. 290)

The resolution of this problem is not achieved in structural or semiological terms (which Gonos tends to treat as interchangeable) but rather by reference to a sophisticated interactionist perspective. Goffman continues:

> What, then, is talk viewed interactionally? It is an example of the arrangement by which individuals come together and sustain matters having a ratified, joint, current and running claim upon attention, a claim which lodges them together in some sort of inter subjective mental world. (1976a, p. 308)

This is, surely, about as far as it is possible to get from the semiotic injunction to treat the social world as a text; it recommends treating apparent texts as part of the social world. Goffman's treatment of 'reality', then, is not usefully classified as structuralist, but, rather in terms of its systematic ambiguity between a view of frame-as-structure and frame-in-use.

CONCLUSION

If the question, 'What is going on here?' is not to become a metaphysical demand for an exhaustive account of every aspect of a

248 *The View from Goffman*

situation described at every possible level of generality, it must be a demand for an account which is adequate to some practical matter at hand. Frame analysis cannot, and does not, aim to capture the activity-in-itself in all its infinite variety; it seeks to account for the sense generated in activities which gives enough interpretation to enable actors to keep on acting. In other words, frame analysis can only begin where accounts of activities begin. Goffman hints at this when discussing primary frameworks; in daily life, he tells us: 'a multitude of frameworks may be involved or *none at all*', (1974, p. 26; emphasis added) and we would argue that an actor is not using any framework unless he is able to account for what he is doing (to preserve symmetry and universality, one could introduce a 'doing nothing in particular' frame, but *that's* an account as well). Frame organises accounting possibilities rather than 'actual activity' *per se*, and to frame an activity is to offer an account of it which excludes other possible accounts. The necessary articulateness of frame-analytic categories is perhaps the genuine core of Goffman's concern with language. Frames must be languaged both from the perspective of the actor who employs them and from that of the analyst concerned with their structure.

In the light of these considerations it can be argued that the figures of frame analysis owe what illuminative power they have to their ambiguity; an ambiguity between frame-in-use and frame-as-structure, or in a different 'key', between communication and meta-communication. But it is important to remember that even frame-in-use is a formal organisational phenomenon, it might grasp the real world but is not equivalent to it; frame does not catalogue actual experiences, it classifies experiential possibilities. The balance between the organising formalism of frame-in-use and the meta-organisational formalism of frame-as-structure finally gives us some purchase upon the ambiguities of Goffman's treatment of 'reality'. What is to be accounted for first of all is the 'sense of reality' at play in experience and this is done by reference to the relation which all framing practices must bear to primary frameworks which frame 'real' events. The meta-communicative messages of transformations ensure that their communicative messages can convey the sense of reality. This sense of reality, produced by frame-in-use, is *itself* guaranteed by the reality of frame-as-structure; as we have seen, Goffman claims that frame is more than a matter of mind and the world somehow 'urges' frame analysis upon us. Now, this might be interpreted as straightforward realism, but it is a realism with distinctly Platonic overtones, as is clear in this quotation from *Frame Analysis*:

> ordinary conduct, in a sense, is an intimation of the proprieties, a gesture at the exemplary forms, and the primal realisation of these ideals belongs more to make-believe than to reality. (1974, p. 562)

Frame Analysis is not presented as an heuristic tool, or work of imagination, it is offered as the map to the territory of objective experiential possibilities which have a real, if imperfect, presence in the social world. This formalism – this lack of reference to the actual events which might routinely be apprehended through a dramatic, ritualistic, or primary framework – is responsible for the emptiness at the centre of the text. There are hundreds of examples of the different possible ways in which events have been experienced, but no suggestion at all as to the principles which might underlie the active selection of a particular framework, or to the cultural considerations which might prompt such a selection.

This failing is most evident in Goffman's attempt to work with the concept of 'engrossment'. Engrossment is similar to James's 'attention'; it lies (literally) at the heart of frame, it is related to our sense of reality and yet it defies explication. Goffman can give no account of *why* people should attend more intently to some features of their experiential 'given', rather than to others. All he can offer is the suggestion that the objective possibility of selection is made available in the range of framing possibilities. This weakness prejudices the ambiguous unity of frame-in-use and frame-as-structure and threatens to reduce frame analysis to a pure formalism with no purchase on the social world.

Goffman does not develop the analytic tools which would allow him to consider the possibility that engrossment might be a function of the significance which a person attaches to the contents rather than the form of experience. Still less is he able to suggest that the 'motivational relevencies' which generate such significance might be related to a person's history as part of a social rather than an experiential structure. But he needs to be able to do so. To state the matter in it's crudest possible form; if ordinary sociology works with a dichotomy between social subject and objective social structure, frame analysis places in the nexus of these two categories another objective reality, that of social experiential possibility. Goffman

examines the formal relations between the subject and this new
objectivity at some length, but he seems to regard as either
uninteresting or unproblematic the equally important relations
between experiential possibility and social structure. Without any
internal analytic warrant, this omission effectively autonomises the
study of social experience in the same way that James autonomised
the study of individual experience. Perhaps this is *Goffman's* 'cop
out'.

EDITIONS OF GOFFMAN'S WORK USED IN THIS CHAPTER

(The dates are taken from the bibliography provided in the *Editor's
Introduction*; the pagination for quotations cited in this chapter from
the editions shown below).

(1959)   *The Presentation of Self in Everyday Life*, (Harmondsworth;
          Penguin Books).

(1974)   *Frame Analysis: An Essay on the Organisation of Experience*,
          (Harmondsworth; Peregrine).

(1976a)   'Replies and Responses', *Language in Society*, Volume 5,
          No. 3, (December, 1976) pp. 257–313.

CHAPTER ENDNOTES

1. This theme was also mentioned earlier, when Goffman says:

   For what a speaker does usually is to present for his listeners a version of what
   happened to him. In an important sense, even if his purpose is to present the cold
   facts as he sees them, the means he employs may be intrinsically theatrical, not
   because he necessarily exaggerates or follows a script, but because he may have
   to engage in something that is a dramatisation in the use of such arts as he
   possesses to reproduce a scene – to replay it. (1974, pp. 503–4)

2. See, Ditton, (1974 R4), p. 331. [For a fuller list, see: *A Sampler of Reviews* in the
Editor's Introduction].

3. William James, *The Principles of Psychology*, Volume II, (London; Macmillan,
1890) p. 290.

4. Ibid., p. 291.

5. Ibid., p. 293.

6. Ibid., p. 300.

7. See, for example, Goffman, (1974) pp. 81, 156, 560.

8. It is important to notice that phenomena interpreted through a primary framework are held to be 'meaningless' without the mediation of the framework in question. It is a constant theme of *Frame Analysis* that the meaningfulness of experience is a function of the general ordering concepts which give it form; indeed, at one point, Goffman makes the strong and severely Kantian claim that to find no form is to be no experience.

9. Gregory Bateson, 'A Theory of Play and Fantasy', American Psychiatric Association, *Psychiatric Research Reports*, (1955); quoted from Gregory Bateson, *Steps to an Ecology of Mind: Collected Essays in Anthropology, Psychiatry, Evolution and Epistemology*, (St. Albans; Paladin, 1973) pp. 150–66.

10. Ibid., p. 153.

11. Ibid., p. 161.

12. Ibid., p. 159.

13. Ibid., p. 160.

14. Ibid., p. 166.

15. See, Jameson, (1974, R1), p. 119. [For a fuller list, see: *A Sampler of Reviews* in the *Editor's Introduction*].

16. Ibid., p. 122.

17. Ibid., p. 127.

18. Jaques Lacan, *Ecrits*, (Paris; Editions de Seuil, 1966) p. 498.

19. Roland Barthes, *Mythologies*, (Paris; Editions de Seuil, 1957) pp. 218–19.

20. George Gonos, ' "Situation" versus "Frame": The "Interactionist" and the "Structuralist" Analyses of Everyday Life', *American Sociological Review*, Volume 42, No. 6, (1977) pp. 854–67.

21. Ibid., p. 859.

9: Goffman's Framing Order: Style as Structure

By Peter K. Manning

Built into language, written and spoken, are the means by which we can talk about language, and built into social life are the means by which we define the world, and communicate to others the world we are defining. But the world is actually constituted of multiple worlds with somewhat clear norms within them in which we are erstwhile dwellers. Erving Goffman has published over the course of twenty years or so a series of remarkable volumes on these social worlds and interactions within them. Each focuses and defocuses an aspect of social life. Earlier works investigated performances, their honourings, and the structure in which they were cast; later work, *Frame Analysis* in particular, concerns the organisation of experience. *Frame Analysis* draws on earlier work, and could not in fact have been written without the earlier work. In this review of Goffman's style, I will start 'backwards' by considering the issues raised in *Frame Analysis*, explicating them as matters of style, seeing how much style is structure in most of social interaction, then considering the generic Goffman socio-literary method and procedure, and return to *Frame Analysis*, its strengths and limits as a form of structuralism.

STYLE

Style is a mode of expression that points to something else, much like the shadow from the pin of a sundial points to the time. Structure, on the other hand, indicates a pattern or ordering of categories of things that gives category distinctiveness. So consider the first problem of discussing a writer's style and the structure of his work:

the style utilised by an author can indeed be the structure by which that author attains distinctiveness and distinction. Insofar as the work becomes only style, it may be seen as lacking substance. Substantive work, of course, can lack style, or emanate it. Think of a tightly constructed legal statute, a sparsely outlined memorandum, or a set of operating procedures.

Set this distinction aside for the moment and consider that between the 'empirical world', that exists as social structure in the sense attributed to it by the English anthropologist Radcliffe-Brown,[1] and conceptualisations of that social world developed by social scientists, e.g., role, status, bureaucracy, social change, authority. Nominalists have obviated the problem by dissolving the world into a conceptual edifice. Goffman, often viewed as a nominalist of the worst sort (a kind of diabolical taxonomist), eschews this view. For example, he says in *Frame Analysis*:

> This book is about the organisation of experience – something that an individual actor can take into his mind – and not the organisation of society. I make no claim whatsoever to be talking about the core matters of sociology – social organisation and social structure. Those matters have been and can continue to be quite nicely studied without reference to frame at all. I am not addressing the structure of social life but the structure of experience individuals have at any moment of their social lives. I personally hold society to be first in every way and any individual's current involvements to be second; this report deals only with matters that are second. (1974, p. 13)

Thus, in an interesting twist of the word, he encourages us to see a work of importance as dealing with 'secondary' matters. This is, the substance of social life is what he is not dealing with, but what he is dealing with becomes the substance of social life precisely because we are so rarely aware of 'primary matters'. To say that people define situations, and that they are thus real, is not to say that they alter the world they define in such a way, for the world is too infinitely complex to be altered by a definition. Rather, he asks, what can definitions produce when believed? Goffman does not argue for a totally constructed world, yet attributes great significance to the definition of situations. Earlier in *Frame Analysis*, he says:

Defining situations as real certainly has consequences, but these may contribute very marginally to the events in progress. All the world is not a stage – certainly the theatre isn't entirely. (Whether you organise a theatre or an aircraft factory, you need to find places for cars to park and coats to be checked, and these had better be real places, which, incidentally, had better carry real insurance against theft.) Presumably, a 'definition of the situation' is almost always to be found, but those who are in the situation ordinarily do not *create* this definition, even though their society often can be said to do so; ordinarily, all they do is to assess correctly what the situation ought to be for them and then act accordingly. True, we personally negotiate aspects of all the arrangements under which we live, but often once these are negotiated, we continue on mechanically as though the matter had always been settled. So, too, there are occasions when we must wait until things are almost over before discovering that what has been occurring and occasions of our own activity when we can considerably put off deciding what to claim we have been doing. But surely these are not the only principles of organisation. Social life is dubious enough and ludicrous enough without having to wish it further into unreality. (1974, pp. 1–2)

What occurs to persons as a result of assuming that a definition is real is substantial. To a considerable degree, one misses the structure of social life because we style it away again and again and mistake or misplace that styling for the structure. But this leaves much to be understood, as this example from Goffman displays:

observers actively project their frames of reference into the world immediately around them, and one fails to see their so doing because events ordinarily confirm to these projections, causing the assumptions to disappear into the smooth flow of activity. Thus, a properly dressed woman who closely examines the frame of a mirror on sale at an auction house and then stands back to check on the trueness of the mirror's reflection can well be seen by others present as someone who hasn't really been seen. But if she uses the mirror to adjust her hat, *then* others present can become aware that only a certain sort of looking had all along been what was expected and that the object on the wall was not so much a mirror-for-sale; and this experience can be reversed should she appraisingly examine a mirror in a dressing room instead of examing herself in the mirror. (1974, p. 39)²

Now, let us be clear to this point. Goffman does not see the real world as being composed by words, labels, or semantic conundrums (or non-conundrums), and does not thus join phenomenologists who are interested only in that which is constructed or created (with narrowed, circumscribed, biological limits, cf., Berger and Luckmann).³ Nor does he see sociological style as the act of *creating* social structure, as Garfinkel does, for example.⁴ On the other hand, he does not see the mandate of his form of analysis to be that of explicating the social structure that we have loosely referred to as 'the world'.

What is at issue when we call on Goffman to clarify the style/structure problem, is that although one can analytically carve up the world into limits, constraints structure and style, everyday life is not so carved. Rather, it is *reflexive*, it produces that which it takes to be immutable, and the immutabilities are in some degree in existence because they are affirmed by events that are mutable, or because when they are recognised as mutable they stand mute until events close on them, reproducing them again and again. Think again of the woman at the mirror. People define her behaviours in one version (or interpretation) as 'looking at a mirror in order to buy it', therefore not looking into it to see herself. (Goffman writes, she is seen as someone, 'who hasn't really been seen'. That is, she has not been defined by others as looking at herself in the mirror, but looking at the mirror as something that might reflect whatever comes before it). He contrasts this with a second interpretation of her actions where she is seen because she attends to an item of personal concern, or front, her hat, as someone using a mirror in a personalised manner and not as a customer. The versions available are merely made more reflexive by the choice of example, for the woman directly 'sees' her behaviour in the mirror, and modifies her conduct in accord with what she sees. But the mirror substitutes in Goffman's example for the audience which it reflects and stands for. People watching her are being performed for, they take her behaviour to mean something, they frame it, and this definition is used by her to convey a state of mind, a cultural attitude, a role, perhaps a mood. She in a sense acts to produce a frame that is available, and presumed by others viewing (at least some of them). When she gives off other signals by adjusting her hat, she produces cues that can be organised to yield another version of her actions and symbolisations.

Social life contains available frames or definitions, ways to organise experience; they are real because we both display for each other and recognise them when others produce them for us. We do mirror each other to a degree, and this degree is what is at issue in most of Goffman's stylised writings. Since we mirror each other, but unlike mirrors do not produce faithfully all that is reflected/ deflected toward us, social life is both problematic and reflexive. It is both *literal* in the sense that we communicate messages and information like machines and mirrors to each other, and *metaphorical* in the sense that we act toward each other in terms of what we believe the situation to be, or what the other wants us to believe. This latter is done primarily through symbolic codes, linguistic and non-linguistic, a messy business at best. Now we can see, I think, that what Goffman is concerned about is not the structure of the world, the primary matters to which he refers above, and which he says can be interpreted within several frameworks (1974, Chapter 2), but the fact that the social world alway involves the production of performances. These performances, for example, lying or truth-telling, are different at the epistemological and ethical level, but ironically, they present the same problem with regard to displaying a performance. Each demands the successful display of conduct judged by an audience to be a credible performance.[5] Goffman says for example:

> While the performance offered by imposters and liars is quite flagrantly false and differs in the respect from ordinary perform-ances, both are similar in the care their performers must expert in order to maintain the impression that is fostered . . . Whether an honest performer wishes to convey the truth or whether a dishonest performer wishes to convey a falsehood, both must take care to enliven their performances with appropriate expressions, exclude from their performances expressions that might discredit the impression being fostered, and take care least the audience impute unintended meanings. (1959, p. 66)

Follow this line further into the problems of sociological analysis. The sociologist must *describe* the conduct before him/her, or reported to him/her, and must constantly draw upon vocabularies of motive, or assessments of others (if the level of explanation is at the small group of individual level), and for the most part, upon analogies and metaphors. This means that to speak of the world as theatre (a metaphor) one must hold lightly to the notion simultaneously that this is a metaphor, that, as Goffman wrote in *Frame Analysis*, 'All the world is not a stage – certainly, the theatre isn't entirely'. (1974, p. 1) He means here that the theatric convention is one among many conventions that are used in the world, that we do *not* see all events as 'theatre' e.g., experiments, games, ceremonials, and that, on the other hand, in order to experience theatre *as* theatre, we must draw on more than that metaphor e.g., we must be able to distinguish the stage from the house, find seats and places to hang our coats, discount non-relevant talk, body positioning, and to see that a play within a play is that. Further, if we can see these elements, and hold metaphors lightly, we can also appreciate that what begins as one thing in our frame, for example, a joke, can be transformed into something quite different: a dream, an experiment, a mistake and so on. In such transformings or changes from one definition to another, we do not set aside the first sense of an event, but rather *add* the second to it. And one can alter involvement from one to the other, again retaining the reality of both. In this way, the reflexive (one aspect of life reflects another and changes it; our behaviour as we perform it, is shaped by what we perceive others think of our performance) aspects of life, and it's multiple-layered aspects are seen. One does share the problem of framing experience with others, and one is aware that to make sense one must both be able to see things as others do, and to understand how it is they come to similar working understandings. And one does change, redefine things, while retaining the sequence as a factor in the on-going events. To unravel this process one must attend to matters of style, or of the framing of events, the organisation of experience. Unravelling may mean that one will discover ironies, the ironies Goffman so likes to play with such as the definition of an event as 'unreal' (a dream) can of course be very real in its consequences (such as a dream of killing someone which precipitates the dreamer to be a killer). Conversely, the definition of an event as a dream does not change the dreamer's life status when he sleepwalks out of a window. Or consider that stage or screen lovers do 'fall in love' as a result of playing at it. The limits on such re-definitions of events are strewn around us, and we return to them.

These conceptual concerns, etched in the latest Goffman writing, carry within them a solution to earlier problems in his writing.

Before we can consider the solution advanced in *Frame Analysis*, let us further examine the problem. We can do so by reviewing some terminological and definitional problems which characterise Goffman's work and indeed are thought by many to be the characteristic feature of it.

TERMINOLOGICAL AND DEFINITIONAL PROBLEMS[6]

Goffman does not consistently employ terms defined in earlier essays in later ones, and may, without warning or explanation, develop new terms or use a concept in a different way in subsequent essays. 'Self', for example, is defined in *The Presentation of Self in Everyday Life* as a produce of a scene, an imputation made by others to a person which the person may or may not affirm:

> The self, then, as a performed character ['character' is defined above as a 'figure . . . whose sterling qualities the performance was designed to evoke', (1959, p. 252)] . . . is not an organic thing that has a specific location, whose fundamental fate is to be born, to mature and to die; it is a dramatic effect arising diffusely from a scene that is presented, and the characteristic issue . . . is whether it will be credited or discredited. (1959, pp. 252–3)

In *The Presentation of Self in Everyday Life* and latter essays, Goffman elaborates his analysis of the self. The focus is, 'the little salutations, compliments, and apologies which punctuate social life'. 'The little interactions that are forgotten about as soon as they occur', and that 'serious students of society never collect'; 'the gestures which we sometimes call empty', but which 'are perhaps in fact the fullest of all'.[7] Goffman, using irony in these passages, intends the reader to understand that these phenomena are all that he suggests they are *not*. They are neither little, empty, *nor* forgotten. By a process of stylised inversion they are meant to be seen as a focal concern in social life and as a basis for constructing systematic empirical social science. In these mundane little gestures, according to Goffman, the common man's claims to a self are displayed, his ritual 'face' is offered, and his honour is put to a test of the moment. A claim proffered for others to accept is not who 'one really is' (that is in fact a moot point), for one tries to dramatise elements of performance by selectively presenting symbolic cues indicative of the self one wants others to impute to him.

Whenever one commits oneself to a line of symbolic expression: a speech, a game, or a seduction pitch; one risks the possibility that the relevant others will not listen, will disattend one's claims, or will actively reject them. By expressing a view, one puts forth a possible self, a self which will continue to exist only if it is affirmed by the cooperation of others. This self at risk can be polluted by minor remarks, broken eye contact, coughs, or abrupt changes in conversational content – and any of these eruptions can occur at any time, in the company of anyone. Consequently, there is precious little one can do to invariably avoid them. Risks to the self are virtually always a potential feature of public social relations. Each claim is a risk, each affirmation a tribute, so that a series of exchanges can build into a kind of ritual dance. One reviewer has claimed:

> This perspective sees every encounter as a masked dance; it infuses everyday life with a sacred magical power. In order to possess the power, we must take sacred vows: each encounter requires an accommodative process, a tacit convenant by which everyone agrees 'to conduct himself so as to main both his own face and the faces of other participants'. These oaths of 'mutual acceptance', these miniature social contacts, reenacted by everyone of us, unthinkingly, hundreds of times everyday, keep the forces of doubt, hate, chaos away.[8]

The self, as a very fluid 'diffuse' product of others' imputations (always contraposed in some fashion in Goffman's writing with the individual's image of himself – that which requires the least 'energy' one might say to display), is transformed in later writings into a 'product' of 'social arrangements' rather than of others' imputations. Later Goffman says:

> The self . . . can be seen as something that resides in the arrangements prevailing in a social system for its members. The self in this sense is not a property of the persons to whom it is attributed, but dwells rather in the pattern of social control that is exerted in connection with the person by himself and those around him. This special kind of institutional arrangement does not so much support the self as constitute it. (1961c, p. 168)

The self referred to here is at least in some significant fashion a feature of the pattern of social control within an organisation. Goffman's term, the moral career of the mental patient, suggests that the self changes shape and content as organisationally generated control is exerted. ('Socially sanctioned expectations', 1961c, pp. 127–8). In *Asylums* the self emerges, as in Hughes' discussion of careers,[9] from the interplay of 'subjective' (self-definitions) and 'objective' contingencies (rules, and normative constraints). The institution is seen as a foil *against* which a self is shaped. Again, *Asylums*:

> Our sense of being a person can come from being drawn into a wider social unit; our sense of selfhood can arise through the little ways in which we resist the pull. Our status is backed by the solid buildings of the world, while our sense of personal identity often resides in the cracks. (1961c, p. 320)

In the above quote 'self' implies what one defines as one's view of one's own conduct. 'Person' now refers to that which he previously had defined as the 'self' (cf. 1961c, p. 168 as previously quoted). Goffman seems to intend the term person to refer to the entity which the sociologist infers when he sees an actor behaving in the guise of his several selves. The term person is meant to refer to the individual's synthesis or capacity to view his own actions reflexively, and to refer to the locus of integration of organisational and self-definitions. Such a reading is supported by Goffman's definition of person as, 'a stance-taking entity, a something that takes up a position somewhere between identification with an organisation and opposition to it, and is ready at the slightest pressure to regain its balance by shifting its involvement in another direction' (1961c, p. 320).

The self, changing from an imputation to an individual definition, becomes however, more a function of situational constraints in Goffman's writing. The tensions between self-definition and imputation, mediated by the person, are reduced in salience. The characteristics Goffman attributes after 1961 to actors are derived from the *situations* in which Goffman-as-observer chooses to observe them, while organisational arrangements fade to the background. He claimed:

> Social situations at least in our society, constitute a reality *sui generis* as He used to say, and therefore need and warrant analysis

in their own right, much like that accorded other basic forms of social organization. (1964a, p. 134)

And then, somewhat later:

> I assume that the proper study of interaction is not the individual and his psychology, but rather the syntactical relations among acts of different persons mutually present to one another . . . not, then, men and their moments. Rather, moments and their men. (1967, pp. 2, 3)

The tendency to make changes in centrality and definitions of concepts can also be illustrated through a close analysis of *Relations in Public*.[10]

Changes in the definitions of concepts and in relative emphases upon their implications are frequently found in Goffman's work. Some of the problems that his concepts portend for social research are a result of his almost systematic elusiveness. As we have seen, Goffman often confuses the reader by employing multiple concepts to refer to the 'same thing', (his uses of person and self), and at other times uses one concept to refer to more than one thing (self to refer both to imputations or attributions and to one's own quasi-unique view of his own situated conduct). Goffman sometimes rests his case with a series of definitions rather than analyses (1959, pp. 15-16; 252-3; and 1971, pp. 29-41), and tends to present taxonomies and classification rather more than to seek to construct explanatory conceptual schema. Most significantly, he has shifted from the perspective of an observer to the perspective of the actor (as in his vague definitions of person, selfhood and identity *supra*, where he blurs the actor/observer perspective by using terms such as, 'We obtain our sense'). It is possible to argue, however, on the basis of *Frame Analysis* that this most perplexing of Goffman's conceptual problems has been obviated by yet another set of concepts, definitions, and focusings. In *Frame Analysis*, the concern with situations, and with the structure of experience, is made clearly dominant over the self, and over the individual's definitions as they bear on self.

Some of the clever ambiguities in conceptualisation (some might say they are too clever by half) will be of concern later in this chapter, following an overview of two other aspects of Goffman's style: his socio-literary method and his procedural approach to his materials. In both of these matters, the abiding issue is his struggle to encompass *both* the social reality and facticity of social life, and the variations introduced by the problematic meanings that are so frequently a part of the individual's perception and definition of the situation. Perhaps too much has been made of the data and approach of Goffman, because he has repeatedly eschewed any identification with conventional methods of social scientific data gathering, analysis or assessment (see: 1959, p. xii; 1971, p. 1; and, 1974, p. 15). On the other hand, he has repeatedly claimed a generic validity for his work, and urged others to test it (1959, p. xii). Without question, he sees social life in a Durkheimian manner, as external to individuals, as constraining upon their actions, as existing through time, and as continuing on after the death of individuals. This conception of social life, an issue addressed in the last segment of this chapter, makes more crucial an understanding of precisely how his method and procedure enables himself and others to uncover and reveal much that otherwise would remain unseen.

A SOCIO-LITERARY METHOD AND PROCEDURE[11]

The critical success and continuing impact and significance of Goffman's writing both in and outside the social sciences does not rest solely on its content, a content shared with others who have written on similar issues (e.g., deviance, complex organisations, mental illness). Although the writing is sometimes precious, and at others almost pedantic, (and is not invariably clear) it radiates verisimilitude. One sees oneself playing social games, being clever or witty, and sometimes suffering embarrassment. How does Goffman achieve his original and often startling effect? Clues to his force and present fame may be uncovered by an investigation of his literary style, particularly his use of metaphor. He employs *metaphor* to describe at length (allegorically and oxymoronically) objects, persons, social organisations and places in terms generally reserved to describe other objects, persons, social organisations and the like. It creates powerful images and evokes painful effects. He uses what the literary critic Kenneth Burke terms 'perspective by incongruity':

the placing of special stress upon the kinds of hermeticism, or stylistic mercureality, that are got by the merging of categories once felt to be mutually exclusive.[12]

Certainly, no other social scientist would call psychiatrists 'tinkerers', or refer to the medical professions as the 'tinkering trades', as Goffman does in the last essay in *Asylums*. (1961d) Audaciously, he has made reference to Durkheim (seen by some as the patron saint of sociology) as 'He', using the form of capitalisation conventionally restricted to indicating members of the Holy Trinity, and once classified as analytically equivalent: absence of vision, a leg, and sphincter control!

Two features of this method may be pinpointed. Firstly, Goffman creates *incongruity* when he juxtaposes dissimilar ideas or concepts in the same sentence. John Lofland has already cited some examples of this procedure in play in the second section of chapter one of this book. The examples used there were taken exclusively from the early Goffman, however. Consider the following examples, selected from Goffman's later work, and notice thus that Goffman uses the device consistently through his writings:

> The deepest nature of an individual is only skin-deep, the deepness of his others' skin (1971, p. 363).

> So although it might be taken that the individual in unstaged, face-to-face conversation plays his cards behind his face, so to speak (1974, p. 514).

> during the disorganisation phase, the family will live the current reality as in a dream, and the domestic routine which can now only be dreamt of will be seen as what is real (1971, p. 382).

> We are vehicles of society; but we are also overheated engines prone to keep firing even though the ignition is turned off (1974, p. 552).

Secondly, the incongruity is heightened by his choice of a substantive or root imagery. His use and choice of a particular metaphor is not simply a matter of convenience or artifice. It would appear to be a deliberate choice of weapons by which to assail the fictional facades that constitute the assumptive reality of conventional society.[13] He claims that what is taken to be 'reality' or the outlines of the possible is quite simply the result of socialisation within a given social structure. To this often reified body of conventional wisdom he juxtaposes the weak, uncertain, somewhat befuddled person possessing the potential for humanity and dignity. Socialisation, however, shapes and modifies humanity 'universal human nature is not a very human thing' (1955, p. 231). That is, once one learns to accept conventional assumptions, and define events within the frame of reference, one loses a degree of humanity. One is quite prepared to accept constraints, orders, persuasion and even humiliation. One gladly accepts what by transcendental moral standard of judgement would be unconscionable. To dramatise the extent to which we are 'victims' of the assumptions implicit in *social* worlds, he specifically marshalls what appears to many sociologists to be absurd and extreme examples. 'Excessive' contrasts are constructed. In so doing, he retains a sense of the socially sanctioned nature of the examples: they are meant to be more significant because they are so common, yet placed (and seen) in a new context. He meticulously selects that which is to be *transformed* e.g., a person with problems of managing interpersonal relations and *that to which it is transformed* e.g., an 'official self', or 'paper self', a compressed version of a previously alive being now lying dehumanised in the files of a mental hospital. By this literary means he can convert persons lacking full bladder or sphincter control into 'brave little troops of colostomites and ileostomites [who] make their appearance disguised as nice, clean people.' (1971, pp. 551–2).

By tearing these items from one context and placing them in another, or by contrast making an absurdity of what appears to be quite 'reasonable', he is reproducing for our appreciation the same process by which society molds, shapes and in many cases dehumanises individuals. He consciously employs stark metaphors to show how brutally and inappropriately people are used one another in American society. (If his rendition of the consequences of society's vicissitudes violates our sensibilities, what might [should] the experience produce for individuals who actually suffer them?) For example, Goffman implies in a particularly powerful essay, the appendix to *Relations in Public* that family members condemn a person, perhaps excluding him from little familial appreciations and affirmations and calling him mentally ill, for doing what is the human thing to do:

Public life is entered through its least guarded portals; volunteer work; letters to politicians, editors and big corporations; celebrity hunting; litigation. Critical national events, such as elections, war policy statements, and assassinations are taken quite personally. (1969c, p. 370)

Thus, Goffman dramatises the relativity of the interests of those who possess the quite arbitrary authority to define humanity and propriety and provides a subtle but very radical warrant for attempts to alter structures in order to produce more authentic human relationships. Consider two selections from *Relations in Public*:

> and there are a multitude of reasons why someone who is not mentally ill at all, but who finds he can neither leave an organization nor basically alter it, might introduce exactly the same trouble as is caused by patients. (1971, p. 387)

> [Discussing the occupation by students of the office of Grayson Kirk, the then President of Columbia University, and Kirk's remark upon seeing the disorder in his office, 'My God, how could human beings do a thing like this?']
> The great sociological question is, of course, not how could it be that human beings would do a thing like this, but rather how is it that human beings do this sort of thing so rarely. How come persons in authority have been so overwhelmingly successful in conning those beneath them into keeping the hell out of their offices? (1971, p. 288, fn. 44)

For a variety of reasons, Goffman reserves his most cutting ironies and examples for the most legitimate of social institutions, medicine. Psychiatrists and psychiatry merit even more severe condemnation through incongruity. Goffman, in a series of papers (1957; 197b; 1959a; 1961d; 1961e; 1964a; and, 1969c), has ridiculed and indignantly criticised the assumptions and operation of conventional medicine and psychiatry. His critical attitude grows from a conceptual and sociological analysis of the implicit assumptions of western biomedicine.[14] I believe they deserve a brief review. Goffman believes that mental illness is a violation of 'situational proprieties', rather than deviation from physical or organic levels of functioning. The label is derived from perceived alterations in subtle aspects of the self in a particular social context ('an expressive matter confirmed by a place in social organisation', 1969c, p. 366). The treatment of mental illness intends to modify or reshape the self (with and often without the permission of the person viewed as ill). Alterations in levels of physical functioning, on the other hand, are derived from measures of organ systems, signs, and structural modifications of the body. Treatment is directed toward a restoration of the body function. In western societies, the latter treatment has been defined by physicians as having little bearing on the 'mind' or self, reflecting the dualistic orientation of western medicine. Goffman tries to show, especially in 'The Insanity of Place' (1969c) that such dualism overlooks the qualitatively different impacts on the self which issue from these quite logically distinctive conceptual frameworks and related treatment modalities.[15] The psychiatrist merits special attention for his work, which Goffman sees as one way in which families attempt to preserve their power equilibrium, outer boundaries and perhaps existence against the especially 'florid' manic. He notes:

> whereas ordinary relationships give rise to collusive coalitions, the therapeutic situation (Where the family hires a psychiatrist to defend its interests against the claims and interests of the 'sick' member) is a collusion that gives rise to a relationship. This resembles a domestic handicapping system, whereby the weakest team in the family tournament is given an extra man. Let me add that collusion for hire seems a rum sort of business to be in, but perhaps more good is done than harm. (1969c, p. 384)

He then comments, 'We can all agree that everything should be done to patch up bodies and keep them alive, but certainly not that social organisations of all kinds should be preserved' (ibid., p. 387). By example and by explicit criticism, Goffman suggests the horror that results from the medical profession's tendency to treat both literally and figuratively deviations from norms as matters of disease and therefore qualitatively comparable. He personally parodies this (by treating 'face' in both its usual literal, and in his own figurative sense) when he tells us (ibid.), 'there is no disfigurement of the body that cannot be decorously covered by a sheet and apologised by a face; but many disfigurements of the face cannot be covered without interfering with communication.' Consider the following two juxtapositions from the same essay.

A person with carcinoma of the bladder can, if he wants, die with more social grace and propriety, more apparent inner social normalcy, than a man with a harelip can order a piece of apple pie. (1969c, p. 353)

When an amputee fails to rise to greet a lady, it is perfectly evident that this failure is only an incidental and unintentional consequence of his condition; no one would claim [as they do in the case of mental illness] that he cut off his leg to spite his courtesies. (1969c, p. 354)

This shocking effect is achieved by extending the medical model such that its most profound implications are not concealed by one's acceptance of the conventional wisdom. When discussing mental health he remarks, 'All the terms I have used to describe the offensive behavior of the patient – and the term "patient" itself are expressions of the viewpoint of parties with special interests. Quotation marks would have been in order, but too many of them would have been necessary.' (1969c, p. 387) For Goffman, the psychiatric therapeutic relationship is a kind of grotesque of the service relationship (1961c, p. 340). He says so when discussing the costs of commitment to mental hospitals for the person who, in effect, violates a form of social organisation, not a physical thing. 'This has not been merely a bad deal; it has been a grotesque one' (1971, p. 336). Such harshness, when combined with the brilliant satiric metaphor work that accompanies it, has the intended effect of producing a sense of shocked disbelief in the reader. More significantly, it acts to corrode the authoritative hegemony of meanings wrapped around their conduct by members of powerful institutions.

It has yet another effect. His style virtually teeters near a plunge into hyperbole and excess and threatens to launch readers into a seamy voyage into the absurb. He is aware of this tendency, and frequently obliquely qualifies his claims by admitting his penchant for exaggeration – 'now it should be admitted that this attempt to press a mere analogy so far was in part a rhetoric and a manœuvre' (1959, p. 254). In addition, a degree of ambiguity is inherent in metaphoric communication. Which of the features of psychiatry resembles 'the tinkering trades?' Are all mental hospitals 'total institutions', or to what degree are they? Could it be that he meant the idea to apply only to the large federal hospital that he studied?

Are people 'really' (i.e., always and in essence) 'sacred social objects'? It is difficult as a result to attempt to delineate the intention of the concepts, their logical interconnections, and to ascertain whether the concepts are 'primitive' (simply assumptive or stipulative) or analytic, intended to be applied to other instances of 'the same thing'.[16]

Goffman's procedure is to first contrast (a) what is taken for granted in a situation with (b) *either* what can be shown to occur in a series of encounters when a particular perspective or metaphor is utilised by those in power or by himself, e.g., the tinkering trades 'analogy' and in viewing the path to the mental hospital as 'betrayal funnel', *or* what occurs in selected vignettes culled from plays, biographies, short stories, novels for ethnographies, e.g., the recently returned seaman who asks his mother to 'pass the fucking butter' (1959, pp. 14–15).

By selecting precisely these types of shattered frames (or shattered/repaired) frames, Goffman shows that a focus of his attention is problematic features of everyday life (which, in turn, highlight the normal, expected, and taken-for granted features).[17] Goffman seeks situations which will make problematic what is assumed within an observer's perspective. His abiding concern is with making apparent the implicit structure and nature of everyday experience as it is enacted in routine permutations of mutually shared activity. He gives small attention in his writing to the way given persons might live through or manage a sequence of or combination of encounters.

Since encounters have a variety of features to which actors attend, Goffman's sociology is done much as one does a jigsaw puzzle. Having arrayed a variety of examples, he peers at the pieces (encounters) first in one way and then in another, and in so doing is able to apprehend that first this piece and then that one might be fitted together. When looked at differently, they may more properly fit in another place to form still another pattern. He is not, therefore, as much concerned with developing one *inclusive* set of tools or concepts as with *what* any single set of concepts, adopted for a purpose (analysis of stigma, strategic interaction, or face-work) can produce. An author's note in *Relations in Public* reveals his unwillingness to claim a logical structure integrating or systematising his sociology. The essays in the volume bear on 'a single domain of activity', were intended to be published together, and are sequentially related, 'except for the two on interchanges – each develops its own perspective starting from conceptual scratch – and taken together, the six do not purport to cover systematically, exhaustively, and without repetition what is common to them. I snipe at the target from six different positions unevenly spaced; there is no pretence of laying down a barrage.' (1971, Author's Note). There is an even more explicit, if not more satisfying, rationale for the kind of convoluted reasoning that Goffman often employs, stacking concept upon concept, example upon example, qualification and reservation upon stipulation. He sees this mode as replicative of the structure of experience, and by extension, of social interaction. As he puts it, when confronting experience in particular:

> In dealing with conventional topics, it is usually practical to develop concepts and themes in some sort of logical sequence: nothing coming earlier depends on something coming later, and, hopefully, terms developed at any one point are actually used in what comes thereafter. Often the complaint of the writer is that linear presentation constrains what is actually a circular affair, ideally requiring simultaneous introduction of terms, and the complaint of the reader is that concepts elaborately defined are not much used beyond the point at which the fuss is made about their meaning. In the analysis of frames, linear presentation is no great embarrassment. Nor is the defining of terms not used thereafter. The problem, in fact, is that once a term is introduced (this occurring at the point at which it is first needed), it begins to have too much bearing, not merely applying to what comes later, but reapplying in each chapter to what it has already applied to. Thus each succeeding section of the study becomes more entangled, until a step can hardly be made because of what must be carried along with it. The process closely follows the horrors of repetition songs, as if – in the case of frame analysis – what Old MacDonald had on his farm were partridge and juniper trees. (1974, p. 11)

His formalistic method owes much to Simmel; a type of analysis in which an event, occurrence, or rule is stipulated as being a form in the world. As John Lofland has already pointed out in chapter one, in one essay are listed these social forms:

3 types of face
4 consequences of being out of or in the wrong face

2 basic kinds of face work
5 kinds of avoidance processes
3 phases of the corrective process
5 ways an offering can be accepted (1955, pp. 213–211).

Later, in *Frame Analysis* these (at least) are found in a 19 page span:

4 kinds of playful deceit
6 types of benign fabrications
3 kinds of exploitive fabrications
5 sorts of self-deception (1974, pp 87–116)

Such lists of items do not always fall out so neatly in a text, they may accrue in an almost shadowy fashion. The purpose of these lists is unstated and often elusive. He does not infer or deduce from them, does not claim that these types are exhaustive, explicate the degree of kinds of possible logical interconnections between them, nor does he always relate his current efforts to previous ideas of himself or others.[18] His formalistic version of analysis is accomplished by identifying the *shape* of an activity – the encounter – a single class or type of event involving face to face involvement and the exchange of verbal or non-verbal communication then delineating *subtypes* or near versions of the same thing. In interactional analyses, he then notes sources of *tension*, disruption, or intrusion and points out permutations of moves or *tactics* involved in maintaining an equilibrated state of affairs. He often generates lists of kinds or types of consequences. This analysis is not dependent, it should be emphasised, upon the substantive content of the examples – blindness, racial, age or sexual identity, a lost nose, a harelip, or flatulence may all be seen as stigmatising by someone, sometime, someplace. A waiting line operates as a mechanism for assigning turns whether people await a bus or gassing at Dauchau; apologies are expected and must be adequate whether a person runs over another's line in conversation, his foot, or his dog. This formalistic style, like that of Mauss and Simmel, can be captured in the form of 'if/then' propositions which John Lofland has already described in chapter one.

  Having said this about the method and procedure of Goffman, one is still left with the problem in the pre-1974 Goffman corpus of substituting just such stylistic delicacies (and rude awakenings), and accompanying rich descriptive material, especially of a microsegment of everyday life, for an abstract analysis. As Rock has insightfully noted, Goffman's formalism has not been acknowledged, but is rather 'unobtrusively woven into the larger reportings (ethnographies) so that it may retain some semblance of intimate connectedness to that subjective life.'[19] Rock claims in the same essay that much interactionist writing (in which he includes Goffman's work) is 'thus governed by a stylistic delicacy which suggests faithfulness that is actually lacking.' Similar claims have been made by others.[20] However, it is in *Frame Analysis* that much of the preciousness of style receeds; and substance, as defined above, superceedes style. Let us return to the issues with which we began: the organisation of experience and the framing of these phenomena.

ASPECTS OF THE SOLUTION TO THE CONCEPTUAL PROBLEM: *FRAME ANALYSIS*

In order to better understand the criticisms of Goffman that have been made, in part reflected in the previous brief overview, one must first appreciate, I should think, the misunderstandings of Goffman's work by his interpreters. A variety of commentaries hardly require attention, while others misplace the tradition of Goffman by overemphasizing the 'Meadian' basis, or the symbolic interactionist basis of this theoretical work. Although Goffman makes polite bows in the direction of symbolic interactionism, and cites with favour Mead and Blumer, his primary debt is to formal sociology as seen in the work of Mauss, Durkheim, Simmel, and more recently in his affection for and citation from structural semanticists. Other clues can be found in his oblique dedication of *Relations in Public* to A. R. Radcliffe-Brown, his frequent citation of Durkheim and Africanists, and concepts found in earlier work such as transformational rules, face, strategies, interaction ritual: all matters of the moral geometry of social life, not of its emergence, collective action, process and sequelae.[21] The Meadian emphasis on individual selves, rather than upon the constraints provided on interaction by the social forms in which it occurs, Goffman's emphasis even prior to the publication of *Frame Analysis* (cf. *Encounters*), differentiates Meadian and Goffmanian perspectives.

In *Frame Analysis*, his thematic question (taken from William James) is: 'Under what circumstances do we think things are real?'

His view of his work is that it addresses 'secondary matters', (1974, p. 13). The perspective is summarised there:

> situational . . . concern for what one individual can be alive to at a particular moment, this often involving a few other particular individuals and not necessarily restricted to the mutually monitored arena of a face-to-face gathering. I assume that when individuals attend to any current situation, they face the question: 'What is it that's going on here?' Whether asked explicitly, as in times of confusion and doubt, or tacitly, during occasions of usual certitude, the question is put and the answer to it is presumed by the way the individuals then proceed to get on with the affairs at hand. Starting, then, with that question, this volume attempts to limn out a frame-work that could be appealed to for the answer. (1974, p. 8)

Another aim is also offered: 'to try to isolate some of the basic frameworks of understanding available in our society for making sense out of events and to analyse the special vulnerbilities to which these frames of reference are subject.' (1974, p. 10)

The extent of the differentiation and of the extension of previous concerns is apparent in *Frame Analysis*, where Goffman confronts the problem touched on above: social life always contains at least two kinds of understandings, a literal one (what is going on?) and a metaphoric one (what is the meaning of what is going on). As Ditton has pointed out:

> At critical points, any analogically based analysis becomes extremely awkward. In trying to dramatically describe the occupational life of the entertainer, for example, we are faced with the irritating paradox of descriptive category exhaustion. Here, the literal sense of performance coincides with the metaphoric sense in which it is drama. The metaphor exhausts all available common-sense descriptions and leaves nothing for the literal meaning. The result? The analyst has to milk two meanings from one ward – either by analytic regression (handling one's relaxation from a performance as a performance) or by tenacity in bracketing techniques coupled with cumbersome phraseology to produce such barbarous neologisms as 'staged play.'[22]

To talk about experience in several social worlds, then, one cannot use the language originating in only one of them, expecially when the world of theatre has been among the most rich of all metaphors for social life, *and* provides a great many of the more pointed examples of social roles, values, dilemmas, situations and re-solutions. Goffman aims for an analysis of the organisation of experience, and for the similarities *between* the worlds of experience in which we participate. They are both different and the same.

In order to do the work of separating and analysing social worlds, Goffman borrows from several sources. Primary among these is Gregory Bateson, one of the most innovative minds in con-temporary social science, who first introduced the term 'frame' into social science.[23] Bateson uses the term, as does Goffman, in at least two ways at once. Firstly, it refers to the literal way in which persons mark events one from another by physical boundaries, or the way in which frames hang around pictures to mark both the picture (by separating it from non-picture), and that which is not picture (including itself). It stands thus for itself and for something else. It also refers, secondly, to the capacity that concepts have for referring to themselves as for example when 'gaming' can refer to the activity of making social life a game. Thus, the term refers to something conceptual which in turn refers to something in the world. When we think of the term 'gaming' we can think of the literal meaning of it (as in playing a game), as well as the metaphoric meaning of it (calling something a game and giving the activity and 'as-if' status by so doing). And in these activities we can be aware that by labelling something literal with this language we are able to think of it conceptually. Concepts allow us, like social relations, to both see and to do, to act and reflect on the acting by naming it, and further producing consequential acts as a result of the first sequence. Goffman seeks by borrowing from Bateson, and elaborating to be sure, to use the concept of a frame to: (a), indicate the reflexive nature of social life; (b), to show that simultaneous meanings are present in life as they are in language (such as when we change the meaning of a term from literal to metaphoric by placing it in quotation marks); and (c), to show that as actions change our definitions (or frames), we can alter our principal or original meanings and confer new ones, or add them to the first set. A frame, then, in Goffman's terms, contains principles of organisation: 'definitions of situations are built up in accordance with principles or organisation which govern events – at least social ones – and our subjective involvement in them; frame is the word I use to refer to such of these basic elements as I am able to identify.' (1974, p. 10) Evidence is presented in 'strips', 'arbitrary slices cut from streams of ongoing activity', e.g., cartoons, films, vignettes, newspaper articles, etc. Given these sorts of data, *Frame Analysis* attempts to outline what from the actor's perspective constitutes the principal distinctions among social worlds and between those social worlds and everyday life. Assuming that all knowledge is derived from contrast, and that everyday life, although not more 'real' than other worlds, is the ground against which other worlds are contrasted, Goffman asks: How can everyday life be contrasted with other self-recognised activities such as games, ceremonies, plays, novels, the cinema? How can they, in turn, be characterised formally with regard to their recognition, transformation, and the division of dramatic labour? How are these types of experience not only different from, but also like, everyday life? What do distinctions between everyday life and other forms reveal, obscure, or blur about such generically applied concepts as persons, characters, roles, bodies and selves? In each case, a *pirmary framework*, either 'natural' (where natural causation is evoked to explain or anticipate events) or 'social', is *keyed* (indicated for participants to be patterned on that world of reality but as something else), or *transformed* into another reference frame. For example, ceremonials are characterised by marked beginnings and endings that set them apart from other sorts of experience, and this marking is termed keying. Within an episode, keyings (or *fabrications*, which are intentional efforts to produce a false belief in what is going on), can be themselves transformed, re-keyed or re-fabricated. A play can contain inside its frame a second frame which marks a 'play within a play' which we are to understand as a part of the play, yet seen within another frame. The first play is the outer rim, the defining external frame, while re-keying is the process by which we define the play within a play. Social life is laminated, constituted of strips of activity, laid one on top of the other, each of which can be unpacked using this analytic scheme. The analysis presented is said to be that which competent actors undertake insofar as the argument presents recognisable features of our work of doing and seeing social episodes. The argument permits the sorting out self-induced errors from fabrications and keyings, and Goffman provides an understanding of the transformation of readings of events (fabrications can be re-fabricated; keys can be fabricated, etc.).[24]

Perhaps an example from research will be helpful. The data are taken from observation of police officers who enforce narcotics laws, who work largely 'undercover', i.e., not in uniform and with persons who do not know that they are the police when interacting with them.

Several officers were discussing a narcotics deal that they hoped would 'go down'. They outlined various strategies that they might employ: they might try to meet the 'bad guys' in a parking lot, and then drive with them to make the transaction (exchange the marijuana for cash) in the desert; they might meet the bad guys and 'front' them money so that the bad guys could rent a truck and bring the load (nearly a ton) of marijuana somewhere where the deal might result; they might bring trucks, driven by other officers 'disguised' as Mexican campesinos, to a preselected site to haul away the grass. While the first group was discussing this activity [which could be keyed as a game], a second group of officers was discussing a deal they were working on which involved a large cocaine purchase and possible buy-bust (an arrest would be made at the time the drugs were handed over and while the money and the sellers were on the scene). The two groups overheard each other talking. The second group were *fabricating* a story [re-keying the events discussed above] that they would lay out for the bad guys concerning why they had to do the deal at a particular time and place. This was necessary because the buy-bust situation required surveillance (observation by other officers during the course of the events) both for the protection of the officers and the money, and to insure an arrest occurred. [The first, or literal activity, viewed or keyed as a game was then being re-keyed, from their perspective, but became a fabrication when viewed from the observer's perspectives]. They intended to deceive the 'bad guys' with the story and the bad guys did not have the information necessary [to transform or refabricate (re-key and thus re-frame) the events]. When the second group heard the first group talking, they realised that the timing of the two events would make them competitive for the time and personnel of the unit and that the unit could not simultaneously execute the 'buy-bust' *and* the one ton grass deal.

The two activities were virtually mutually exclusive. One of the officers in the second group made a suggestion to members of the first group, [that they reveal *their* fabrication to the one ton grass dealers] by saying, 'We really can't meet then, because we're narcs, and we have to be back to the station to cover some other guys on a "buy-bust" '.[25]

Several points can be made here, in order to illustrate the power of Goffman's technique for uncovering social process. First, telling this story is keying it as an 'example'. Now, within that example, narcs are telling tales, treating their literal work as a game (keying it for each other). When they outline for each other the sort of frame they want to produce for the 'bad guys', they are *fabricating* (creating an *exploitative fabrication* in Goffman's terms), thus, *re-keying* them, or altering their meaning by inducing others to have a false belief in what is going on. When group two suggests to group one that they tell the villains that they are really narcs, they are suggesting that they *re-key* the events for others, thus *containing* a *containment* (or altering a definition by placing an alternative around it, even while the first still stands as a possibility). Such framing, of course, produces ambiguities in the framers and the framees, for if group one accepted the suggestion as so outrageous that it might work, they would be turning a keying, fabricated, back into a keying. Thus, as Goffman discusses at length in his chapter on fabrications (1974, chapter six), any containment (a frame that is based on fabrication) can be recontained (re-defined) because its vulnerable by its very elements to be manipulated by both parties without the outer knowing it.[26]

A bust in a parking lot planned by narcs to be a place where they can cover it, provide adequate personnel to rush to the car and arrest people, can also be a place where dope dealers hope to place their people, rush the car and rip-off (rob) the police of their flashroll or buy-money. And so on and so forth. (It should be noted that just these kinds of contingencies add uncertainties of timing, effort, planning, personnel and money occupy vast amounts of time in narcotics units).

In earlier work, Goffman suffered from two principal weaknesses. It was said that he had not fixed upon a set of analytic tools that were consistent and that allowed him to capture both the actor's definition of a situation and the structural, normative, or external constraints under which the actor worked even when attaining minimal concensus in situated encounters. Secondly, the problem identified by Ditton was a form of 'descriptive category exhaustion': when one writes about a social world by means of a metaphor derived from it, then literal description becomes difficult, awkward and misleading.[27] It certainly reduces one of the Goffman's most effective tools, the use of perspective by incongruity. *Frame Analysis* has moved a considerable distance toward resolving these weaknesses. The power results directly from the use of the concept of a frame. It is produced because of the following line of reasoning. In written and oral (as well as in non-verbal) communication, persons are able to convey to each other meta-messages (messages about what they are doing). People can carry on mock-fights, for example, where it is understood that people are 'not really angry'; they can speak ironically, conveying by a tone of voice, a facial grimace, a body posture, that what they have said is to be understood as precisely the opposite of it's literal meaning; words can be placed in texts (as I have above, and as this material in this parenthesis is) in quotes and brackets to alter their meaning. Written devices such as brackets, quotes, parentheses, the use of space, and ellipses convey by conventional rhetorical means a changed textual meaning. In interaction, frames act in this way, both to act literally to frame or set apart an event, and in a metaphoric way to provide a meaning. Think, for example, of obvious frames of a literal sort like the door to a sanctuary with holy water which, when crossed, alters the role of the person, the meaning of his actions, the symbols and vocabulary available to him, and the consequences of the experience. This frame is both literal and metaphoric, as are many of the more subtle meaning-transforms we experience in interactions. The frame that is shared is available in the world, while the particular usage put to it can be indicated in writing by punctuation, and in social interaction by other cues and clues. Reflexivity is provided because when one wants to comment on what one is doing, one can do so by indicating altered meanings. Goffman's chapters on the frame analysis of talk (1974, Chapter 13), and out of frame activity (1974, Chapter 7), are virtuoso performances, and contain some of the most subtle reasoning in the social sciences. The clarity of definition is aided by stylistic matters such as a one paragraph summary of the major focus of the chapter and the key terms placed on the first page of the chapter (old Goffmanians will think this makes it all too easy to appreciate 'what's going on here' after the rambling of *The Presentation of Self in Everyday Life* and the barely-hung-together essays in *Relations in Public*). Within bracketing that such an organisation physically provides, the lists and examples fall more readily into place as part of an explanatory scheme. Cross references to previous Goffman work may be somewhat excessive to some, but obviate the previous criticism that the ideas were non-cumulative, or further, that they 'hung in the air' without connection to other ideas and themes in social science.

The second major problem that attends his shift in root imagery or substantial metaphor from the theater to something approaching a cinematic notion (frame as in a frame or slide, or individual picture – recall that a picture has a frame, and it itself framed as a phenomenon), is less clearly resolved. There is something naggingly vague about the concept frame in Goffman's work, (as there is an even more uneasy feeling one gets from Bateson's *pas de deux* with it over a number of years), in part because the examples, strong as they are, depend on the capacity of the observer to analyse and categorise the events. They are presented as done. Even the detailed discussion of out of frame activity and of negative experiences depend heavily on pre-established definitions (framing activity), and one wonders whether one could do the same sort of analysis. It is possible to do the sort of processual analysis that is advocated here? *Frame Analysis* is not a frame analysis, but is a book *about* frame analysis, a kind of sociology of knowledge.

STYLE AND SOCIAL REALITY

Social sciences are, as many have pointed out, reflexive sciences, sciences that depend for their insights on the phenomena they study. They are particularly susceptible to trends in language and metaphor current among the social and cultural groups they study. They ape the style of their subjects. Metaphors are two-sided: they provide insights into those aspects of social reality that are like the metaphor, and conceal those that are not. Each of these aspects of the metaphor, insofar as people act upon them as guides, has real consequences. If narcs think of the enforcement of narcotics laws as a game with fictional rewards and stereo-typic 'good guys and bad guys', this will allow them some distance and self-protection concerning their own identities (no one takes a game completely seriously, and this is a crucial consideration when the game itself requires betrayal, lying, self-deception, the playing of discredited roles, the buying and selling of people's loyalty, the use of force and fraud). It may also encourage imagination and creativity in the planning of scenarios (such as those outlined above). On the other hand, the limits of the metaphor become constraining, as when people start 'acting like cops' (in the cops and robbers game), therefore re-keying their own view of themselves as something they are not. Contradiction can pile on contradiction: i.e., if you begin to view what you do as something you are not, then doing is not doing. Not doing is then a way of doing; psychic immobilisation or exhaustion can result. Likewise, the theatric metaphor has limits, especially when referring to itself as a literal activity. If this occurs, that is if the metaphor overcomes the capacity of the analyst to see its limitations, then style can indeed become the principal message. Rock, for example among others, has claimed that style has assumed this position in symbolic interactionist writings, including Goffman's work (prior to *Frame Analysis'* appearance). Rock writes:

> The rhetoric and phrasing practiced by the members of the school is as important as the more obvious features of their work. It is in this sense that a successful piece of symbolic interactionism is prestigious art, blending artifice and illusion with the trappings of simplicity and naturalism. As an artistic accomplishment, it defies analytic dismemberment. Its basic appeal is to the sensibilities of its reader, being capable of enlightening him without appearing to radically disfigure the social life it describes.[28]

When the particularly dramatic anecdote carries the weight of an argument, it may overcome, temporarily at least, the analytic point that is being made. The power of the metaphor, as in the case of the narcs' game, may allow both analyst and actor to overlook the fact that the game keys life, and vice-versa, thus building into our very understanding of events structured incapacities. There are limits on the power of substantive analogy (how long can one think of a courting relationship as a game before it trivialises and dehumanises the participants?), and there are limits to the informational capacity and to the tolerance of individuals for endless redefinition of events (1974, pp. 530, fn. 27). We do not know what the informational limits are, but there are suggestions.[29] In Anglo-American society there are also limits to altering the meanings of events grounded in sex, money, power, and competition (more true perhaps in America than in Canada and England). Events in the primary key that involve such matters are more enduring and less easily transformed than others. The examples chosen, of conmen, spies, police, and criminals of various sorts may overrepresent to the reader a certain kind of 'operative looseness of frame' that is not in fact generic.

These limits on metaphoric communication, both substantive and real in the sense that thinking in such a way produces real consequences, are very real limitations of Goffman's work. From the metaphors he has used, as was pointed out, comes the much-emulated stylistic qualities of his writing, the critical or debunking capability of the work, and its popular appeal outside professional social science audiences. The style, combining vivid anecdotes, sharp oxymorons and other clashing combinations of imagery, phrasing and vocabulary, dramatises social life in the ways that talk can, but also trades on ambiguity. Of course, we all trade on ambiguity; for some of us that is our trade indeed. But the irony of Goffman's style, being I think, his attempt to capture features that he sees really in social life and not merely epiphenomena, in his commitment to a structuralism that sees codes or orders beneath the surface, only occasionally presented for our appreciation. He is Durkheimian to the extent that the playness of his writing, wordwork, is not reality, but the belief that his words capture a part of reality is.

EDITIONS OF GOFFMAN'S WORK USED IN THIS CHAPTER

(The dates are taken from the bibliography provided in the *Editor's Introduction*; the pagination for quotations cited in this chapter from the editions cited below).

(1955)   'On Face-Work: An Analysis of Ritual Elements in Social Interaction', in Goffman, (1967).

(1956a)   'The Nature of Deference and Demeanour', in Goffman, (1967).

(1959)   *The Presentation of Self in Everyday Life*, (Garden City, New York; Doubleday Anchor).

(1961c)   *Asylums: Essays on the Social Situation of Mental Patients and Other Inmates*, (Chicago; Aldine).

(1961d)   'The Medical Model and Mental Hospitalisation: Some Notes on the Vicissitudes of the Tinkering Trades', in Goffman, (1961c).

(1964a)   'The Neglected Situation', *American Anthropologist*, Vol 66, No. 6, Part II [Special Issue], (1964) pp. 133–6.

(1967)   *Interaction Ritual: Essays on Face-to-Face Behaviour*, (Chicago; Aldine).

(1969c)   'The Insanity of Place', in Goffman, (1971).

(1971)   *Relations in Public: Microstudies of the Public Order*, (New York; Basic Books).

(1974)   *Frame Analysis: An Essay on the Organisation of Experience*, (Cambridge; Harvard University Press).

CHAPTER ENDNOTES

1. A. R. Radcliffe-Brown, *A Natural Science of Society*, (Glencoe, Illinois; Falcon's Wing Press, 1957); and see the comment by Edmund Leach, 'Social Anthropology: A Natural Science of Society', *Proceedings Of the British Academy*, Volume LXIV, (Oxford; Oxford University Press, 1976).

2. Goffman elaborates this with a fine, qualifying footnote. He says: 'I do not mean to imply that no stable meaning is built socially into artifacts, merely that circumstances can enforce an additional meaning. Cannon shells, five-gallon jars, and bits of disused plumbing can be transformed from utilitarian goods into decorative lamps, but their value as the latter depends on their never quite ceasing to be the former. At best the result is not a lamp but an interesting lamp. In fact, a certain amount of sport can be found in subordinating an official use to an irreverently alien one, as when pranksters manage to play pushbutton phones for tunes, not numbers, a possibility opened up by the fact that each button, when pushed, produces its own distinctive tone (*Time*, March 1972). Here again I argue that the meaning of an object (or act) is a product of social definition and that this definition emerges from the object's role in the society at large, which role then becomes for smaller circles a given, something that can be modified but not totally re-created. The meaning of an object, no doubt, is generated through its use, as pragmatists say, but ordinarily not by particular users. In brief, all things used for hammering in nails are not hammers.' (1974, p. 39, fn. 25).

3. Peter Berger and Thomas Luckmann, *The Social Construction of Reality*, (New York; Doubleday Anchor, 1966).

4. Harold Garfinkel, 'Common-Sense Knowledge of Social Structures: A Documentary Method of Interpretation', pp. 689–712, in J. Scher (ed) *Theories of the Mind*, (New York; Free Press, 1962).

5. See, Peter K. Manning, 'Police Lying', *Urban Life and Culture*, Volume 3, (1974) pp. 283–306.

6. The following section draws heavily upon my previously published essay, 'The Decline of Civility: A Comment on Erving Goffman's Sociology', *Canadian Review of Sociology and Anthropology*, vol 13, No. 1, (February, 1976) pp. 13–25.

7. The final snippet being from Goffman, (1956a) p. 91.

8. Berman (1971, R2). [See: *Editor's Introduction* for a full reference to this, together with a list of other reviews in the section, *A Sampler of Reviews*].

9. See, Everett C. Hughes, *Men and Their Work*, (New York; The Free Press of Glencoe, 1958).

10. See, Manning, 1976, op. cit., p. 18. Unlike the gamelike encounter-oriented sociology Goffman fostered and popularised in a dramatically rendered series of volumes published in the sixties, *Relations in Public* contains a deeply disturbing picture of everyday life. [However, note the forboding remarks in Goffman, (1967) pp. 147–8]. This shift is also discussed by Berman (1971, R2) op. cit., and by Alan Dawe, 'The Underworld View of Erving Goffman', *British Journal of Sociology*, volume 24, (1973), pp. 246–53.

11. In this section I am indebted to the ideas of John Lofland, and have drawn heavily upon his insightful paper, published for the first time as chapter one of this volume.

12. Kenneth L. Burke, *Permanence and Change*, 2nd. and rev. ed., (Indianapolis; Bobbs-Merrill, 1965) p. 65.

13. I do not think it wise to cast Goffman as a provocative writer in the political sense. He is far too subtle and sensitive to the nuances of language and meaning to attempt that, even if that were his intent. One passage is particularly revealing of his view of the 'practical' implications of his work. While freely admitting the 'conservative' aspects of his work since it 'does not catch at the differences between the advantaged and disadvantaged classes and can be said to direct attention away from such matters', Goffman riposts: 'I can only suggest that he who would combat false consciousness and awaken people to their true interests has much to do, because the sleep is very deep. And I do not intend here to provide a lullaby but merely to sneak in and watch the way the people snore.' (1974, p. 14).

14. See, Peter K. Manning and M. Zucker, *The Sociology of Mental Health and Illness*, (Indianapolis; Bobbs-Merrill, 1976).

15. And here see: Manning and Zucker, ibid.; H. Fabrega Jnr., *Disease and Social Behaviour*, (Cambridge; M.I.T. Press, 1974); H. Fabrega Jnr., and Peter K. Manning, 'Disease, Illness and Deviant Careers', in R. A. Scott and J. D. Douglas (eds) *Theoretical Perspectives on Deviance*, (New York; Basic Books, 1972); and, Peter, K. Manning and H. Fabrega Jnr., 'The Experience of Self and Body: Health and Illness in the Chiapas Highlands', in G. Psathas (ed) *Phenomenological Sociology*, (New York; J. Wiley and Sons, 1973).

16. See George Psathas, chapter two in this volume.

17. This technique can result in misreading Goffman's aim, as S. Messinger, R. Sampson and R. Towne point out in their article, 'Life as Theatre: Some Notes on the Dramaturgic Approach to Social Reality', *Sociometry*, volume 25, (September, 1962) pp. 98–110. For it is possible to infer that Goffman's analytic actors are like stage players, actors always conscious of the threat of disruptions, failures, mistakes and the like, and therefore in some sense always well prepared (rehearsed) in order to avoid or minimise their possible effects. If people were actors in this sense, they would be 'on' or acutely self-aware of the need to appear 'normal'. According to Messinger, Sampson and Towne, only mental patients constantly question what others assume will be/is taken for granted normal behaviour. Goffman assumes that people *aren't* self-aware in this way. As a result, they continue to place themselves at risk.

18. For an exception, see Goffman (1974) Chapter 1. However, generally Goffman's footnotes frequently indicate ritual debts, friendship ties or are marks indicating intellectual predecessors. They have highly variable utility as informational sources.

19. Paul Rock, 'Symbolic Interactionism', in R. B. Smith and Peter Manning (eds) *Social Science Methods* Volume I: *Qualitative Methods*, (New York; Irvington Press, Forthcoming).

20. Sharrock (1974, R5). [See: *Editor's Introduction* for a full reference to this, together with a list of other reviews in the section, *A Sampler of Reviews*].

21. See, Peter Manning, 'Existential Sociology', *Sociological Quarterly*, volume 14, (1973) pp. 283–306; and Tiryakian (1967, R3) [See: *Editor's Introduction* for a full reference to this, together with a list of other reviews in the section, *A Sampler of Reviews*].

22. Ditton (1974, R4), p. 329. [See: *Editor's Introduction* for a full reference to this, together with a list of other reviews in the section, *A Sampler of Reviews*].

23. Gregory Bateson, *Naven*, (Stanford; Stanford University Press, originally published, 1936); 2nd ed., (1958); and also his, *Steps to an Ecology of Mind*, (San Francisco; Chandler, 1972). The term frame, and analogous concepts with the same salutory ambiguity are found in several other works, but none has developed the idea as fully as has Goffman in *Frame Analysis*. Among the more important writers using and developing the term are, Mary Douglas, Basil Bernstein, Pierre Bourdieu, Clifford Geertz and Victor Turner. The idea is used in sociolinguistics (sometimes as 'context'), and some clues to the tradition are found in B. N. Colby *et al.*, 'Ethnographic Semantics: A Preliminary Survey', *Anthropology*, volume 7, (February, 1966) pp. 3–32. These writers all seek to refine a concept which simultaneously captures the literal and metaphoric aspects of social life, and their works vacillate in emphases between these two. Unfortunately, a critical review of the use of the concept and its refinement by Goffman is beyond the scope of this chapter.

24. Remaining chapters of *Frame Analysis* (not dealt with extensively here) discuss: the out-of-frame activity upon which the meaning of the framed activity depends (subordinate activity, or 'tracks', which indicate, for example, who is talking, what

is to be considered concealed and the relationships between the framed activity and outer activity); 'troubles' (ambiguities and errors in framing); 'breaking frame' and 'the manufacture of negative experience' (a description of what happens when something is not what it is framed to be by the actor, and the resulting limbo). Goffman relies heavily upon argument by analogy, and he attempts to show that people understand activities because they are like others, and that they cling to such analogic thinking even when the activities appear to depart from the model. Considerable space is devoted to exploring the limits and powers of the theatrical analog (chapter 5, *et passim*).

25. The example is drawn from a study on which I am working (LEAA/NILECJ Grant Number, 76-NI-99-0109) on police and illicit substance control with Jay Williams of the Research Triangle Institute; and Lawrence J. Redlinger of the University of Texas, Dallas.

26. Goffman commented much earlier: 'It was suggested earlier that an audience is able to orient itself in a situation by accepting performed cues on faith, treating these signs as evidence of something greater than or different from the sign-vehicles themselves. If this tendency of the audience to accept signs places the performer in a position to be misunderstood and makes it necessary for him to exercise expressive care regarding everything he does when before the audience, so also this sign-accepting tendency puts the audience in a position to be duped and misled, for there are few signs that cannot be used to attest to the presence of something that is not really there.' (1959, p. 58)

27. Ditton (1974, R4) op. cit.

28. Rock (forthcoming) op. cit.

29. Cf. G. A. Miller, 'The Magical Number Seven, Plus or Minus Two: Some Limits on our Capacity for Processing Information', *Psychological Review*, volume 63, (1956) pp 81–97, Peter McHugh, *Defining the Situation*, (Indianapolis; Bobbs-Merrill, 1968); and, A. F. C. Wallace, 'One Just Being Complicated Enough', *Proceedings of the National Academy of Science*, volume 47, (1961) pp. 458–64.

Goffman Citation Index

The dates are taken from the bibliography provided in the *Editor's Introduction*. Numbers followed by an 'n' indicate a footnote citation, and those in italics a bibliographic citation.

Author Index

Numbers followed by an 'n' indicate a note citation, and those in italics a bibliographic citation.